NONNATIVE ENGLISH-SPEAKING TEACHERS OF U.S. COLLEGE COMPOSITION: EXPLORING IDENTITIES AND NEGOTIATING DIFFERENCE

INTERNATIONAL EXCHANGES ON THE STUDY OF WRITING

Series Editors: Steven Fraiberg, Joan Mullin, Magnus Gustafsson, and Terry Myers Zawacki

Series Associate Editor: Anna S. Habib

The International Exchanges on the Study of Writing Series publishes books that address worldwide perspectives on writing, writers, teaching with writing, and scholarly writing practices, specifically those that draw on scholarship across national and disciplinary borders to challenge parochial understandings of all of the above. The Latin America Section of the International Exchanges on the Study of Writing book series publishes peer-reviewed books about writing, writers, teaching with writing, and scholarly writing practices from Latin American perspectives. It also offers re-editions of recognized peer-reviewed books originally published in the region.

The WAC Clearinghouse and University Press of Colorado are collaborating so that these books will be widely available through free digital distribution and low-cost print editions. The publishers and the series editors are committed to the principle that knowledge should freely circulate and have embraced the use of technology to support open access to scholarly work.

Recent Books in the Series

Estela Inés Moyano and Margarita *Vidal Lizama (Eds.), Centros y Programas de Escritura en América Latina: Opciones Teóricas y Pedagógicas para la Enseñanza de la Escritura Disciplinar* (2023)

Jay Jordan, *Grounded Literacies in a Transnational WAC/WID Ecology: A Korean-U.S. Study* (2022)

Magnus Gustafsson and Andreas Eriksson (Eds.), *Negotiating the Intersections of Writing and Writing Instruction* (2022)

L. Ashley Squires (Ed.), *Emerging Wrioting Research from the Russian Federation* (2021)

Natalia Ávila Reyes (Ed.), *Multilingual Contributions to Writing Research: Toward an Equal Academic Exchange* (2021)

Cecile Badenhorst, Brittany Amell, and James Burford (Eds.), *Re-imagining Doctoral Writing* (2021)

Bruce Morrison, Julia Chen, Linda Lin, and Alan Urmston (Eds.), *English Across the Curriculum: Voices from Around the World* (2021)

Alanna Frost, Julia Kiernan, and Suzanne Blum Malley (Eds.), *Translingual Dispositions: Globalized Approaches to the Teaching of Writing* (2020)

NONNATIVE ENGLISH-SPEAKING TEACHERS OF U.S. COLLEGE COMPOSITION: EXPLORING IDENTITIES AND NEGOTIATING DIFFERENCE

Edited by Mariya Tseptsura and Todd Ruecker

The WAC Clearinghouse
wac.colostate.edu
Fort Collins, Colorado

University Press of Colorado
upcolorado.com
Denver, Colorado

The WAC Clearinghouse, Fort Collins, Colorado 80523

University Press of Colorado, Denver, Colorado 80203

© 2024 by Mariya Tseptsura and Todd Ruecker. This work is licensed under a Creative Commons Attribution-NonCommercial-NoDerivatives 4.0 International License.

ISBN 978-1-64215-214-2 (PDF) | 978-1-64215-215-9 (ePub) | 978-1-64642-617-1 (pbk.)

DOI 10.37514/INT-B.2024.2142.

Library of Congress Cataloging-in-Publication Data

Names: Tseptsura, Mariya, 1987– editor. | Ruecker, Todd Christopher, editor.

Title: Nonnative English-speaking teachers of U.S. college composition : exploring identities and negotiating difference / edited by Mariya Tseptsura and Todd Ruecker.

Other titles: Nonnative English-speaking teachers of United States college composition

Description: Fort Collins, Colorado : The WAC Clearinghouse ; Denver, Colorado : University Press of Colorado, [2024] | Series: International exchanges on the study of writing series | Includes bibliographical references.

Identifiers: LCCN 2024016816 (print) | LCCN 2024016817 (ebook) | ISBN 9781646426171 (pbk.) | ISBN 9781642152142 (adobe pdf) | ISBN 9781642152159 (epub)

Subjects: LCSH: English language—Composition and exercises—Study and teaching (Higher)—United States. | Academic writing—Study and teaching (Higher)—United States. | English language—Study and teaching (Higher)—Foreign speakers—Social aspects. | Multilingualism.

Classification: LCC PE1405.U6 N68 2024 (print) | LCC PE1405.U6 (ebook) | DDC 808/.042071073—dc23/eng/20240624

LC record available at https://lccn.loc.gov/2024016816

LC ebook record available at https://lccn.loc.gov/2024016817

Copyeditor: Don Donahue

Design and Production: Mike Palmquist and Heather M. Falconer

Cover Photo: Istock Photo ID 1287264491 by Kubkoo. Used with permission.

Series Editors: Steven Fraiberg, Joan Mullin, Magnus Gustafsson, and Terry Myers Zawacki

Series Associate Editor: Anna S. Habib

The WAC Clearinghouse supports teachers of writing across the disciplines. Hosted by Colorado State University, it brings together scholarly journals and book series as well as resources for teachers who use writing in their courses. This book is available in digital formats for free download at wac.colostate.edu.

Founded in 1965, the University Press of Colorado is a nonprofit cooperative publishing enterprise supported, in part, by Adams State University, Colorado State University, Fort Lewis College, Metropolitan State University of Denver, University of Alaska Fairbanks, University of Colorado, University of Denver, University of Northern Colorado, University of Wyoming, Utah State University, and Western Colorado University. For more information, visit upcolorado.com.

Citation Information: Tseptsura, Mariya, and Todd Ruecker. (2024). *Nonnative English-Speaking Teachers of U.S. College Composition: Exploring Identities and Negotiating Difference*. The WAC Clearinghouse; University Press of Colorado. https://doi.org/10.37514/INT-B.2024.2142

Land Acknowledgment. The Colorado State University Land Acknowledgment can be found at https://landacknowledgment.colostate.edu.

§ Contents

1. Introduction 3
   Mariya Tseptsura and Todd Ruecker

2. Constructing a Professional Identity: Nonnative English-Speaking Teachers in First-Year Writing Courses 23
   Marcela Hebbard

3. Multilingual Writing Teacher Identities and Institutional Ecologies: A Collaborative Narrative Inquiry 45
   Su Yin Khor, Cristina Sánchez-Martín, Lisya Seloni, Md Mijanur Rahman, and Demet Yiğitbilek

4. Dismantling Racial Microaggression: Translingual, Nonnative Identities as Pedagogical Resources 63
   Nabila Hijazi

5. Cultural Adaptation and Building Authority As a NNES: A Reflective Study 79
   Mariya Tseptsura

6. "What Authority I Have?": Analyzing Legitimation Codes of English Composition ITAs 97
   Aleksandra Kasztalska and Michael Maune

7. Native English-Speaking Students' Perceptions of a Nonnative English-Speaking Writing Teacher, Teaching Effectiveness, and Language Performance 115
   Lan Wang-Hiles

8. A Corpus Study on Written Comments by Nonnative English-Speaking and Native English-Speaking Teachers of First-Year Writing 137
   Wen Xin

9. (Re)framing Uncertainty as Opportunity: A Study of International Teaching Assistants in Writing Classrooms Across the Curriculum ... 157
   Tamara Mae Roose, Min-Seok Choi, and Christopher E. Manion

10. Identity and Professional Development of First-year NNES Teachers: Two Case Studies 175
    Xin Chen

11. NNESTs, Teacher Education, Language Diversity, and Equality 195
    Melinda Reichelt

Contents

12 Building Confidence as NNESTs of Writing through Pre-service
   Training and Professional Development 207
   Anastasiia Kryzhanivska and Tetyana Bychkovska

Afterword 227
   Mariya Tseptsura and Todd Ruecker

Contributors 231

NONNATIVE ENGLISH-SPEAKING TEACHERS OF U.S. COLLEGE COMPOSITION: EXPLORING IDENTITIES AND NEGOTIATING DIFFERENCE

1 Introduction

Mariya Tseptsura
UNIVERSITY OF ARIZONA

Todd Ruecker
UNIVERSITY OF NEVADA, RENO

The issues of linguistic diversity and linguistic justice have generated a lot of discussion, research, and debate in writing studies over the last half century, and the last two decades have seen a stronger interest in addressing linguistic prejudices with the wider impact of translingual approaches and anti-racist movements. But while this shift is timely and necessary, writing studies as a field has largely ignored the growing diversity of teachers of writing just as it has been attracting increasing numbers of graduate students and international scholars and expanding its reach around the world. For instance, all the chapters in Shirley Rose and Irwin Weiser's (2018) excellent collection *The Internationalization of US Writing Programs* focused on serving students, and references to instructors were limited to how to prepare them to support international student writers. Elsewhere, work on translingualism has overwhelmingly focused on supporting students through curricular and pedagogical changes (e.g., Canagarajah, 2013; Horner et al., 2011; Horner & Tetreault, 2017; Lee & Jenks, 2016). This collection offers a deeper insight into the experiences of nonnative English speaking teachers (NNESTs) at a variety of postsecondary institutions in different U.S. geographical contexts and suggests ways that writing programs can support the success of not only increasingly diverse students but also increasingly diverse teachers of writing.

While the fields of TESOL and applied linguistics have seen a substantial number of studies addressing and challenging the native speaker fallacy as it relates to nonnative English-speaking professionals in these fields (we offer a more detailed overview of this work in the next section), the field of writing studies has not fully acknowledged the extent of linguistic diversity among writing instructors, nor has it fully explored how writing pedagogies can draw on this diversity as our field strives towards greater linguistic inclusivity and justice. This collection brings together a number of voices, most of whom are nonnative English speakers, that represent a great multiplicity in terms of the authors' nationalities, genders, career stages, and cultural, religious, and racial backgrounds. Many of the authors draw on their unique positionality within writing studies to explore their own and their students' experiences

DOI: https://doi.org/10.37514/INT-B.2024.2142.2.01

through an intersectional lens. The accounts presented in these chapters aim to move our field towards a greater understanding of linguistic diversity of our instructor population while also promoting greater inclusivity in our research and pedagogical practices.

A Note on Terminology

Before we continue, it is important to note that the terms native English speaker (NES) and nonnative English speaker (NNES) have seen a considerable amount of debate within TESOL, applied linguistics, and writing studies alike. Vivian Cook (1999) and Claire Kramsch (1997) argued that the NES/NNES dichotomy is unclear. While native speaker is often conflated with fluency in a language, it only really refers to the language a speaker learned first (Cook, 1999); as we have learned in our own work, defining one's first language is often complicated for those growing up in multilingual contexts. More importantly, it is an unattainable status for someone not born learning a particular language, and scholars have found it more productive to focus on the unique competencies of L2 users such as their ability to code switch. George Braine, in his introduction to his 1999 collection *Non-Native Educators in English Language Teaching*, acknowledged the problematic history and implications of the "NNES" term, admitting that it provided legitimacy to the very native-nonnative dichotomy that the collection strove to prove as false or misconstrued. Braine also cited a list of suggested alternatives, among which were "second language speaking professionals" and "non-native teachers of English," yet the collection retained both "NES" and "NNES" terms while simultaneously pointing, like Cook (1999) and Alan Davies (1991), to the difficulties in defining what either a native or a nonnative speaker actually is or difficulties in assigning either one label to multilingual speakers of English in some cases (e.g., Brutt-Griffler & Samimy, 2001; Liu, 2005). The NNES/NES terms then became widely used in the publications appearing after Braine's volume, and it is our intent in using them in this collection to connect and expand on this existing body of literature. As Lucie Moussu and Enric Llurda (2008) also pointed out, many language users who consider themselves either native or nonnative speakers self-align with either linguistic group as "a way of positioning themselves as members or as aliens in a particular social community" (p. 318).

NNES Teachers of English in TESOL

The NNEST movement in professional TESOL circles started gaining recognition in the 1990s (e.g., Medgyes's *The Non-Native Teacher* published in

1994) and grew exponentially in the late 1990s throughout the 2010s. The first colloquium on NNES professionals in TESOL organized by Braine at the 1996 TESOL Convention featured a number of prominent NNES scholars, including Ulla Connor, Suresh Canagarajah, and Jacinta Thomas. Two years later, the NNESs in TESOL Caucus was formed (headed by Braine), which evolved in 2008 into the NNES Interest Section with the goal to promote wider awareness of and research into NNES issues as well as fight discriminatory practices in the profession (Kamhi-Stein, 2016; also see Brady, 2018, for more on this history). Numerous publications have contributed to the movement, with a number of books and edited collections including Braine's 1999 *Non-Native Educators in English Language Teaching*, Lia D. Kamhi-Stein's 2004 *Learning and Teaching from Experience* and Llurda's 2005 *Non-Native Language Teachers*, Ahmar Mahboob's 2010 *NNES Lens*, and Bedrettin Yazan and Nathaniel Rudolph's (2018) *Criticality, Teacher Identity, and (In)Equity in English Language Teaching*—bringing together an impressive number of NNES and NES voices. As of 2015, Kamhi-Stein counted 356 publications on the topic, a number that had accelerated in recent years, with 32% of those appearing since 2010—she also noted that the *TESOL Encyclopedia of English Language Teaching*, published in 2018, would include an entire volume with 45 entries on NNEST issues.

Some of the earlier studies, like Péter Medgyes's (1994) *The Non-Native Teacher* or his earlier articles, focused on comparisons between NNES and NES teachers of English. Medgyes viewed NES and NNES as fundamentally different teachers, mostly on the basis of the differences in language proficiency, and investigated how these linguistic differences translated into differences in teaching practices and self-perceptions. However, an important strand of NNES research focused not on the perceived differences between NES and NNES teachers but rather on dismantling the artificially constructed divides between the two groups. Publications like Robert Phillipson's (1992) *Linguistic Imperialism*, Alastair Pennycook's (1994) *The Cultural Politics of English as an International Language*, Henry G. Widdowson's (1994) "The Ownership of English" (1994) and Cook's (1999) "Going Beyond the Native Speaker in Language Teaching" paved the way for many researchers to question the privileged status of English varieties from what Braj Kachru (1986) called the "inner circle" or "center" English speaking countries (the UK, the US, Australia, New Zealand, and Canada) and the privileged status of the teachers who claim these varieties of English as their native language.

Phillipson (1992) coined the term "native speaker fallacy" and traced its origins to a 1961 conference on TESOL held in Uganda where the status of NESs as superior teachers of English was widely legitimized. He also demonstrated how upholding the native speaker teacher status helped the "center" countries to maintain control over the TESOL industry, as well as how native speaker fallacy was tied in with racial discrimination and the history of colonialism for languages such as English, French, Spanish, Russian, and Portuguese.

As touched on earlier, Cook (1999) demonstrated how various definitions of a native speaker contain a number of incidental characteristics such as complete knowledge of the language (far from all native speakers are completely competent in it) or belonging to a speech community (native speakers might want to disassociate themselves from the community of native speakers). The only unquestionable characteristic of a native speaker is that they speak the language learned first in childhood. Thus, the native speaker competence is by definition an unattainable goal for second language learners: "Adults could never become native speakers without being reborn" (Cook, 1999, p. 187). They can, however, attain native-like levels of proficiency in their second language and become indistinguishable from native speakers in their language use. Furthermore, Cook argued that a "native speaker" in traditional understanding is a monolingual speaker of that language; thus, comparisons between bilingual speakers or L2 learners and monolingual native speakers are inherently fallacious because the minds of these speakers are "qualitatively different" in a number of ways, including language and thought processing (1999, p. 191). Nonetheless, comparisons between NS and NNS persist in language learning pedagogy and have a negative effect on both students and NNS teachers as these comparisons are drawn not from the perspective of difference, as Cook argued, but from the viewpoint of deficit, whereby NNSs are by default inferior to their NS counterparts. Multiple studies have pointed out that this deficit view is widespread in contexts across the globe and among English language learners, educational administrators and employers, and NNES teachers themselves.

A number of studies looked into the ways prejudices against NNES teachers present employment challenges for these teachers. For instance, in Mahboob's studies (2003 and 2004), the majority of Intensive English Program administrators in the US considered NES status to be an important factor in hiring ESL teachers. In EFL contexts, it has not been uncommon for many countries to hire ESL teachers on condition of holding an "inner circle" country citizenship or directly requiring native speaker status or native-like proficiency in teacher job ads (Lengeling & Pablo, 2012; Ramjattan, 2015; Ruecker & Ives, 2014; Selvi, 2010). Thanks to advocacy by NNESTs within TESOL, TESOL released the "Position Statement Against Discrimination of Nonnative Speakers of English in the Field of TESOL" in 2006, which has led to a number of practices by the organization, including prohibiting native speaker requirements in hiring practices on its jobs listings and at its national convention. Members of the NNEST movement have also raised awareness of these issues via social media, encouraging members to contact employers practicing discriminatory practices in order to educate them about the problem of focusing on nativeness over other, more relevant qualifications (Ruecker & Ives, 2014).

Equally important, deficit discourses and native speakerism affect NNES teachers' self-perception and self-positioning. NNES teachers' self-perception became the central focus of a number of studies looking at teachers' perceived language skills and these perceptions' effect on teaching strategies and teachers' self-positioning in the classroom and in the ideological and political debates (e.g., Huang, 2018; Llurda & Huguet, 2003; Matsumoto, 2018; Reves & Medgyes, 1994; Samimy & Brutt-Griffler, 1999). Medgyes (1994) was one of the first to point out that NNESTs suffer from a kind of inferiority complex as they often feel they cannot attain the same level of proficiency in English or have a native-like accent. Some publications presented NNESTs' autobiographical accounts of navigating academic writing in English and professionalization in the TESOL field, and some presented case studies of effective collaboration (e.g., Connor, 1999; de Oliveira & Lan, 2012; Liu, 2005). Other studies documented NNESTs' evolving identities and self-perception through a variety of quantitative and qualitative methods. For instance, participants in Keiko Samimy and Janina Brutt-Griffler's study (1999), NNES TESOL students, thought that NESs were more proficient users of the English language, but the participants also saw benefits in their knowledge of students' L1 and appreciated EFL contexts more than ESL ones where their competence was more likely to be questioned. Participants in Sibel Tatar and Senem Yildiz's (2010) study in Turkey recognized a variety of strengths of NNESTs, including their ability to draw on shared culture and language, their experiences as a language learner, and their ability to manage the classroom better. Overall, investigations of NNESTs' self-perceptions have painted a complicated picture where NNESTs' sense of confidence is shaped by a number of factors including previous education and exposure to the U.S. higher education, their race, and their students' backgrounds.

Some scholars have documented student perceptions of NNESTs (Amin, 1997; Aslan & Bailey, 1983; Benke & Medgyes, 2005; Lipovsky & Mahboob, 2010; Ma, 2012; Pacek, 2005; Rubin, 1992; Timmis, 2002; Thompson, 2017). Donald Rubin (1992) found that race/ethnicity and language are often conflated by listeners when they played a recording for undergraduate students accompanied by a picture of an Asian instructor and a Caucasian instructor—comprehension levels dropped when the recording was accompanied by the picture of the Asian instructor. While earlier work (e.g., Timmis, 2002) found that students generally held negative attitudes towards NNESTs, more recent work has indicated more balanced attitudes. Lai Ping Florence Ma (2012) found that the 30 secondary students she interviewed in Hong Kong saw unique advantages to having both NNES and NES teachers. For instance, a number of students said that NNES teachers benefited from knowing and using students' L1, better understood student needs and challenges as language learners, and were more easily understood. On the other hand, NES teachers were praised for having good English proficiency, having a more relaxed classroom, and motivating presence which facilitated learning. Studies in English as a second language (ESL) contexts (as opposed to English as a foreign language (EFL) contexts) have also found more balanced student attitudes. In a study of 19 Japanese students in the US, Caroline Lipovsky and Mahboob (2010) found that students appreciated the complementary knowledge and abilities of their NNESTs and NESTs. Elsewhere in the US, Erhan Aslan and Amy Thompson (2017) found in a survey of 76 ESL students that what respondents "seem to be paying attention to the most is the professional and personal qualities of their teachers rather than their native/nonnative status" (p. 289).

Linguistic Diversity in Writing Studies

Despite this robust body of literature on the experiences and challenges of NNES teachers of English in TESOL and applied linguistics, writing studies overall has yet to recognize and explore the full scale of implications of linguistic diversity among writing instructors in the US, partly due to the complicated history of linguistic pluralism in the field. Bruce Horner and John Trimbur (2002) argued that postsecondary writing instruction in the US has been historically shaped by a "tacit language policy of unidirectional English monolingualism" (p. 594) as writing instruction in English came to replace, in the late nineteenth century, the classical curriculum of Latin and Greek. While other historians of composition (e.g., Crowley, 1998; Miller, 1991) pointed to the policing and elitist motives that facilitated the establishment of college composition, Horner and Trimbur showed how at the birth of composition, English was severed from other modern languages into its own entity, assuming the role of the only language of writing. The special place assigned to English also helped solidify the "social identity of U.S. Americans as English speakers" (Horner & Trimbur, 2002, p. 607). While the United States today is no less multilingual and multicultural than it was in the late nineteenth and early twentieth centuries, the same reified notions of language and nationality and monolingual culture are evident today in many English-only policies and arguments and, as Horner and Trimbur maintained, in writing studies at large when language learning is commonly portrayed as moving unidirectionally towards a monolingual native speaker ideal.

Writing studies' attempts to acknowledge and account for the linguistic diversity in composition classrooms and in the wider U.S. social landscape are most visible in the publication of the CCCC 1974 resolution "Students' Rights to Their Own Language" (*SRTOL*). The resolution was developed in response to the changing student demographics, growing Civil Rights and other political movements in and outside of academia, and the efforts of researchers like James Sledd (1969) or Geneva Smitherman (1977; 1995) who strove for acknowledgement of the legitimacy of English dialects commonly deemed substandard. *SRTOL* maintained that all students, regardless of their socioeconomic or racial background, had the right to "their own patterns and varieties of language—the dialects of their nurture or whatever dialects in which they find their own identity and style."

Perhaps in response to visible changes in student demographics and also in the field's growing embrace of anti-racism, issues of language diversity have been more prominent in the composition circles for the last decade with the advent of translingual approach. Following earlier work by Canagarajah (2006), Horner and his co-authors (2011) published their influential opinion piece "Language Difference in Writing: Towards a Translingual Approach," which was signed by fifty composition and second language writing scholars. Drawing on *SRTOL* among other resources, "Language Difference in Writing" called for a paradigm shift in writing studies, urging its researchers and practitioners to see "difference in language not as a barrier or as a problem to manage, but as a resource for producing meaning in writing, speaking, reading, and listening" (2011, p. 303). Rejecting the myth of a fixed, universally accepted entity called "standard English," the authors offered a number of propositions focused on accepting and promoting multiple languages and dialects in the composition classroom and beyond—propositions that have been explored and expanded in numerous publications since then, including Horner and Tetreault's more recent edited collection (2017) on translingual pedagogies and writing programs.

Working from a different perspective, Shawna Shapiro proposed another framework for approaching language differences in the writing classroom in her more recent book on critical language awareness (2022), calling for more explicit attention to the "power dynamics in and around language variation and use" (Shapiro & Leonard, 2023, p. 3). Shapiro's work actively seeks to offer concrete and practical ways for enacting linguistic justice in the language or writing classroom; similarly, more pedagogy-oriented suggestions appeared in another recent collection (Losey & Shuck, 2021) that brought together scholars working at the intersection of writing and second language acquisition studies.

Nonetheless, as scholars have increasingly turned their attention to supporting linguistically diverse students, the "disciplinary division of labor" (Matsuda, 1999), a gap between writing studies and TESOL, has largely remained (Atkinson et al., 2015). Scholars such as Christine Tardy (2017) continue to call for truer inter/transdisciplinary scholarship, arguing that much of the work on language diversity in writing studies ignores decades of work in other fields. Because of this persisting divide and the predominantly white English L1 speaking field's traditional aversion to discussing issues of difference (Garcia de Müeller & Ruiz, 2017), it is unsurprising that writing studies' focus on language diversity has remained narrowly focused on students and that the dominant image of composition instructor as a white, monolingual English speaker has also remained widely unchallenged. As we will discuss in the next section, scholars in applied linguistics and TESOL have long explored and challenged the prejudice, linguistic and otherwise, faced by teachers in their profession. Within writing studies, the history of this work is comparatively brief. A number of writing studies scholars have explored the prejudices scholars of color have faced during their graduate studies and advancing in their career (e.g., Martinez, 2014; Royster & Williams, 1999; Villanueva, 1993). We have found the use of counterstory and counterspaces (Martinez, 2014; Yosso et al., 2009) especially productive in addressing the marginalized status of NNESTs in writing studies, arguing the importance of creating a "community of people with shared experiences and thus a greater opportunity to create counterspaces where they can safely share each other's experiences and create counterstories in marginalizing environments" (Ruecker et al., 2018, p. 636). Also, as evident from the recommendations of many authors in the present collection, NNESTs in writing studies have found the implementation of translingual approaches in writing programs as a way to promote discussions about linguistic difference that challenge student beliefs of NESTs as ideal writing teachers.

In one of the earliest publications focused specifically on NNES teachers of writing, Liu (2005) explored the challenges and coping strategies of four international TAs from China teaching first-year writing (FYW) at a Southwestern U.S. university. He described the surprise and self-doubt the TAs experienced upon learning about their teaching assignments and the challenges they faced in their classrooms that stemmed from NES students' resistance towards instructors "who are not even American" as well as "such factors as different sets of cultural expectations for teachers and learners, intercultural miscommunication and misunderstanding, and disjuncture in teaching and learning styles" (2005, p. 173). Around the same time, Kevin DePew (2006) shared a single case study of a Chinese international teaching assistant (ITA) of FYW—while a large number of students in the class faulted the teacher's spoken accent, they valued the teacher's ability to convey instructions clearly via writing. DePew (2006) concluded the chapter by pointing to the outdated focus on oral training for ITAs, calling for more robust training in writing. In our more recent study (Ruecker et al., 2018), we surveyed and interviewed a much larger sample of NNES writing instructors and found that while NNES instructors tended to feel more confident compared to the participants in Liu's (2005) study, many of them still faced microaggressions and negative bias from students and sometimes colleagues. We urged writing programs to provide sufficient support for their NNES instructors in the form of pedagogical and community support as well as a stronger focus on language diversity at the programmatic level.

With the increased attention to linguistic pluralism within writing studies in the last decade, the field can benefit from engaging the multiple resources and literacies brought by the NNES members of the profession. As Jun Liu phrased it in his 2005 piece, having NNES teachers of writing in North America "is encouraging as it creates opportunities for intercultural communication, and enhancement of the globalization of English" (p. 173). Yet, some NNES professionals, like Monika Shehi (2017), pointed out that while these writing instructors are uniquely positioned to advocate for marginalized varieties of English and challenge the privileged positioning of Standardized U.S. English (commonly referred to as Standard American English, SAE), in doing so they risk losing their hard-earned positions as language and writing experts in front of their NES students. As Shehi (2017) put it,

> students can be frustrated in a class where SAE is not privileged, particularly if they believe that the reason the privilege of SAE is challenged is to accommodate "foreign" instructors whose language skills they believe to be inferior to their own and a sign that the instructors have not succeeded in achieving native-like proficiency. (p. 267)

As this passage confirms, the problem of students' negative attitudes towards language diversity and NNESTs remains one of the central challenges in NNESTs' professional lives. This collection draws attention to these attitudes and explores strategies NNESTs and writing programs can adopt to address them.

Across different fields, there have been multiple efforts to mitigate the challenges NNESTs face. One major shift, building on related work in world Englishes and English as a lingua franca scholarship, has been increased scholarship on English as an international language (EIL). EIL recognizes that English has become a global language that is not linked to a particular culture or social context, unlike a language such as Czech or Korean. Along those lines, any student of English should work on building intercultural competence so that they can use English in a variety of social contexts (McKay, 2018). Similarly, English teachers should be prepared to teach EIL, which has been the subject of another edited collection (Matsuda, 2017). One possibility is the development of a Global English course for teachers in training as described by Ali Faud Selvi (2017). This course helps future teachers recognize the diversity of English users, challenges native speaker privilege in ELT, and "problematizes the ownership of English" (p. 118). While not all programs may have a separate course in this area, they can also infuse these ideas and topics throughout teacher training programs.

Elsewhere, scholars have stressed the importance of helping students recognize the unique linguistic, cultural, and societal knowledge and contributions that NNESTs bring while also taking steps to boost students' ability to understand speakers of EIL (Aslan & Thompson, 2017; Bailey, 1983; Kang & Rubin, 2012; Timmis, 2002). For instance, in a very early study of student perceptions of ITAs at U.S. universities, Kathleen Bailey (1983) suggested student training in the form of "programs designed to help underclassmen deal with the diversity of people to be encountered in higher education" (310). Similarly, Aslan and Thompson (2017) emphasized the importance of raising students' awareness about the processes involved in language learning and the need to deemphasize and problematize labels like "native" and "nonnative" for students. Some, like Okim Kang and Donald Rubin (2012), have developed programs to boost students' comprehension of NNESTs.

Several scholars have provided focused recommendations to support NNEST ITAs that are particularly relevant to the discussions in the present collection—these were especially present in a special 2012 issue of the *Journal on Excellence in College Teaching* focused on supporting NNEST ITAs. A number of scholars in this issue and elsewhere have emphasized the importance of group or individualized mentoring opportunities for new ITAs (de Oliveira & Lan, 2012; DePew, 2006; Liu, 2005; Reis, 2012). For instance, Davi S. Reis (2012) has argued for the need of "meditational means and spaces both to externalize [NNESTs] everyday conceptualizations and, potentially, to internalize the available scientific knowledge and discourses about these concepts," noting that it is "essential that NNESTs working in various higher education institutions have a space where linguistic and cultural legitimacy issues can be acknowledged, expressed, and deconstructed by peers and supervisors" (p. 52). In a different form of mentoring, Liu (2005) suggested that new GTAs spend their first semester taking a teaching seminar and observing the classes they are to teach but hold off on teaching until at least their second semester.

Limited research into the experiences of NNES professionals teaching writing has begun to explore the multiple challenges these instructors face due to their NNES status, but this research has remained scant compared to the robust body of publications on NNEST issues in other fields. This may stem in part due to writing studies' history of being a U.S.-based field dominated by monolingual White scholars, compared to a field like TESOL, which has long been international and, by its very nature, included a large number of multilingual professionals. This separation means that a growing population of NNES writing teachers continue to face challenges and discrimination that remain largely unacknowledged in their workplaces and underexplored in research, even as the field has increasingly turned its eye to creating inclusive learning environments for multilingual students. Indeed, some of the chapters in this collection report on prejudices and challenges the authors faced that are dishearteningly similar to the ones described in much earlier literature within the NNEST movement in TESOL. Recently, there have been attempts to change the status quo with a few publications in well-known venues (e.g., Ruecker et al., 2018; Shehi, 2017; Youssef, 2023) and the establishment of the NNES Writing Instructors standing group at the 2015 Conference on College Composition and Communication. This growing group of NNES educators seeks to increase awareness of NNES writing instructors' presence and challenges across U.S. institutions and advocates for these instructors' rights in the face of possible bias and discrimination. However, more efforts are necessary to shift the discipline's attention towards its NNES members and support further research into the challenges they face and the resources they bring to the profession. This collection provides a better understanding of the experiences of NNESTs of writing and suggests multiple ways to promote programmatic and institutional change towards more equitable working conditions.

Collection Overview

This collection is the first publication of its kind situated within writing studies. Just as writing studies as a field has been historically U.S.-based, this collection focuses on the experiences of NNES teachers of writing working in the United States, where the majority of the authors of this collection teach and conduct research.

The themes of the chapters that follow often overlap and support each other; the thematic trajectory of the volume overall shifts the focus from the level of the individual to the communal and institutional issues. While the first few chapters explore NNES teacher identity in relation to issues of professionalization and growth, chapters in the middle of the collection focus more on student perceptions and teacher-student interactions. The last few chapters explore programmatic and institutional contexts and suggest ways writing programs can build support for NNES instructors' professional development. The chapters in this volume represent a variety of voices—from NNESs of diverse backgrounds to NESs and from established professors to relative newcomers in the profession, as well as a variety of methodological approaches ranging from mixed-methods research to autobiographical narratives and narrative inquiries.

In Chapter 2, Marcela Hebbard offers a look at teacher identity as she traces the professional identity construction of five NNES writing instructors over the course of two years. Drawing on Martha Pennington's (2002) identity framework as well as notions of subjectivity (Alsup, 2006), Hebbard's exploration focuses on three areas: the impact of previous educational experiences, the importance of social support when integrating into a new academic community, and the impact of rank and disciplinary divisions. In concluding comments, she makes recommendations for WPAs and the field more broadly, such as the importance of integrating the perspectives of NNESTs in mainstream research literature and recognizing NNESTs' potential as transnational literacy brokers in writing programs and classrooms.

Next, in Chapter 3, Su Yin Khor, Cristina Sánchez-Martín, Lisya Seloni, Mijan Rahman, and Demet Yiğitbilek use collaborative narrative inquiry to demonstrate how the institutional ecologies influence NNES instructors' multilayered identities. The five authors, who are at different stages in their academic careers, use identities-as-pedagogy framework (Motha et al., 2012) to demonstrate how writing programs can use NNES instructors' identities as resources in building translingual spaces at their institutions. The chapter also contributes to the studies on language learner identity that interrogate the interconnections between identity formation and institutional ecologies.

In the next chapter, "Nonnative Teacher of Writing Navigating Multiple Forms of Student Resistance," Nabila Hijazi, a Muslim NNES female instructor, describes her experiences as a "double minority" in U.S. academic culture. While some researchers have argued that NNES instructors are uniquely positioned to facilitate the recent turn towards "translingual dispositions" in writing studies as they possess heightened metalinguistic awareness and multifaceted rhetorical competence (Canagarajah, 2011; Horner et al.,

2011; Lee & Jenks, 2016; Lu & Horner, 2013), Hijazi's reflective study provides a useful, practice-oriented look at how NNES instructors can make their identity central in a pedagogy that seeks to question many of our students' preconceived notions about language, identity, and related power dynamics. In closing, she makes a strong argument for the increased use of reflective practice in writing studies as a teacher development tool while also describing ways that NNESTs can claim their authority as writing teachers.

In Chapter 5, Mariya Tseptsura reports the results of a year-long auto-ethnographic study that followed critical reflective inquiry approach and used a combination of classroom video recordings and reflective teaching journals. Tseptsura argues for the benefits of adopting this method for professional development for NNESTs on a wider scale. In her case, the results of the study highlight the challenges NNESTs face in constructing a legitimate professional authority (Pace & Hemmings, 2007) in the classroom and draw attention to how the limited types of authority available to NNESTs might exacerbate already existing conflicts between different cultural and ideological stances international teachers have to navigate.

The next chapter also addresses the question of teacher authority: the authors, Aleksandra Kasztalska and Michael Maune, apply Karl Maton's (2014) legitimation code theory to analyze professionalization paths of fifteen international NNES TAs teaching composition. Kasztalska and Maune's data suggest that within composition community, legitimation is often based on members' attributes (like being born a NES) and not on specialized knowledge. The authors also argue that to support ITAs and successfully challenge the native speaker fallacy, writing programs need to reframe composition as a knowledge code in which legitimacy and authority are based on learned skills and knowledge.

Chapter 7 shifts focus onto students' perceptions of their NNES instructors. Lan Wang-Hiles opens by describing the biases she faced as a foreign-born NNEST when taking over writing classes full of NESs mid-semester. This experience led to a mixed-methods study in which Wang-Hiles surveyed 71 of her students over the course of three semesters to investigate their acceptance levels of her linguistic and rhetorical skills, teaching styles and methods, and personal and cultural factors (following the design in Mahboob, 2004). Wang-Hiles explores the range of student attitudes towards her status as an NNES, from skepticism to appreciation. In addition to pedagogical recommendations for NNESTs, she calls for a joint effort by institutions, writing programs, and writing instructors to help make students aware that English is not the sole exclusive domain of native English speakers.

While a number of studies discussed above focused on students' perceptions of their NNES instructors, Wen Xin adopts a different angle in Chapter 8 and uses corpus analysis to explore NNES and NES instructors' perceptions of their students. Following Ken Hyland's (2005) conceptualization of metadiscourse, Xin analyzes instructors' written comments on their students' papers to shed light on instructors' relationships with students, their self-positioning in the classroom, and how NESTs and NNESTs may comment differently on their students' writing. In discussing the differences between NES and NNES instructors' comments, Xin offers suggestions for training and professional development programs, such as workshops that help NNES teachers comment more effectively on student writing while also developing strategies to deal with student resistance to their feedback.

In Chapter 9, Tamara Mae Roose, Min-Seok Choi, and Christopher E. Manion seek to reframe the familiar narratives of international teaching assistants (ITAs) struggling with teaching at U.S. universities. Drawing on interviews with three ITAs of writing, the authors analyzed how their participants responded to instances of uncertainty (defined as value-neutral moments where the lack of prior knowledge makes it difficult to predict the outcomes of a situation) and constructed them as opportunities for growth rather than obstacles to their professional success. In closing, they argue that WPAs should work to create spaces in which ITAs and TAs can share their lived experiences of teaching rather than rely on formal training; they also make recommendations for how ITAs can draw on their experience living and working in different cultures as an asset in their programs and classrooms.

In Chapter 10, Xin Chen explores the relationship between identity and professional development as she traces the evolution of teacher identity of six NNES teaching assistants who were teaching ESL academic writing and courses on their first language at the same time. Chen shows how teaching their first language and forming multiple peer support groups facilitated the NNES instructors' introduction into the new discourse community and profession. Chen concludes by emphasizing the importance of a focus on critical pedagogy and cross-cultural competence in classes and programs focused on writing teacher development for both NNESTs and NESTs while joining other authors in calling for increased collaboration among teachers.

In Chapter 11, Melinda Reichelt shares her perspective and expertise as a NES WPA who has trained both NES and NNES novice teachers to teach ESL writing for more than 17 years. Reichelt makes a number of recommendations to writing programs, including expanding TA preparation curriculum to focus explicitly on teaching L2 writing, fostering equality between NES and NNES teachers, and providing in-depth training on issues of language diversity. The chapter offers a detailed account of successful teacher training course designs and mentorship programs that followed such recommendations.

In Chapter 12, Anastasiia Kryzhanivska and Tetyana Bychkovska draw on their experiences developing their teacher identities during graduate studies and in their subsequent experiences teaching at different universities. In the form of a reflective narrative, they detail the experiences that contributed to their sense of confidence and preparedness for teaching academic writing, focusing in particular on the following: pre-service training, tutoring writing and training tutors, observing other teachers, collaboration and mentoring, gaining experience in the classroom, and additional professional development.

Finally, in the Afterword, we offer some reflections on the labor that went into the publication of this collection and what this long process has taught us about the current state of our field.

References

Alsup, J. (2005). *Teacher identity discourses: Negotiating personal and professional spaces.* Routledge.

Amin, N. (1997). Race and the identity of the nonnative ESL teacher. *TESOL Quarterly, 31,* 580–583. https://doi.org/10.2307/3587841.

Aslan, E. & Thompson, A. S. (2017). Are they really "two different species"? Implicitly elicited student perceptions about NESTs and NNESTs. *TESOL Journal, 8*(2), 277–294. https://doi.org/10.1002/tesj.268.

Atkinson, D., Crusan, D., Matsuda, P. K., Ortmeier-Hooper, C., Ruecker, T., Simpson, S. & Tardy, C. (2015). Clarifying the relationship between L2 writing and translingual writing: An open letter to writing studies editors and organization leaders. *College English, 77*(4), 383–386.

Bailey, K. (1983). Foreign teaching assistants at U.S. universities: Problems in interaction and communication. *TESOL Quarterly, 17*(2), 308–310. https://doi.org/10.2307/3586658.

Benke, E. & Medgyes, P. (2005). Differences in teaching behaviour between native and non-native speaker teachers: As seen by the learners. In E. Llurda (Ed.), *Non-native language teachers* (pp. 195–215). Springer.

Brady, B. (2018). NNEST Caucus/Interest Section of the TESOL International Association. *The TESOL encyclopedia of English language teaching,* 1–7. https://doi.org/10.1002/9781118784235.eelt0036.

Braine, G. (1999). *Non-native educators in English language teaching.* Lawrence Erlbaum Associates.

Brutt-Griffler, J. & Samimy, K. K. (2001). Transcending the nativeness paradigm. *World Englishes, 20*(1), 99–106. https://doi.org/10.1111/1467-971X.00199.

Canagarajah, A. S. (2006). The place of World Englishes in composition: Pluralization continued. *College Composition and Communication, 57*(4), 586–619. https://www.jstor.org/stable/20456910.

Canagarajah, A. S. (Ed.). (2013). *Literacy as translingual practice: Between communities and classrooms*. Routledge.

Connor, U. (1999). Learning to write academic prose in a second language: A literacy autobiography. In G. Braine (Ed.), *Non-native educators in English language teaching* (pp. 29–42). Lawrence Erlbaum Associates.

Cook, V. (1999). Going beyond the native speaker in language teaching. *TESOL quarterly, 33*(2), 185–209. https://doi.org/10.2307/3587717.

Crowley, S. (1998). *Composition in the university: Historical and polemical essays*. University of Pittsburgh Press.

Davies, A. (1991). *The native speaker in applied linguistics*. Edinburgh University Press.

de Oliveira, L. & Lan, S. (2012). Preparing nonnative English-speaking (NNES) graduate students for teaching in higher education: A mentoring case study. *Journal on Excellence in College Teaching, 23*(3), 59–76.

DePew, K. E. (2006). Different writers, different writing: Preparing international teaching assistants for instructional literacy. In P. K. Matsuda, C. Ortmeier-Hooper & X. You (Eds.), *The politics of second language writing* (pp. 168–187). Parlor Press.

Garcia de Müeller, G. I. & Ruiz, I. D. (2017). Race, silence, and writing program administration: A qualitative study of U.S. college writing programs. *WPA: Writing Program Administration, 40*(3), 19–39.

Horner, B., Lu, M., Royster, J. & Trimbur, J. (2011). Language difference in writing: Toward a translingual approach. *College English, 73*(3), 303–321. https://www.jstor.org/stable/25790477.

Horner, B. & Tetreault, L. (Eds.). (2017). *Crossing divides: Exploring translingual writing pedagogies and programs*. University Press of Colorado.

Horner, B. & Trimbur, J. (2002). English only and U.S. college composition. *College Composition and Communication, 53*(4), 594–630. https://doi.org/10.2307/1512118.

Huang, I. (2018). Power and ownership within the NS/NNS dichotomy. In B. Yazan & N. Rudolph (Eds.), *Criticality, teacher identity, and (in) equity in English language teaching* (pp. 41–56). Springer.

Hyland, K. (2005). *Metadiscourse: Exploring interaction in writing*. Continuum.

Kachru, B. (1986). *The alchemy of English: The spread, functions, and models of non-native Englishes*. Pergamon.

Kamhi-Stein, L. (2004). *Learning and teaching from experience: Perspectives on nonnative English-speaking professionals*. University of Michigan Press.

Kamhi-Stein, L. D. (2016). The non-native English speaker teachers in TESOL movement. *ELT Journal, 70*(2), 180–189. https://doi.org/10.1093/elt/ccv076.

Kang, O. & Rubin, D. L. (2012). Intergroup contact exercises as a tool for mitigating undergraduates' attitudes toward nonnative English-speaking teaching assistants. *Journal on Excellence in College Teaching, 23*(3), 159–166.

Kramsch, C. (1997). The privilege of the nonnative speaker. *PMLA, 112*(3), 359–369.

Lee, J. & Jenks, C. (2016). Doing translingual dispositions. *College Composition and Communication, 68*(2), 317–344. https://www.jstor.org/stable/44783564.

Lengeling, M. & Pablo, I. M. (2012). A critical discourse analysis of advertisements: Inconsistencies of our EFL profession. In R. Roux (Ed.), *Research in English language teaching: Mexican perspectives* (pp. 91–105). West Bow Press.

Lipovsky, C. & Mahboob, A. (2010). Appraisal of native and non-native English speaking teachers. In A. Mahboob (Ed.), *The NNEST lens: Non-native English speakers in TESOL*, (pp. 154–179). Cambridge Scholars Publishing.

Liu, J. (2005). Chinese graduate teaching assistants teaching freshman composition to native English-speaking students. In Llurda, E. (Ed.), *Non-native language teachers: Perceptions, challenges, and contributions to the profession* (pp. 155–177). Springer.

Llurda, E. & Huguet, N. (2003). Self-awareness in NNS EFL primary and secondary school teachers. *Language Awareness, 12*(3–4), 220–233.

Losey, K. & Shuck, G. (Eds.). (2021). *Plurilingual pedagogies for multilingual writing classrooms.* Taylor and Francis.

Lu, M.-Z. & Horner, B. (2013). Translingual literacy, language difference, and matters of agency. *College English, 75*(6), 582–607.

Ma, L.P. F. (2012). Advantages and disadvantages of native- and nonnative-English-speaking teachers: Student perceptions in Hong Kong. *TESOL Quarterly, 46*(2), 280–305. https://doi.org/10.1002/tesq.21.

Mahboob, A. (2003). *Status of nonnative English-speaking teachers in the United States* [Unpublished doctoral dissertation]. Indiana University, Bloomington.

Mahboob, A. (2004). Native or non-native? What do students enrolled in an intensive English program think? In Kamhi-Stein, L. (Ed.), *Learning and teaching from experience: Perspectives on nonnative English-speaking professionals* (pp. 121–148). University of Michigan Press.

Mahboob, A. (2010). *The NNEST lens: Non-native English speakers in TESOL.* Cambridge Scholars Publishing.

Martinez, A, Y. (2014). A plea for critical race theory counterstory: Stock story versus counterstory dialogues concerning Alejandra's "fit" in the academy. *Composition Studies, 42*(2), 33–55. https://www.jstor.org/stable/43501855.

Matsuda, A. (Ed.). (2017). *Preparing teachers to teach English as an international language.* Multilingual Matters.

Matsuda, P. K. (1999). Composition studies and ESL writing: A disciplinary division of labor. *College Composition and Communication, 50*(4), 699–721. https://doi.org/10.2307/358488.

Matsumoto Y. (2018). Teachers' identities as "non-native" speakers: Do they matter in English as a lingua franca interactions?. In B. Yazan & N. Rudolph (Eds.), *Criticality, teacher identity, and (in) equity in English language teaching* (pp. 57–79). Springer https://doi.org/10.1007/978-3-319-72920-6_4.

McKay, S. L. (2018). English as an international language: What it is and what it means for pedagogy. *RELC Journal, 49*(1), 9–23. https://doi.org/10.1177/0033688217738817.

Medgyes, P. (1994). *The non-native teacher.* Macmillan.

Miller, S. (1991). *Textual carnivals: The politics of composition.* Southern Illinois University Press.

Motha, S., Jain, R. & Tecle, T. (2012). Translinguistic identity-as-pedagogy: Implications for language teacher education. *International Journal of Innovation in English Language Teaching and Research, 1(1)*, 13–28.

Moussu, L. & Llurda, E. (2008). Non-native English-speaking English language teachers: History and research. *Language Teaching, 41*(3), 315–348. https://doi.org/10.1017/S0261444808005028.

Pace, J. L. & Hemmings, A. (2007). Understanding authority in classrooms: A review of theory, ideology, and research. *Review of Educational Research, 77*(1), 4–27. https://doi.org/10.3102/003465430298489.

Pacek, D. (2005). "Personality not nationality": Foreign students' perceptions of a non-native speaker lecturer of English at a British university. In E. Llurda (Ed.), *Non-native language teachers: Perceptions, challenges and contributions to the profession* (pp. 243–262). Springer.

Pennington, M. C. (2002, October 18). *Teacher identity in TESOL* [Paper presented]. Quality in Teacher Education Seminar, London, UK.

Pennycook, A. (1994). *The cultural politics of English as an international language.* Longman.

Phillipson, R. (1992). *Linguistic imperialism.* Oxford University Press.

Ramjattan, V. A. (2015). Lacking the right aesthetic: Everyday employment discrimination in Toronto private language schools. *Equality, Diversity and Inclusion: An International Journal, 34*(8), 692–704. https://doi.org/10.1108/EDI-03-2015-0018.

Reis, D. S. (2012). "Being underdog": Supporting nonnative English-speaking teachers (NNESTs) in claiming and asserting professional legitimacy. *Journal on Excellence in College Teaching, 23*(3).

Reves, T. & Medgyes, P. (1994). The non-native English speaking EFL/ESL teacher's self image: An international survey. *System, 22*(3), 353–357.

Rose, S. & Weiser, I. (Eds.). (2018). *The internationalization of U.S. writing programs.* Utah State University Press.

Royster, J. & Williams, J. (1999). History in the spaces left: African American presence and narratives of composition studies. *College Composition and Communication, 50*(4), 563–584. https://doi.org/10.2307/358481.

Rubin, D. L. (1992). Nonlanguage factors affecting undergraduates' judgments of nonnative English-speaking teaching assistants. *Research in Higher Education, 33*(4), 511–531. https://doi.org/10.1007/BF00973770.

Ruecker, T., Frazier, S. & Tseptsura, M. (2018). "Language difference can be an asset": Exploring the experiences of nonnative English-speaking teachers of writing. *College Composition and Communication, 69*(4), 612–641. https://www.jstor.org/stable/44870978.

Ruecker, T. & Ives, L. (2014). White native English speakers needed: The rhetorical construction of privilege in online teacher recruitment spaces. *TESOL Quarterly, 49*(4), 733–756. https://doi.org/10.1002/tesq.195.

Samimy, R. & Brutt-Griffler, J. (1999). To be a native or nonnative speaker: Perceptions of "nonnative" students in a graduate TESOL program. In G. Braine (Ed.), *Nonnative educators in English language teaching* (pp. 127–144). Lawrence Erlbaum Associates.

Selvi, A. F. (2010). All Teachers are equal, but some teachers are more equal than others: Trend analysis of job advertisements in English language teaching. *WATESOL NNEST Caucus Annual Review, 1*, 156–181.

Selvi, A. F. (2017). Preparing teachers to teach English as an international language: Eeflections from northern Cyprus. In A. Matsuda (Ed.), *Preparing teachers to teach English as an international language* (pp. 114–128). Multilingual Matters.

Shapiro, S. (2022). *Cultivating critical language awareness in the writing classroom*. Routledge.

Shapiro, S. & Leonard, R. L. (2023). Introduction to the special issue: Critical Language Awareness (CLA) as a lens for looking backward, outward, and forward in Second Language Writing. *Journal of Second Language Writing, 60*.

Shehi, M. (2017). Why is my English teacher a foreigner? Re-authoring the story of international composition teachers. *Teaching English in the Two-Year College, 44*(3), 260–275.

Sledd, J. (1969). Bi-dialectalism: The linguistics of White supremacy. *English Journal, 58*(9), 1307–1315. https://doi.org/10.2307/811913.

Smitherman, G. (1977). *Talkin and testifyin: The language of Black America*. Houghton Mifflin.

Smitherman, G. (1995). "Students' right to their own language": A retrospective. *The English Journal, 84*(1), 21–27. https://doi.org/10.2307/820470.

Tardy, C. M. (2017). Crossing, or creating divides? A plea for transdisciplinary scholarship. In B. Horner & L. Tetreault (Eds.), *Crossing divides: Exploring translingual writing pedagogies and programs* (pp. 181–189). Utah State University Press.

Tatar, S. & Yildiz, S. (2010). Empowering nonnative-English speaking teachers in the classroom. In A. Mahboob (Ed.), *The NNEST lens: Non-native English speakers in TESOL* (pp. 114–128). Cambridge Scholars Publishing.

TESOL (2006). Position statement against discrimination of Nonnative speakers of English in the field of TESOL. https://www.tesol.org/media/d2gfeisk/position-statement-against-nnest-discrimination-march-2006-1.pdf.

Thomas, J. (1999). Voices from the periphery: Non-native teachers and issues of credibility. In G. Braine (Ed.), *Non-native educators in English language teaching* (pp. 5–14). Lawrence Erlbaum Associates.

Timmis, I. (2002). Native-speaker norms and international English: A classroom view. *ELT Journal, 56*(3), 240–249.

Villanueva Jr., V. (1993). *Bootstraps: From an American academic of color*. National Council of Teachers of English.

Widdowson, H. (1994). The ownership of English. *TESOL Quarterly, 28*(2), 377–389. https://doi.org/10.2307/3587438.

Yazan, B. & Rudolph, N. (Eds.). (2018). *Criticality, teacher identity, and (in)equity in English language teaching*. Springer.

Yosso, T., Smith, W., Ceja, M. & Solórzano, D. (2009). Critical race theory, racial microaggressions, and campus racial climate for Latina/o undergraduates. *Harvard Educational Review, 79*(4), 659–691. https://doi.org/10.17763/haer.79.4.m6867014157m7071.

Youssef, S. (2023). International teaching assistants' needs and undergraduate native English-speaking students' expectations: Meaning negotiation as a rhetorical strategy. In W. J. Macauley, Jr., L. R. Anglesey, B. Edwards, K. M. Lambrecht & P. K. Lovas (Eds.), *Threshold conscripts: Rhetoric and composition teaching assistantships (pp. 239–266)*. The WAC Clearinghouse; University Press of Colorado. https://doi.org/10.37514/PER-B.2023.1626.

2 Constructing a Professional Identity: Nonnative English-Speaking Teachers in First-Year Writing Courses

Marcela Hebbard
UNIVERSITY OF TEXAS RIO GRANDE VALLEY

Research on nonnative English-speaking teacher (NNEST) identity has been well-documented in the fields of second language acquisition (SLA) and TESOL (Cheung et al., 2015; De Costa & Norton, 2017; Tsui, 2007; Varghese et al., 2016; Yuan, 2018; Zhang & Zhang, 2015). On writing teachers' professional identity development, a body of research has grown in the "symbiotic field" of second language (L2) writing (Kim & Saenkhum, 2019; I. Lee, 2013; Racelis & Matsuda, 2015; Sánchez-Martín & Seloni, 2019). In mainstream composition, however, research on NNESTs' identities remains underexplored despite the fact that the number of nonnative English-speaking teachers of writing is increasing (Ruecker et al., 2018; Zheng, 2017)—I am one of them.[1] There are at least three contributing factors for this under exploration. First, the history of the notion of identity in composition scholarship is elusive because various concepts such as "self" and "representation" have been used to refer to writer identity (Cox et al., 2010). Second, while issues related to L2 writing have been acknowledged and received by the field, in practice, they are still perceived as special interest issues (Matsuda, 2012). Third, a raciolinguistic bias which assumes that faculty who teach college writing in English are linguistically and racially homogeneous is still prevalent (Alim et al., 2016; Geller, 2011; Martinez, 2020; Ruiz & Sánchez, 2016). Thus, to advance scholarship in this area, this chapter reports on a qualitative study that began as a graduate thesis work and extended two years after graduation that investigated

---

[1] In this work, NNESTs are individuals who either grew up speaking languages other than English at home, are Generation 1.5 (immigrant students who came to the US as children or adolescents), international visa students, or naturalized citizens (Matsuda, 2011). I am a Mexican-born Hispanic woman and U.S. citizen by paper (Viera, 2016). English is my additional language and has become my dominant academic language. I began learning it in Mexico City at the age of 13. I emigrated to the US as a visa international student at the age of 23.

factors that contribute to NNESTs' professional identity construction in FYW courses. Results suggest that in order to develop and sustain a professional teacher identity, NNESTs of writing should achieve and maintain an alignment between the personal subjectivity and the cultural expectations of the profession, as well as to develop an openness and awareness to disciplinary identity reinvention. These findings are important because they can elucidate a better understanding of NNESTs of writing professional identity formation. For writing programs that employ NNESTs, the findings can assist in developing initiatives that help sustain their professional identities. And for NNESTs themselves, these findings shed light on the different factors that can help or hinder the development and balance of a professional identity.

Conceptual Framework and Literature Review

Operational Definition of "Professional Identity" in Composition

Defining "professional identity" within mainstream composition studies is challenging because the field has become highly interdisciplinary, many different theories and approaches come from areas inside and outside English studies (Fulkerson, 2005; Matsuda, 2012). As a result, teachers of writing from disciplines outside composition may develop a professional identity that aligns more with their community of practice (e.g., education, sociology, literature) (Wenger, 1998). Nonetheless, in 2013, *College Composition and Communication* published a special issue that explored what *profession* means to those of us in writing studies. The collection contains six vignettes and four empirical articles. While only one article explicitly investigated the concept of professional identity and suggested that teaching writing at a two-year college is a related but different profession than teaching at a four-year university (Toth et al., 2013), most of the individual narratives offer insights of the variegated lived experiences within the profession. For example, Ethna Dempsey Lay (2013) shared how her professional identity as a writing instructor was questioned by some colleagues who did not see her journey as legitimate because she was a Wall Street employee by day, graduate student by night, and part-time writing instructor before fully embracing academia. Kate Pantelides (2013), on the other hand, wrote about having a hyphenated identity where "mother" preceded her identity as teacher of writing, and Cruz Medina (2013) noted how welcoming his first child gave him a new understanding of the value of professionalism in the teaching of writing.

When read as a whole, this special issue highlights how the profession raises and complicates career expectations for its members (Hesse, 2013), and how our professional identities are always in contact with other subjectivities (Pantelides, 2013), but it does not address the concerns and issues related to NNESTs' construction of their professional identities. To expand our understanding of NNESTs identity construction, we draw on scholarship in the field of English language teaching.

In second language acquisition as well as allied fields, research on nonnative English language teachers has materialized since the 1990s (Braine, 1999; Moussu & Llurda, 2008). Most studies, however, have centered around "(non)nativism," that is, "whether a teacher identifies (or is identified by others) as a native-speaker (NEST) or nonnative speaker (NNEST)" (Ellis, 2016, p. 597) despite the fact that language is only one aspect of one's identity (Motha et al., 2012). Fortunately, research published in recent years has begun to explicitly expand beyond linguistic identity to include class, gender, privilege, emotions, and race in teacher identity work (Appleby, 2016; Charles, 2019; Ruecker & Ives, 2015; Varghese et al., 2016). Not that these issues were not present before, they were. Jacinta Thomas (1999), for example, wrote about how as a nonnative English teacher in Canada, she faced issues of credibility related to race, gender, and her Indian-accented English. However, although race and gender are mentioned in Thomas' piece, they are not salient concepts as language is.

In TESOL and the broader field of applied linguistics it is now accepted that "a teacher's identity cannot be viewed as the aggregation of a set of innate, acquired or ascribed attributes, but should be conceptualized as a socially constructed, contextually situated and continually emerging (and changing) sense of self that is influenced by myriad factors" (Cheung et al., 2014, p. 18). From this perspective, a teacher's identity is fluid and among the factors that constitute such identity is the integration of the personal and professional levels.

In this work, a professional identity refers to the complex ways NNES writing faculty build, interpret, position, negotiate and enact their multiple roles as teachers-scholars in manners consonant with the constantly evolving professional structures and projections of the discipline itself at the macro, meso, and micro levels, and how these roles interact, influence, conflict, challenge, intersect, shape, and/or connect with their other subjectivities. In short, constructing a professional identity requires balancing one's personal subjectivities against the cultural expectations of the profession (Cheung et al., 2014; The Douglas Fir Group, 2016).

Defining Personal Subjectivity

Personal subjectivity originally refers to the incorporation of the various identity strands that make up the self with other personal subjectivities or ideologies (e.g., students, family, peers, even internal dialogues) through discourse (Alsup, 2006). The goal of engaging in dialogue is not to reach consensus among subjectivities, but coexistence. In this work, I use the term to refer to the various moments a NNES writing instructor realizes it is okay to acknowledge their translinguistic histories and pedagogical ideologies and see not only their linguistic identity but also other subjectivities such as racial, ethnic, religious, and gender as positive contributions to the profession even when tensions and discomfort occur.

The concept "translinguistic histories" refers to how our life experiences, including our linguistic and social identities, interact with our pedagogical practices (Motha et al., 2012). In other words, who we become as teachers is a function of the life-stories we bring to the profession. While all teachers have translinguistic histories, there are differences between NES and NNES teachers (Motha et al., 2012). NNESTs, in comparison with NES, undergo complex cognitive processes for developing proficiency in an additional language which allows them to develop translinguistic identities. By traversing between languages, NNESTs draw on a broader range of concepts and interpretative frames that ultimately impact their pedagogical practice and their understanding of their relationship to the world (Norton, 2013). Therefore, recognizing that something more than language skills is at play in constructing a professional identity is imperative. Mariya Tseptsura's (this volume) autoethnography demonstrates these connections. She shows how her identity was shaped by her educational background and how it manifests itself in her teaching practices and shapes the relations of power in the classroom.

The Cultural Expectations of the Profession

The cultural expectations of the profession refer to the attitudes and beliefs, knowledge, and skills the discipline expects writing specialists to embody in the everyday context of their classrooms and in the interactions with the different stakeholders such as students, administrators, and colleagues (Pennington, 2015). These cultural expectations are in constant contact with the personal, forcing NNESTs to continually (re)organize themselves and to co-create their professional identities (Kim & Saenkhum, 2019). However, because identities are complex and fluid lived experiences (Block, 2007; Norton, 2000, 2013; Norton Peirce, 1995), an alignment between the personal and the cultural expectations is never neutral or permanent once it happens. Instead, this alignment constantly shifts in different degrees and assumes reflection, tension, and constant negotiation with the macro (societal) and meso (institutional), context (The Douglas Fir Group, 2016).

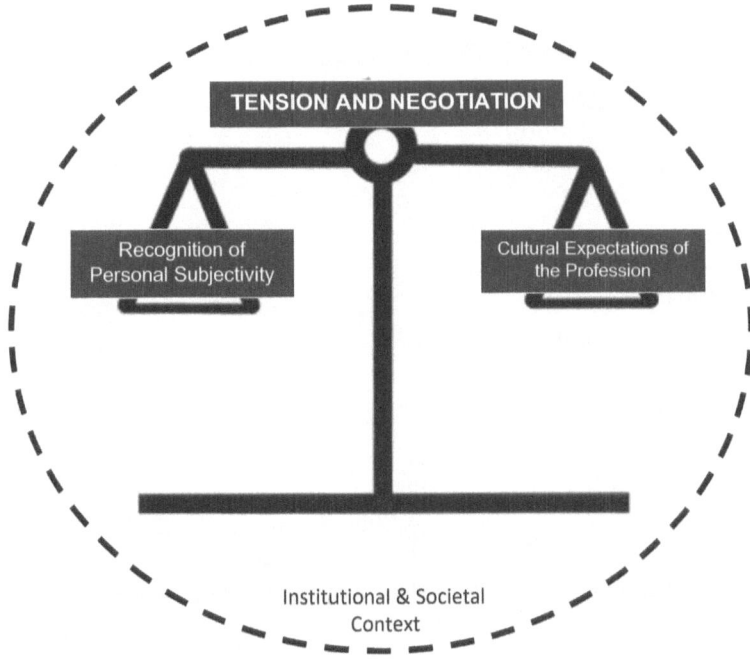

Figure 2.1. A Balanced Professional Teacher Identity[2]

A figure that helps to represent this synergy is a double-pan scale. The components of the scale are a base, a pivoted horizontal lever with arms of equal length and two weighing pans attached to each arm (see Figure 2.1). For the scale to work properly, the pivoted horizontal lever needs to be centered. While a scale rests at neutral, once an object is placed on either pan, to find and maintain balance, objects must be added on the other pan until equilibrium is achieved and the pans level off. The dotted line represents the influence of the institutional and societal context.

In this illustration, imbalance will occur when the cultural expectations of the profession pan is heavier than the personal subjectivity pan and/or the pivoted horizontal lever is misaligned thus creating unequal tension or negotiation. In other words, when NNESTs of writing suppress, ignore, neglect or are denied embodying their translinguistic identities, imbalance will happen. This imbalance can manifest itself in various negative ways. For instance, if NNESTs make their linguistic identity their sole identity-marker, they may

---

2   I conceptualized the scale for my thesis work which reflects my understanding of identity then (Hebbard, 2012). In this work, I revised the scale and added the dotted line to point out that both the personal and professional identities function and interact within specific sociocultural, historical, and ecological contexts.

constantly question their professional and pedagogical qualifications and unintentionally reinforce for themselves (and for their students) the native vs nonnative stereotypes. An unbalanced scale can also prevent or block engaging in effective negotiation skills. In extreme cases, a decision to opt out of the profession can also happen (Alsup, 2006).

In contrast, when NNESTs recognize their translinguistic histories as a strength, they can deploy alternate identities that challenge, complicate, counter, or problematize commonly held assumptions about what it means to be an NNEST of writing which can help maintain a more balanced professional identity. Nabila Hijazi (this volume) offers a narrative that serves as a positive example of what happens when NNESTs translinguistic histories are recognized as a strength.

On the other hand, when the individual aspect is overemphasized, a cultural disconnection with the profession might result and can affect performance in the classroom ultimately inhibiting not only the development of a professional identity but also student learning. A study on eight white and monolingual pre-service high school teachers in Australia exemplifies this point. The study showed that when participants assumed their privileged cultural, ethnic, and linguistic positions uncritically, they marginalized their multilingual students and negatively impacted their learning (Santoro, 2009). Another study on non-White and multilingual faculty revealed similar findings. The study investigated ESL tertiary students' writing attitude and the learning problems they faced in a writing course at a university in Malaysia (Ismail et al., 2012).[3] Findings indicated that the multilingual writing instructors perceived the multilingual students' writing and language skills as deficient.

When looking at these studies through the professional identity scale, one can argue that when NESTs and NNESTs alike place their own subjectivities above their students and fail to interrogate their own variegated subjectivities (e.g., ethnic, gender, racial, religious, and linguistic assumptions), they are at risk of neglecting the cultural expectations of the profession that calls for an ethical treatment of all students' agencies (Silva, 1997). In sum, a balance between the personal subjectivity and the cultural expectations of the profession ought to exist to (re)construct or (re)invent and maintain a balanced professional identity scale. Achieving this balance requires that NNESTs develop critical awareness of their translinguistic histories, position their pedagogies in the richly relevant and complex context of their own lives, and interact with stakeholders within their specific institutional and social location.

---

3   The authors do not provide background information of the lecturers in their article. I emailed the authors who replied stating that all four instructors are NNES.

Study Description

This qualitative study began in 2011 as a graduate thesis work in a mid-size university located along the Mexico/U.S. border where more than 80% of enrolled students are Hispanic. My interest in conducting this research arose from my personal experience. Having taught ESL for thirteen years, I felt very comfortable teaching *in* English *the* English language. However, when I was hired as a TA to teach freshman English composition, I suddenly felt insecure and questioned *my identity* as a teacher. Since there were other non-native English-speaking instructors in the first-year writing program, I wonder if they too have gone through similar experiences. Four female lecturers who self-identified as NNES and who hold MAESL degrees accepted to participate. The questions investigated were: How do nonnative speakers of English teaching composition classes develop a professional identity? How do they view their role as teachers? And how do their students perceive them? Data collection from instructors included class observations, semi structured interviews, and a questionnaire. Student data included a survey administered at the end of the semester.

Two years later I returned to the same university. I wanted to follow up with participants and investigate whether their respective professional identity scale had suffered any shifts. Upon inquiring, I learned that three of the participants had left the institution and moved out of the area; one of them had left the profession entirely. Only one of the original four participants remained. I contacted her and requested an interview. She accepted.

In order to expand the first study, I invited two new participants, a newly hired Hispanic NNES female instructor with a Ph.D. in rhetoric and composition and the recently appointed White male writing program administrator (WPA) who self-identified as English monolingual and he/his/him pronouns. The purpose of interviewing the Ph.D. instructor was to explore whether disciplinary background, degree, and rank play a role in how NNESTs develop a professional identity. My interest in interviewing the WPA was to learn about his experience working with NNESs teaching composition, his perceptions on them, and the kind of support, if any, the program offers them. Both of them agreed to participate. In comparison with the first study, I did not conduct class observations or collect a questionnaire from the female instructor. I only carried out individual semi-structured interviews using the same protocol from the previous study. Each of the interviews lasted over an hour.

To analyze previously collected and new interview data, I used an In Vivo coding approach. This approach allows me to prioritize and honor the participant's voice (Saldaña, 2016). I coded each participant's narrative separately twice and identified essential elements such as specific situations, memories, reflections, or interactions that assisted, challenged, or hindered their construction of their professional identities in FYW courses. Codes were then clustered according to similarity and regularity. After that, the clusters were combined into categories that resulted into three major themes. I refer to these themes as factors impacting NNESTs' professional identity construction which are: the impact of prior educational experiences, the impact of social support; and the impact of rank and disciplinary knowledge.

Participants' Description

The information in Table 2.1 provides a snapshot of the participants' backgrounds. It shows that most participants began acquiring English as children and have used it alongside their native languages. For three participants, English is their third or fourth language. Participants are from different ethnic and linguistic groups. Two participants are Generation 1.5, they arrived in the US as children and three arrived as international visa graduate students. Three participants have previous teaching experience in an area other than writing and two have undergraduate studies in disciplines outside English studies. All participants worked as TAs in the writing program for a year while pursuing their respective master's degrees.

The participants' backgrounds are rich and diverse, therefore, analyzing their experiences is important because they can shed light on ways NNESTs of writing (re)construct their professional identities.

Findings and Discussion

Before discussing results obtained for this study, I will summarize the findings from the original study. This information can assist the reader to better understand later on the discussion about the factors impacting the construction of a professional identity of the participants. Data analysis from the first study showed that Priscilla and Michelle had balanced professional identities, albeit that balance was being challenged due to changes in their personal subjectivities. Anita had a tilted scale where more of the weight had fallen on the cultural expectations of the profession. She was contemplating leaving the profession. For Rielle, results suggested her professional identity scale was going through a period of tension and negotiation. She reported she still had a hard time relating to students' experiences in writing courses (Hebbard, 2012). Andrea is the new participant. Next, I discuss the first factor.

Table 2.1. Participants' Backgrounds

Characteristics	Rielle	Priscilla	Anita	Michelle	Andrea
Rank	Lecturer	Lecturer	Lecturer	Lecturer	Associate Professor
Area/Country of Origin	European France	Slovenia	Japan	Overseas French Département	México
Languages spoken	French, English, and Spanish	Slovenian, English, and Italian	English and Japanese	French, Creole, English, Spanish, and Japanese	English and Spanish
Age they began learning English	11 years old	10 years old	12 years old	—	10 years old
Arrived in the US	As a graduate student	As a graduate student	With her parents at age 16	As a graduate student	With her parents at age 8
Academic Background Undergraduate (UG)	MA in Literature (earned in native country) MAESL	UG in Geography (earned in native country) MAESL	UG in English MAESL	UG in business (earned in native country) MAESL	UG in English MA in English Ph.D. Rhet & Comp
Years as TA	1 year	1 year	1 year	1 year	1 year
Previous teaching experience before becoming a TA	None	Taught ESL in private school for three years in her home country	Student-teacher in a local high school	Taught French in Ireland and U.K. to students with psychological problems	Student-teacher in a local high school

Factor 1: The Impact of Prior Educational Experiences

When asked about life experiences that influenced their self-perceptions as composition teachers, all five referred to prior educational experiences, corroborating previous research (Racelis & Matsuda, 2015). However, the analysis revealed that how they perceive these educational experiences either helps balance or destabilize their personal subjectivities. Michelle mentioned that teaching students with psychological issues in Ireland and the UK taught her that facing difficult situations in the classroom is not tied to her nonnativeness. She expressed, "I could be a native English speaker and still have challenging situations with students." She saw this experience as a positive contribution to balancing her sense of self as a writing teacher. In contrast, for Priscilla and Rielle, it was the lack of specific educational experiences that impacted their subjectivities. Both noted that in their native countries, there is no college class solely focused on teaching writing. This lack made it extremely difficult for them to understand the purpose of teaching composition, even after taking the required graduate class to become a TA in composition. They viewed writing as an integral element of any subject.

While other researchers have reported similar experiences (Park, 2012; Zheng, 2017), Priscilla and Rielle's respective experiences raise important considerations about the intersection between learning and NNESTs' identity formation. Ambrose and colleagues (2010) have defined learning as "a process that leads to change, which occurs as a result of experience" (p. 3). The principle of prior knowledge is part of this process. The authors wrote:

> Students come into our courses with knowledge, beliefs, and attitudes gained in *other courses and through life*. If students' prior knowledge is robust and accurate and activated at the appropriate time, it provides a strong foundation for building new knowledge. However, when knowledge is inert, insufficient for the task, activated inappropriately, or inaccurate, it can interfere with or impede new learning (p. 4). (Emphasis mine).

In this context, we can assume that Rielle and Priscilla did not arrive in the US as blank slates. They entered the required graduate class with robust knowledge about writing, including perceptions, models, and values acquired in their native countries. They viewed writing not as a compartmentalized skill but as an integrated aspect throughout the university curriculum. As graduate students in the US, they were expected to reverse this order. Whether their prior knowledge was accurately or sufficiently activated is unknown, but the data in this study implies that not having where to anchor their educational experiences created an imbalance in their personal subjectivity pan.

When I interviewed Rielle for the first study, the results suggested her identity scale was going through a period of tension and negotiation. Two years later, she mentioned that she had recently realized that what she had taught in the U.S. writing classroom was being studied by students in her country of origin in high school. Through 'doing,' she was making connections and building new understandings of the teaching and functions of writing. While developing a professional identity through doing is not unique to NNESTs (Ibarra, 1999), Rielle and Priscilla's experiences highlight the need to continue integrating assignments at the curricular level that not only appropriately activate NNES TAs' prior knowledge and experiences with writing but also raise their awareness to perceive their transnational and multilingual identities (Sánchez-Martín, 2020), and mobile literacies (Lorimer Leonard, 2017), as positive contributions in their professional identity formation. One possibility is the use of a transnational literacy autobiography assignment (Canagarajah, 2020).

For Andrea and Anita, it was their educational experiences in the US that impacted their sense of self, yet in opposite ways. In fifth grade, Andrea's non-Spanish speaking teacher encouraged her to speak Spanish at home and to conduct research in Spanish. But, in seventh grade, her English teacher told her parents she would never earn an "A" in English class. These experiences made her question her abilities as a writer and as an English language learner. While she initially saw these as negative experiences, upon reflection, she determined these experiences resulted in a positive outcome. The personal experiences with language difference as a child influenced her current pedagogical approaches in the teaching of writing as well as her research interests.

Anita said she came to the US at the age of 16 and enrolled in high school. She did not like high school and cried almost every day. She was placed in an ESL class where most students came from Mexico and did not have a problem communicating with each other. After graduation from high school, her family returned to Japan, but she decided to stay. She enrolled in the local university and was placed in the remedial English class because she failed the writing part of the THEA test. Reflecting on her experience, she said that if she had been taught the new curriculum she was currently teaching, she believed she would have done much better as an undergraduate student.

Research has shown that classroom environments play a prominent role in the identity formation of language minority students for better or for worse (Harklau, 2000). Andrea and Anita's respective educational experiences attest to this. Andrea's lived experience suggests that having a teacher that did not label her as a perpetual L2 learner of English but who encouraged her to engage in translanguaging, the ability to shuttle between languages (Garcia & Kleyn, 2016), helped her to counter the negative impact she experienced in 7th grade.

Conversely, Anita's compelling experience speaks about the social dimension of the classroom. Sociolinguists have observed that ethnicity and linguistic features are resources used by speakers to construct their social identities. That is, among ethnic groups where a choice of language is available for communication, individuals will choose the language that resonates with their ethnicity and social networks (Holmes, 2013). In Anita's class all the students were considered ESL, but because the majority of the students were ethnically Mexican, Spanish became the dominant language for communication leaving Anita to experience linguistic and cultural isolation. Although she eventually gained fluency in English, her identity shifted again when she was placed in the remedial class. Looking back at her past experience as an undergraduate student, she indicated that the previous curriculum limited her experiences with and knowledge of writing.

Andrea and Anita's prior lived educational experiences show that their professional identities were impacted not only by their own individual translinguistic experiences, but also due to the pedagogical practices believed and practiced by their writing instructors at specific points in time (Kroll, 2000).

Factor 2: The Impact of Social Support

Social network theorists have noted that interpersonal relationships and the patterns formed by these relations serve as the building blocks of social life. An aspect that results from social relations is "social support," defined as "the positive (and negative) outcomes that people received from social relationships" (Shade Wilson, 2017, p. 64). Developing social relationships require NNESTs to successfully integrate themselves into new communities (Mantero, 2007). To do this, they must learn to negotiate and participate in meaning-driven activities. When asked what type of social support they have received that has shaped who they are as teachers, Michelle and Andrea noted receiving support from family. Michelle's parents showed her how to control her nerves in front of an audience; a skill she found useful in the classroom. Andrea's parents motivated her to attend college and her boyfriend (now husband) encouraged her to pursue graduate school and use her education as a platform to advocate for L2 writers. They also said that as TAs they sought and received the support of professors. Michelle shadowed a professor for a semester while Andrea often met with several faculty to discuss teaching strategies and materials. This analysis suggests that both Michelle and Andrea received social support in both areas, the personal and the professional, which might have contributed to developing a more balanced professional identity.

Not so for Priscilla and Anita. Priscilla mentioned that as a TA, she was assigned an instructor of record, but she never received support from that professor. Instead, she said that she asked other TAs for help which she received. Doing this seems to have helped Priscilla prevent imbalance in the cultural expectations of the profession pan which could have negatively impacted her emerging professional identity. Nonetheless, one cannot avoid asking why she did not take the initiative to contact professors like Michelle and Andrea did. Perhaps due to her cultural background. Previous studies have found that cultural disconnect can inhibit identity formation (Hsu, 2009). An example of this disconnection is Anita's experience.

At the time of the first study, Anita was teaching three FYW courses. She was concerned she was spending too much time giving feedback—about 30 minutes per assignment—and was struggling. She took the initiative and met with the former female WPA to seek advice on this issue. According to Anita, the WPA told her she needed to give feedback to each student in each writing assignment. Anita explained that she tried to follow the WPA directive, but it was extremely difficult. With a sad tone she said, "Next semester, I am expected to teach five courses! Right now, I don't have time for myself, and I am very concerned about this. My life revolves around giving feedback. I love my job, but if I don't have time for myself that's going to affect my teaching." How Anita explained her situation to the WPA is not clear. Nonetheless, her compelling narrative suggests conditions of power and investment contributed to a failed communication with the WPA (Darvin & Norton, 2015).

While the WPA might have heard Anita, there seems to be a lack of investment in learning how Anita was doing as a first-time lecturer and to offer suggestions on how to give feedback to many students. The WPA, perhaps, focused only on aspects related to the cultural expectations of the profession—to give individualized feedback. Furthermore, Anita's cultural background impacted her ability to negotiate with her superior. She noted, "In Japan, people do not say what they think. This is considered to be polite." Had the WPA been cognizant that Asian cultures value silence as a virtue and that limited verbal interactions with superiors is a sign of respect, she could have offered Anita the social support needed. Anita's experience painstakingly illustrates an imbalanced identity scale where more attention is given to cultural expectations of the profession. By the time I returned to conduct the follow-up study, I was told Anita had moved to the East Coast and had left the profession despite the fact of receiving some of the highest student course evaluations among the participants. In the first study, student surveys administered in her classes revealed Anita's students perceived her as a highly professional and committed writing instructor.

The other two participants that had left the institution, but not the profession, were Michelle and Priscilla. However, in their case, it was their personal subjectivity pan that impacted their professional identity scale. At the time of the first study, both Michelle and Priscilla's respective spouses, who hold Ph.D.s in other disciplines, were looking for teaching positions outside the area. Priscilla said, "I'm worried. I don't know where we'll end up and how they are going to look at me as a nonnative speaker. What if the English department says 'Sorry, we need a native speaker, we cannot hire you.'" Michelle voiced similar concerns. Their experiences illustrate that alignment between the personal and the cultural expectations is never neutral or permanent. At any point when changes in social support occur or linguistic identity is the dominant identity-marker, they disrupt a NNEST's professional identity scale.

While the decision to relocate is a personal one, the genuine concern faced by 'visible minority women' (Amin, 1999, p. 102) disempowered by the profession is *real*. Studies have shown that minority women scholars in TESOL perceive themselves as less than their NES colleagues and, when compared with men, must navigate more complex and multiple gender identities imposed by sociocultural, sociopolitical, and familial contexts (Thomas, 1999; Park, 2017). A recent study highlights that the rich and diverse literacy repertoires of migrant women in the US do not guarantee social or economic mobility; often, their literate repertoires go unrecognized and undervalued (Lorimer Leonard, 2017). Although the field has made progress, there remains a need for more visible recognition of women classified as NNESTs as assets and capable members in the profession (Alvarez, 2019).

Factor 3: The Impact of Rank and Disciplinary Knowledge

Isabel Baca and her co-authors (2019) have claimed that "while identity is self-defined to an extent, it is also mandated by external forces and experiences in concrete, embodied terms" (p. 3). In academia, factors like rank and disciplinary background act as external forces that can both segregate communities and influence the formation of professional identity. When asked about their perception of themselves as members of the writing teachers' community, all four lecturers expressed that they did not see themselves as 'full' members due to the absence of a Ph.D. degree. For instance, Rielle mentioned, "To some extent I do, but I feel I don't have any authority in sharing what I think, what I've done, or what I've implemented because I don't have a Ph.D." On the other hand, Andrea, holding a Ph.D., felt a part of the profession, but struggled with adjusting to the new expectations of balancing teaching, research, and service. While these experiences are not unique to NNESTs, they underscore the impact of social structures, such as rank, on the construction of professional identity.

In addition to rank, the data indicated that disciplinary background also played a significant role in the formation of professional identity of the

Constructing a Professional Identity

participants. In this context, discipline is defined as a bordered and hierarchically organized intellectual community of practice formed by a network of individuals whose membership is determined by their acceptance of certain ideas, methods, procedures, habits of mind, epistemological assumptions, rhetorical conventions, genre practices, and publication/dissemination procedures (Hall, 2018). As Pennington (2015) notes, "a teacher's disciplinary identity connects the teacher to a specific field and its areas of knowledge and research" (p. 61). To become a member, one must develop discipline-specific knowledge and a sense of allegiance to that discipline. These combined habits of mind and commitment significantly impact one's professional identity.

Furthermore, Soo Hyon Kim and Tanita Saenkhum (2019) argue that in multidisciplinary departments, teaching becomes a prominent mode for communicating disciplinary expertise. When faculty members with related but different disciplinary knowledge are forced or compelled to relegate their disciplinary expertise to the periphery, their ability to establish a professional identity might be constrained. An alternative for such faculty is to develop an *openness to disciplinary identity reinvention*, defined as the imperative to push the methodological and conceptual boundaries of their discipline to foster disciplinary allegiance and connections with other fields (Rademaekers, 2015).

Most writing programs are multidisciplinary. They incorporate instructors from various subfields in English studies, such as literature, creative writing, rhetoric and composition, and/or linguistics. At the time of the study, the freshman writing program had adopted a writing-about-writing approach (Downs & Wardle, 2007), assigning TAs and lecturers to teach it. It is assumed that, over time, the four lecturers with an MAESL degree developed an openness to disciplinary identity reinvention. This reinvention is evident in Michelle's statement, "As an instructor of rhetoric and composition, I have to learn the jargon of the discipline and make it my own." Priscilla explained, "Before, I knew how to write a paper, but as a teacher of composition, I've learned about the rhetorical elements and conventions." Their comments indicate a shift in their disciplinary identities, viewing themselves not as ESL teachers but as teachers of composition.

In addition to the curriculum, the WPA's philosophy of avoiding a segregated community of writing teachers may have influenced the apparent shift in the lecturers' disciplinary and professional identity. When asked about what type of support is given to NNESTs, the WPA explained, "I do a very strategic kind of support. I don't treat ESL teachers any differently than TAs or lecturers because I am concerned with building a community of instructors that give each other feedback." The WPA emphasized, "When a NNEST is coming in and they identify as ESL, I make sure their mentor has that background. But I don't tell them that because I don't want them to see themselves as ESL teachers but as writing, reading, and research instructors."

While the WPA's comment shows a commitment to create a more equitable community of teachers of writing, it also captures the difficulty of achieving this goal. By pairing a NNEST with an ESL faculty, the WPA might be unintentionally reinforcing the NNES vs. NES and disciplinary divide. Furthermore, by emphasizing a type of community, that of writing instructors, the lecturers' ESL disciplinary knowledge is being relegated to a peripheral role hindering the development of hyphenated transdisciplinary identities. Such identities could enable them to see that their language-related expertise as ESL specialists is a positive contribution not only to their professional identity as composition instructors, but it is knowledge that instructors trained in rhetoric and composition, or other English subfields need.

Conclusion and Implications

In this study, we investigated factors contributing to NNESTs' professional identity construction in FYW courses. The results showed that the impact of prior educational experiences, social support, and rank and disciplinary knowledge can either assist or hinder the balance between personal subjectivity and the cultural expectations of the profession. This balance is crucial for NNESTs to develop and sustain a professional identity.

How can we apply this research at the macro and micro levels? One course of action is for the field to fully integrate issues related to L2 writing, including NNESTs' experiences, into mainstream composition scholarship (Kim & Saenkhum, 2019; I. Lee, 2013; Matsuda et al., 2011; Racelis & Matsuda, 2015). A more inclusive scholarship should recognize, from the start, that becoming a writing instructor involves more than performing a writing teacher's role and having the right linguistic identity (Zheng, 2017). The notion of 'non-native English speaker' is a complex term and should not be used to create superior or inferior categories among educators. Instead, it should be used to acknowledge and value differences, not in worth, equality, or ability, but in prior knowledge, embodied experiences, and affective responses gathered across geographies, disciplines, and named languages (E. Lee & Canagarajah, 2019; Sánchez-Martín, 2020). In addition, more inclusive scholarship should continually interrogate and problematize this term. Recently, second language acquisition scholars have called for granting idealized nativeness to both NEST and NNEST by juxtaposing the nativeness of NNESTs' first and local languages against the nonnativeness of NESTs of local and minoritized languages (Yazan & Rudolph, 2018). Scholars claim that doing this can help level the field. Furthermore, research investigating how to strengthen institutional and programmatic infrastructures to unify and reconcile the community of teachers of writing across racial, gender, and linguistic lines needs to be moved from the periphery to the center (Alvarez, 2019; Park, 2017)

At the micro level, writing and graduate programs could initiate two-way social support initiatives. Faculty and graduate students, including both NNESTs and NESTs, should engage in open discussions about their cultural backgrounds (Liu, 2010). This approach aims to challenge and change perceptions that contribute to disenfranchisement and stereotyping of both groups, ultimately fostering social justice on local campuses. Additionally, WPAs and graduate programs should prioritize the design of course assignments that leverage and build upon NNES TAs' antecedent knowledge and literacy brokering skills. These individuals bring valuable insights into rhetorical tools and texts that may be unfamiliar in the U.S. context (Perry, 2009). As transnational literacy brokers with multiple ties and activities, their perspectives can reshape writing studies programs by highlighting the benefits of incorporating non-U.S. writing models (Canagarajah, 2020; Donahue, 2013).

In conclusion, NNESTs and NNESTAs should engage in constant critical reflection and remember that becoming a professional educator is not wrapped up in the ability to conform to the profession, but instead in *integrating* their ever-evolving professional identity to the chain of their other multiple rich subjectivities. Doing this can help maintain their identity scale balanced.

References

Alim, S. H., Rickford, J. R. & Ball, A. F. (2016). *Raciolinguistics: How language shapes our ideas about race.* Oxford University Press.

Alsup, J. (2006). Speaking from the borderlands: Exploring narratives of teacher identity. In B. T. Williams (Ed.), *Identity papers: Literacy and power in higher education* (pp. 109–121). Utah State University Press. https://www.jstor.org/stable/j.ctt4cgp83.10.

Alvarez, N. (2019). On longing and belonging: Latinas in the writing center. In I. Baca, Y. I. Hinojosa & S. Wolff Murphy (Eds.), *Bordered writers: Latinx identities and literacy practices and Hispanic-serving institution*s (pp. 195–212). SUNY Press.

Ambrose, S. A., Bridges, M. W., DiPietro, M., Lovett, M. C. & Norman, M. K. (2010). *How learning works: Seven research-based principles for smart teaching.* Wiley & Sons.

Amin, N. (1999). Minority women teachers of ESL: Negotiating White English. In G. Braine (Ed.), *Non-native educators in English language teaching* (pp. 93–104). Lawrence Erlbaum Associates.

Appleby, R. (2016). Researching privilege in language teacher identity. *TESOL Quarterly, 50*(3), 755–768. https://doi.org/10.1002/tesq.321.

Baca, I., Hinojosa, Y. I. & Wolff Murphy, S. (Eds.). (2019). *Bordered writers: Latinx identities and literacy practices and Hispanic-serving institutions*. SUNY Press.

Braine, G. (1999). *Non-native educators in English language teaching*. Lawrence Erlbaum Associates.

Block, D. (2007). *Second language identities*. Continuum.

Canagarajah, S. (2020). *Transnational literacy autobiographies as translingual writing*. Routledge.

College Composition and Communication (2013). Special issue: The profession, *College Composition and Communication, 65*(1), 1–226. http://www.jstor.org/stable/43490795.

Cox, M., Jordan, J., Ortmeier-Hooper, C. & Schwartz, G. G. (Eds.). (2010). *Reinventing identities in second language writing*. National Council of Teachers of English.

Cheung, Y. L., Said, S. B. & Park, K. (Eds.). (2015). *Advances and current trends in language teacher identity research*. Routledge/Taylor & Francis.

Charles. (2019). Black teachers of English in South Korea: Constructing identities as a native English speaker and English language teaching professional. *TESOL Journal, 10*(4). https://doi.org/10.1002/tesj.478.

Darvin, R. & Norton, B. (2015). Identity and a model of investment in applied linguistics. *Annual Review of Applied Linguistics, 35*, 36–56. http://doi:10.1017/S0267190514000191.

De Costa, P. & Norton, B. (2017). Introduction: Identity, transdisciplinarity, and the good language teacher. *The Modern Language Journal, 101*, 3–14. https://doi.org/10.1111/modl.12368.

Donahue, C. (2013). Negotiation, translinguality, and cross-cultural writing research in a new composition era. In S. Canagarajah (Ed.), *Literacy as a translingual practice: Between communities and classrooms* (pp. 149–161). Routledge.

Downs, D. & Wardle, E. (2007). Teaching about writing, righting misconceptions: (Re)envisioning "first-year composition" as "introduction to writing studies." *College Composition and Communication, 58*(4), 552–584.

Ellis, E. M. (2016). "I may be a native speaker but I'm not monolingual": Reimagining all teachers' linguistic identities in TESOL. *TESOL Quarterly, 50*(3), 597–630. https://doi.org/10.1002/tesq.314.

Fulkerson, R. (2005). Composition at the turn of the twenty-first century. *College Composition and Communication, 56*(4), 654–687.

Garcia, O. & Kleyn, T. (Eds.). (2016). *Translanguaging with multilingual students: Learning from classroom moments*. Routledge.

Geller, A. E. (2011). Teaching and learning with multilingual faculty. *Across the Disciplines, 8*(4). https://doi.org/10.37514/ATD-J.2011.8.4.06.

Hall, J. (2018). Rewriting disciplines, rewriting boundaries: Transdisciplinary and translingual challenges for WAC/WID. *Across the Disciplines, 15*(3), 1–10. https://doi.org/10.37514/ATD-J.2018.15.3.08.

Harklau, L. (2000). From the "good kids" to the "worst": Representations of English language learners across educational settings. *TESOL Quarterly, 34*(1), pp. 35–67. https://doi.org/10.2307/3588096.

Hebbard, Marcela. (2012). *Constructing a professional identity: Non-native speakers as teachers in college freshman composition classes in an American University*. [Unpublished Master's Thesis]. University of Texas - Pan American.

Hesse, D. (2013). Sustainable expectations? *College Composition and Communication, 65*(1), 16–18. http://www.jstor.org/stable/43490797.

Holmes, J. (2013). *Introduction to sociolinguistics* (4th ed.). Routledge.

Hsu, J. (2009). EFL teacher values and identity in tertiary education in Japan. *The Journal of Kanda University of International Studies, 21*, 385–399. http://id.nii.ac.jp/1092/00001273/.

Ibarra, H. (1999). Provisional selves: Experimenting with image and identity in professional adaptation. *Administrative Science Quarterly, 44*(4), 764–791. https://doi.org/10.2307/2667055.

Kim, S. & Saenkhum, T. (2019). Professional identity (re)construction of L2 writing scholars. *L2 Journal, 11*(2), 18–34. https://doi.org/10.5070/L211242088.

Ismail, N., Hassin, S. & Darus, S. (2012). ESL students' attitude, learning problems and needs for online writing. *Journal of Language Studies, 12*(4), 1089–1107.

Kroll, B. (2000). The composition of a life in composition. In T. Silva & P. K. Matsuda (Eds.), *On second language writing* (pp. 1–16). Lawrence Erlbaum Associates.

Lay, E. D. (2013). Making the teacher. *College Composition and Communication, 65*(1), 37–39. http://www.jstor.org/stable/43490804.

Lee, E. & Canagarajah, S. (2019). Beyond native and nonnative: Translingual dispositions for more inclusive teacher identity in language and literacy education. *Journal of Language, Identity & Education, 18*(6), 352–363. https://doi.org/10.1080/15348458.2019.1674148.

Lee, I. (2013). Becoming a writing teacher: Using "identity" as an analytic lens to understand EFL writing teachers' development. *Journal of Second Language Writing, 22*(3), 330–345. https://doi.org/10.1016/j.jslw.2012.07.001.

Liu, Y. (2010). Negotiating with identities as a novice EFL researcher. In M. Cox, J. Jordan, C. Ortmeier-Hooper & G. G. Schwartz (Eds.), *Reinventing identities in second language writing* (pp. 104–112). National Council of Teacher of English.

Lorimer Leonard, R. (2017). *Writing on the move: Migrant women and the value of literacy*. University of Pittsburgh Press.

Mantero, M. (2007). Toward ecological pedagogy in language education. In M. Mantero (Ed.), *Identity and second language learning: Culture, inquiry, and dialogic activity in educational contexts* (pp. 1–11). Information Age Publishing.

Martínez, A. Y. (2020). Counterstory: The rhetoric and writing of critical race theory. *Conference on College Composition and Communication & the National Council of Teachers of English*. Champaign, Illinois.

Matsuda, P. K. (2012). Teaching composition in the multilingual world: Second language writing in composition studies. In K. Ritter & P. K. Matsuda (Eds.), *Exploring composition studies: Sites, issues, and perspectives* (pp. 36–51). Utah State University Press.

Matsuda, P. K., Cox, M., Jordan, J. & Ortmeier-Hooper, C. (2011). *Second-language writing in the composition classroom*. Bedford/St. Martin's.

Medina, C. (2013). The family profession. *College Composition and Communication*, 65(1), 34–36. http://www.jstor.org/stable/43490803.

Motha, S., Jain, R. & Tecle T. (2012). Translinguistic identity-as-pedagogy: Implications for language teacher education. *International Journal of Innovation in English Language Teaching*, 1(1), 13–28.

Moussu, L. & Llurda, E. (2008) Non-native English-speaking English language teachers: History and research. *Language Teaching*, 41(3), 315–348. https://doi.org/10.1017/S0261444808005028.

Norton, B. (2000). *Identity and language learning: Gender, ethnicity, and educational change*. Pearson.

Norton, B. (2013). *Identity and language learning: Extending the conversation* (2nd ed.). Multilingual Matters.

Norton Peirce, B. (1995). Social identity, investment, and language learning. *TESOL Quarterly*, 29(1), 9–31. https://doi.org/10.2307/3587803.

Pantelides, K. (2013). On being a new mother-dissertator-writing center administrator. *College Composition and Communication*, 65(1), 28–29. http://www.jstor.org/stable/43490801.

Park, G. (2012) "I am never afraid of being recognized as an NNES": One teacher's journey in claiming and embracing her nonnative-speaker identity. *TESOL Quarterly*, 46(1), 127–151. https://doi.org/10.1002/tesq.4.

Park, G. (2017). *Narratives of east Asian women teachers of English: Where privilege meets marginalization*. Multilingual Matters.

Pennington, M. C. (2015). Teacher identity in TESOL: A frames perspective, Y. L. Cheung, S.B. Said & K. Park (Eds.), *Advances and current trends in language teacher identity research* (1st ed., pp. 16–30). Routledge.

Perry, K. H. (2009). Genre, contexts, and literacy practices: Literacy brokering among Sudanese refugee families. *Reading Research Quarterly*, 44(3), 256–276. https://doi.org/10.1598/RRQ.44.3.2.

Racelis, J. V. & Matsuda, P. K. (2015). Exploring the multiple identities of L2 writing teachers. In Y. L. Cheung, S. B. Said & K. Park (Eds.), *Advances and current trends in language teacher identity research* (pp. 203–216). Routledge.

Rademaekers, J. K. (2015). Is WAC/WID ready for the transdisciplinary research university? *Across the Disciplines*, 12(2), 1–15. https://doi.org/10.37514/ATD-J.2015.12.2.02.

Ruecker, T. & Ives, L. (2015). White native English speakers needed: The rhetorical construction of privilege in online teacher recruitment spaces. *TESOL Quarterly*, 49(4), 733–756. https://doi.org/10.1002/tesq.195.

Ruecker, T., Frazier, S., Tseptsura, M. (2018). "Language difference can be an asset": Exploring the experiences of nonnative English-speaking teachers of writing. *College Composition and Communication*, 69(4), 612–641. https://www.jstor.org/stable/44870978.

Ruiz, I. D. & Sánchez, R. (2016). *Decolonizing rhetoric and composition studies: New Latinx keywords for theory and pedagogy*. Palgrave Macmillan US. https://doi.org/10.1057/978-1-137-52724-0.

Saldaña, J. (2016). *The coding manual for qualitative researchers* (3rd ed.). Sage.

Sánchez-Martín, C. (2020). Critical autoethnography in TESOL teacher education: A translingual and cultural-historical activity theory perspective for transnational spaces. In O. Barnawi & A. Ahmed (Eds.), *TESOL teacher education in a transnational world: Turning challenges into innovative prospects* (1st ed.) (pp. 105–118). Routledge. https://doi.org/10.4324/9781003008668.

Sánchez-Martín, C. & Seloni, L. (2019). Transdisciplinary becoming as a gendered activity: A reflexive study of dissertation mentoring. *Journal of Second Language Writing, 43*, 24–35. https://doi.org/10.1016/j.jslw.2018.06.006.

Santoro, N. (2009). Teaching in culturally diverse contexts: What knowledge about "self" and "others" do teachers need? *Journal of Education for Teaching, 35*(1), 33–45. https://doi.org/10.1080/02607470802587111.

Silva, T. (1997). On the ethical treatment of ESL writers. *TESOL Quarterly, 31*(2), 359–363. https://www.jstor.org/stable/3588052.

Shade Wilson, J. (2017) The role of social networks and social support in the writing and college planning of multilingual urban adolescents. In C. Ortmeier-Hooper & T. Ruecker (Eds.), *Linguistically diverse immigrant and resident writers: Transitions from high school to college* (pp. 63–81). Routledge.

The Douglas Fir Group. (2016). A transdisciplinary framework for SLA in a multilingual world. *The Modern Language Journal, 100*, 19–47. https://doi.org/10.1111/modl.12301.

Thomas, J. (1999). Voices from the periphery: Non-native teachers and issues of credibility. In G. Braine (Ed.). *Non-native educators in English language teaching*. Routledge. https://doi.org/10.4324/9781315045368.

Toth, C. M., Griffiths, B. M. & Thirolf, K. (2013) "Distinct and significant": Professional identities of two-year college English faculty. *College Composition and Communication, 65*(1), 90–116. http://www.jstor.org/stable/43490808.

Tsui, A. B. M. (2007). Complexities of identity formation: A narrative inquiry of an EFL teacher. *TESOL Quarterly, 41*, 657–680. https://doi.org/10.1002/j.1545-7249.2007.tb00098.x.

Varghese, M., Motha, S., Park, G., Reeves, J. & Trent, J. (Eds.). (2016). Special issue: Language teacher identity in (multi)lingual education contexts. *TESOL Quarterly, 50*(3). https://www.jstor.org/stable/i40211712.

Wenger, E. (1998). *Communities of practice: Learning, meaning, and identity*. Cambridge University Press.

Yazan, B. & Rudolph, N. (Eds.). (2018). Criticality, teacher identity, and (in)equity in English language teaching, *Educational Linguistics, 35*, https://doi.org/10.1007/978-3-319-72920-6_1.

Yuan, R. (2018). A critical review on nonnative English teacher identity research: From 2008 to 2017. *Journal of Multilingual and Multicultural Development, 40*(6), 518–537. https://doi.org/10.1080/01434632.2018.1533018.

Zhang, L. & Zhang, D. (2015). Identity matters: An ethnography of two nonnative English-speaking teachers (NNESTs) struggling for legitimate professional participation In Y. L. Cheung, S. B. Said & K. Park (Eds.), *Advances and current trends in language teacher identity research* (pp. 116–132). Routledge/Taylor & Francis.

Zheng, X. (2017). Translingual identity as pedagogy: International teaching assistants of English in college composition classroom. *The Modern Language Journal, 101*(17), 29–44. https://doi.org/10.1111/modl.12373.

3

Multilingual Writing Teacher Identities and Institutional Ecologies: A Collaborative Narrative Inquiry

Su Yin Khor
COLLEGE OF THE ATLANTIC

Cristina Sánchez-Martín
UNIVERSITY OF WASHINGTON, SEATTLE

Lisya Seloni
ILLINOIS STATE UNIVERSITY

Md Mijanur Rahman
CALIFORNIA STATE UNIVERSITY, LOS ANGELES

Demet Yiğitbilek
ILLINOIS STATE UNIVERSITY

With an increasing presence of linguistically and culturally diverse students and teachers in U.S. institutions of higher education, writing programs are transforming into transnational spaces. As a result, first-year writing (FYW) programs and pedagogies are being adapted to reflect the changing demographics by, for example, instilling in students the awareness of how writing is accomplished differently across communities and helping them recognize the diversity and legitimacy of non-mainstream languages and varieties. In response to these demographic changes, scholars in writing call for a "deep intercultural awareness" (Donahue, 2009, p. 236) and cross-linguistic experience within writing programs (Martins, 2015). Despite the growing number of multilingual instructors in all college courses (Kitalong, 2017) and the emergence of translingualism as a decolonial approach to language difference (Horner et al., 2011), there is still a great need to understand the experiences of this population, as the teachers' backgrounds, identities and life histories are not always considered an asset to the institutions (Zheng, 2017).

Indeed, the struggle to prove oneself as a legitimate English language teacher is well-documented in the nonnative English-speaking teachers (NNESTs) literature. A large body of work contests the native speaker fallacy in educational contexts and extensively discusses the difficulties that NNESTs face in college classrooms (Aneja, 2016; Kamhi-Stein, 2004; Park, 2017). For instance, the literature sheds light on the racial prejudices towards minoritized teachers (Rubin, 1992; Kubota et al., 2021) and job advertisements that regard native English-speaking teachers as the best candidates (Selvi, 2010; Ramjattan, 2015). Recently, more attention has been given to resources and assets that NNESTs bring into university contexts and the importance of institutional support, shifting from a deficit orientation (e.g., see the 2012 special issue of the *Journal of Excellence in College Teaching*). Although these studies contribute to our understanding of the overall NNESTs' experiences in the US, this topic remains underexplored and it was not until recently that their experiences in FYW classrooms have been investigated (e.g., Ruecker et al., 2018; Sánchez-Martín, 2018; Zheng, 2017).

This chapter contributes to the understanding of the role that transnational writing instructors play on college campuses, especially in writing programs. As we demonstrate, these instructors can have a critical role in helping student writers "practice a disposition of openness and inquiry . . . towards language and language difference" (Horner et al., 2011, p. 311) and invite students to develop attentiveness to language issues. With this in mind, we conducted a collaborative narrative inquiry of our stories as five multilingual instructors, primarily sharing our experiences as graduate teaching assistants (Su Yin, Cristina, Mijan, and Demet) teaching FYW at Illinois State University's (ISU) Writing Program and a faculty member (Lisya) who served as a graduate mentor during that time when this chapter came to fruition. Our goal with this chapter is to explore how transnational teachers of English can become instrumental in fostering a multi/translingual disposition among students and supporting their participation with linguistically diverse populations in global communities. We do this by sharing snapshots of our teaching experiences from our autobiographical narratives and classroom materials, particularly exploring how our identities inform our pedagogy, and discuss the role and importance of programmatic infrastructure in creating translingual spaces that meet the needs of all university students in the US. This is accomplished by drawing on an identities-as-pedagogy framework (Motha, Jain & Tecle, 2012) to highlight multilingual instructors' identities as resources rather than deficiencies and how teaching writing deeply involves identity work, influenced by institutional ecologies and practices.

Identity-as-Pedagogy and Institutional Ecology

Pedagogical practices of NNESTs are highly embodied in their identities, as they bring their language experience to the classrooms. While some of these complex identities are situation-specific, conflicting, and learned over time, some are tacitly informed by life histories. In this context, many have argued that multilingual instructors strategically tap into their cultural resources and use their identities as pedagogical resources (e.g., de Oliveira & Lan, 2012; Morgan, 2004; Motha, Jain & Tecle, 2012; Reis, 2012; Seloni, 2012). Viewing teacher identity as "potential pedagogical resources in the classroom," Motha, Jain, and Tecle (2012) use the term "translinguistic identities" to argue for the embodied nature of teaching where language identities play important roles in understanding issues such as privilege, marginalization, and the political role of English in communities (p. 15). They explore their own teaching experiences, using anecdotes to illustrate the complex interplay between racial and linguistic identities embedded in their teaching practices.

Emphasizing the plurality of identities, Alvarez et al. (2017) discussed how transnational instructors' diverse language resources index hybrid ethnicities and caution us to see ethnicity as a ludic identity marker in classroom interactions. They reject viewing identity and ethnicity as predefined constructs, and instead, urge us to recognize their complexities in order to resist perpetuating everyday discourses of language and identity homogenization. Performing one's identity in the classroom is not always optional as the response can be undesired. Therefore, it is paramount to remember that "ethnicity is a complex semiotic achievement" (Alvarez et al., 2017, p. 44) where interlocutors are involved in co-constructing identities.

If the identity-as-pedagogy is one side of the coin of the embeddedness of teaching, the other side would be the institutional ecologies and spaces where these discourses take place. Other scholars (e.g., De Costa & Norton, 2017; Morgan, 2004) have emphasized the embeddedness of identity negotiations within specific sociocultural and institutional contexts, stating that identities "are seen as 'constituted' *within* institutional discourses" (Morgan, 2004, p. 178). In this sense, the notion of ecology, as discussed in writing program scholarship, allows us to understand how our identities are constructed in relation to the environments we inhabit and how our identities shape these environments in a bidirectional movement. For example, Sánchez-Martín and Walker (2021) explained this scenario with reference to their own writing program:

> The philosophies and practices of the program created a space where these teachers could productively make practical and everyday use of these complex identities, with an awareness

> that the program not only valued their work, in theory, but considered this complex and evolving work to understand their literate practice as fundamental to the core work of the program, to their work as teachers, and as part of the significant contribution they were making to the evolution of the program and its practices. (p. 187)

Moreover, an ecological perspective on writing has often focused on the individual writers, but it becomes important to highlight the writing programs themselves as ecologies that are characterized by "interconnectedness, fluctuation, complexity, and emergence" (Reiff et al., 2015, p. 5). For our chapter, we find the first two of these characteristics especially relevant to our context, as interconnection represents the program's relationships and networks with multiple stakeholders and entities (e.g., our department, the writing program, and the TESOL/applied linguistics graduate program), and fluctuation as it points to ongoing transformation due to a variety of factors coming from both within and outside (e.g., new cohort of faculty, new students, and leadership changes). Along these lines, we acknowledge that our teaching of writing takes place in relation to these ecological contexts. The institutional ecologies could challenge, shift, and help re-envision teacher identities and provide spaces for teachers to reflectively and intentionally act on their identities. In more current orientations to language, identity, and interactions, spatiality is increasingly considered, highlighting the discursive-material ecologies in the agency of humans (e.g., Canagarajah, 2018). This move urges us to reexamine our interactions based on the "spatial repertoires," defined as "link[ing] the repertoires formed through individual life trajectories to the particular places in which these linguistic resources are deployed" (Pennycook & Otsuji, 2015, p. 83). While some alternative spaces would be tolerant to the diverse language backgrounds and instructional practices used by transnational instructors, the same practices may not be admissible in spaces that are perceived to be more hegemonic.

As will be explained in the findings section, institutional ecologies are crucial to the types of pedagogies we were able to develop. Specifically, we discuss the importance of turning inclusive beliefs and ideas into concrete actionable steps and practices to create a constructive space for multilingual writing instructors and their writing students.

As illustrated in our collaborative narrative inquiry in this chapter, we embrace the idea that "language teaching is identity work" (De Costa & Norton, 2017, p. 8) and find significant implications of the embeddedness of our NNESTs' identities for our writing classrooms, which are central to the explorations of our own ever-changing narratives. With this in mind, this chapter is guided by the following questions: (i) How do we, as NNESTs, create spaces for our multilingual identities within writing programs? and (ii) What can writing programs do to enable us to bring our evolving, contested, and fluid identities into the classroom as pedagogical resources?

Methodology

In order to answer our research questions, we apply a sociocultural and praxis-oriented framework (e.g., Lantolf, 2012) to illustrate the bidirectional relationship between theory and practice, from an understanding that our lived experiences are linked to our teaching and vice versa. To examine our experiences as multilingual writing teachers, we employed a collaborative narrative inquiry. Narratives are not simply stories and reflections, but they are "social and relational and gain their meaning from our collective social histories" and can't be "separated from their sociocultural and sociohistorical contexts from which they emerged" (Johnson & Golombek, 2002, p. 4). By jointly examining our narratives, we capture and describe our lived experiences, allowing us to "look *inward, outward, backward*, and *forward*" (Johnson & Golombek, 2002, p. 3). By examining our experiences through written narratives, we could collectively relate to and understand them through relevant scholarship on teacher identities.

We conducted recursive analyses of our individually written autobiographical narratives that were written in the fall of 2018 in response to the group-created prompt "Who am I in the classroom?" to reflect the focus of this edited collection and our research questions. In each narrative, we discussed what it means for us to be transnational writing teachers in U.S. higher education and how we reconcile and embrace our identities and language backgrounds. We supplemented our narratives with a variety of teaching materials, such as teaching philosophy statements, pedagogical articles we produced, our course plans that include our first-day syllabi, major assignments and handouts for in-class activities. These data allow us to examine our experiences as writing instructors at a predominantly white institution in the Midwest, drawing attention to the act of making our identities visible in pedagogically productive ways.

For our analysis, we utilized an inductive approach (Hatch, 2002), identifying patterns and relationships in the data by focusing on identity related phrases, words, and stories. For instance, expressions that were central to our narratives were native and nonnative, first language, identity, and multilingual. Common stories concerned fears about being underprepared writing teachers because composition was new to us and our students' potentially disempowering perceptions of us. Each contributor read the other narratives, but was assigned one contributor's narrative, syllabi, and other materials to identify themes that emerge across these documents. We then met and discussed our preliminary themes and findings, identified commonalities and differences, and paid attention to how they related to teacher identity enactment within the ISU Writing Program and in the department in general. In the following section, we present findings from our analysis.

Findings

While multiple themes emerged from the exploration of our autobiographical narratives, we focus on two themes that answer the research questions we posed and are central to using our NNESTs identities as a resource: the first theme, identity-as-pedagogy and its interconnectedness with the second theme, the role of ecology.

Theme 1: Identity-as-Pedagogy

In this section, we share the findings for our first question: How do we, as NNESTs, create spaces for our multilingual identities within programs? As we illustrate below, our multilingual teacher identities translated into pedagogically productive ways after we participated in various professional development activities, completed coursework and other academic interactions. While we are currently at different stages of our academic careers in the US, we draw on our experiences during our time at ISU, our academic home, even though some of us have graduated and taken up positions at other institutions. Both in our current locations and at ISU, we frequently find ourselves not only teaching and developing writing courses in the FYW curriculum and intensive English programs, but also preparing fellow instructors to do the same. As multilingual instructors, we find the characterization of our multilingual selves as nonnatives to be reductive as our writing instructor identities intersect with other aspects of who we are and lived experiences. During different phases of our academic journeys, we all fought against the native speaker ideology that insisted that the ideal teacher is a native speaker. This native speaker fallacy not only impacts the egalitarian nature of interactions in our teaching spaces, it also reinforces asymmetrical power relationships.

For instance, Cristina acknowledges her conflicting identities across the privilege-marginalization spectrum in academia (Park, 2017). In the context of her previous institution (rural U.S. Northeast), she was perceived and constructed as a Latina due to her accent, but she recognizes her white-skin privilege and origin (from Spain rather than Latin America, where European coloniality is particularly present). On the other hand, Demet always tries to be open about her identity as a Turkish woman who studied in an English-medium university and moved on to teach English first in Spain and then in Turkey. She has taught English mainly for academic purposes at colleges, working with many students with varying backgrounds and continues to do so in the US now with a different positionality. Mijan initially identified himself only as a nonnative Bangladeshi academic, who, after seven years of teaching English at a university in his home country, moved to the US to pursue a doctoral degree but now calls himself as a transnational educator of writing. For Su Yin, she is considered "a woman of Chinese descent" by default, but it is an observation that often fails to recognize that she was born and raised in Sweden to Chinese Malaysian parents, and that her subjectivity is multiple as she says: "I am a woman. I am an immigrant. I am a daughter. I have been minoritized. I have been racialized. I am an educator. I am a lifelong learner. I am a scholar. And I am also an activist and I want my work to reflect everything that I am, but also, reflect who my students are." Similarly, Lisya, who has been working with prospective teachers for many years as a faculty member, addresses linguistic diversity, language ideologies, and socio-cultural and political influences on English language learning and teaching in her courses. As an ethnic minority (Turkish woman from a Jewish upbringing) both in her home country and in her adopted country (Turkish-American), she often discusses in her courses how her linguistic, ethnic and cultural practices are contextual and how they play out differently across different communities and geographical locations. She does this by bringing up stories and narratives both from the mainstream Turkish culture she sees herself affiliated with and from her minoritized language and community, Judeo-Spanish. In our chapter, we recognize that our identities are multiple and dynamic, and that they are shaped by sociocultural, historical, political, personal, and professional lives we live and discourses we navigate across (De Costa & Norton, 2017). We also want to underscore and acknowledge the emotional and professional labor required to translate our identities into pedagogical resources and that our chapter provides a glimpse into our journeys rather than a completed process.

Negotiating Inherited NNEST Identities and Discourses

Early on, our NNEST identity presented itself more as a constraint than a resource in our pedagogical enterprise. Most of us started teaching composition in the US, bringing, for instance, internalized discourses of English monolingualism, standard language ideology, and the notion that native speaking teachers are inherently better. This developed a sense of insecurity and concern for student resistance. Consequently, the FYW classroom and other content area courses loomed large as intimidating spaces where the legitimacy of our language and pedagogical expertise is contested and questioned. As Su Yin reflects,

> Before my first day of teaching, I was worried about what my students would think of me. Would my "Asianness" and label as a "non-native" speaker become the big racialized elephant in the room? Would this perception of me as a foreigner negatively affect my teaching? Would they perceive some sort of "Asian" accent and complain about my language proficiency, and by extension, teaching skills?

Demet experienced a similar insecurity as she "was terrified before [her] first class" and contemplated some troubling questions: "What if they do not take me seriously because of my international identity? What if I cannot establish my writing instructor identity in the way that I usually do with my previous students in Turkey?" Mijan also reports a similar disposition, subordinating himself by internalizing the discourse of his accented English as "the native and non-native dichotomy left an indelible print on [his] English teacher psyche." As a result, "the responsibility of teaching writing to the native English-speaking students appeared a very daunting and intimidating task" (Mijan). In the end, in Su Yin's terms, "[We were] not brave enough to bring up social issues that intersected with language and writing" despite "[our] own burning desire to address linguistic inequalities" in composition classrooms as in some ways "[we] found [ourselves] perpetuating the Anglo-monolingual ideology in [our] classroom[s]."

NNEST Identity Transformation

As we took graduate courses in contemporary approaches to teaching composition, cross-cultural issues in TESOL, and language ideologies, our practices and perspectives began to transform. Emboldened by the scholarship on the plurality of English, the problematization of standard language ideology, and translingualism, we progressively claimed ownership of our NNEST identity, accepting teaching as identity work. We navigated our ways through the initially-intimidating spaces, acknowledged the value of alternative rhetorical practices, and revised our course plans to reflect these developments.

As Demet explains in her narrative regarding the graduate courses she took, the intense readings on translingualism, language variations, and identity issues in TESOL had added to my confidence immensely and I revisited my course plan to solidify the concepts I wanted to emphasize more and prepared assignments to address variety and diversity issues in linguistic resources we bring to the classroom both as teachers and students.

Mijan reflects on his experience after reading Henry Widdowson's (1994) article on the ownership of English that problematized the native-nonnative dichotomy, leading him "to feel better in academia." The graduate courses on "language ideology and sociolinguistics further clarified the issues of linguistic diversity, dialects, and accents, [prompting] [him] to take control of [his] writing classroom space." Moreover, as Mijan puts it, "the idea that academic literacy skills are not given to native users of a language and take a lot of time to master also helped [him] overcome [his] doubts about whether [he] could teach writing to the so-called native speakers of English." For Su Yin, she observes that completing coursework in TESOL and engaging in conversations with peers and professors built her confidence to incorporate lessons and units addressing language issues. Lisya, too, remembers that this was the case for her when she was a doctoral student. The courses taught by her mentor, Dr. Shelly Wong, were eye-opening: "Once you learn about the politics of language learning and teaching, you can never unlearn these issues, and you begin to see the field from a critical lens" she says, reflecting back her first exposure to critical applied linguistics during her doctoral program at the Ohio State University. These transformations, we think, are key moments for us as emerging scholars like we once were and still are. It is important to emphasize that while these transformations occurred in different times of our academic growth, the application of this transformation in new contexts is a more complex issue and involves multiple detours. For instance, after moving to new teaching contexts at different institutions, Cristina and Su Yin were, yet again, hesitant to draw on their transnational identities as writing teachers, concerned about how it would be received. These experiences demonstrate that this journey is recursive in nature with no fixed destination.

NNEST Identity Affordances

Our growth as writing instructors and new-found confidence are reflected in our attempts to raise our students' awareness about diverse linguistic practices and support their critical engagement with writing and language issues. Our endeavor, in that sense, is best represented through the materials we include in our course plans and the goals and outcomes we set for our students in major assignments and in-class activities. Demet, for instance, references Gloria Anzaldúa's words "I am my language" (1987, p. 53) in her course to pinpoint the relationship between identity and language use, and urges her students to think about the complexities surrounding linguistic diversity. By using her "personal experiences to talk about writing and how languages and varieties of languages we speak shape the way we think, read, and write and how they show up in our interactions with different people in varying discourses," she asks her students "to think about the past experiences they have had related to languages and varieties they used or encountered" and then "have them relate their multiple aspects of identities to how they can play with the language in different genres." Similarly, Mijan developed a separate unit that takes a social justice perspective on linguistic diversity, making his students investigate how inter- and intralingual diversity prevents people from accessing societies' resources like education, employment and a safe civic life. His students complete a variety of readings on "language ideology, language change and variation, and the social justice issues arising from it" and compose multiple genres of writing (e.g., reading responses and narratives), critically examining their own language ideologies and those around them and reflecting on their own biases, the discriminations they faced, and the privileges they enjoyed while interacting with linguistically diverse people across settings. In a similar fashion, Su Yin redesigned her syllabus and developed "a unit that specifically addressed language diversity in society, and specifically focused on the local" to foreground the students' own language backgrounds in the class as she "wanted them to understand that they, too, despite being 'monolingual', find themselves in translingual spaces where diverse people, codes, and texts merge and interconnect." Cristina, too, defines her "classroom space as a meaning-making resource for [her] and [her] students" about "writing and language practices." Her multilingual self makes her students "curious about [her] language repertoire," triggering discussions about how the L_1-L_2 or native-non-native dichotomy is "limiting" in real world contexts. At her new institution, her international multilingual students (from Nigeria, for example) initiate questions about the complicated power dynamics in world Englishes that prevented them from being in the mainstream composition classes "even though they acquired English as a first language." Presenting herself as an embodiment of "the contradictions and tensions involved in writing across languages," she facilitates "conversations around writing, language and identity" fashioning a unique path for the course's trajectory.

Through these experiences, we try to foster discussions at the theoretical and practical level about language from a variety of (geographical) contexts. These materials and teaching practices are closely connected to our identities as teachers, informed by our backgrounds, unique experiences and how we understand the personal and the academic world. However, it should be noted that a crucial factor that created spaces for us to use our agency to engage critically with writing in our classrooms is the active support from our institution, which we discuss in the next section.

Theme 2: Ecology and the Importance of Programmatic Infrastructures

While we discussed the diverse ways that our multilingual identities inform our pedagogy, a key aspect that often gets overlooked is the role that writing programs and institutions play in creating the types of spaces where we, as NNEST teachers, can draw on our identities to enrich our pedagogical practices. In this section, then, we answer our second question: "What can writing programs do to enable us to bring our evolving, contested, and fluid identities into the classroom as pedagogical resources?" and examine the role that writing programs and institutions play, particularly addressing the impact of ecology and space.

Examining the enactment of teacher identities takes us beyond the classroom and intersects with institutional ecology and programmatic infrastructures. Thus, the space that we occupy becomes central to the discussion of how our identities are enacted in the classroom (Sánchez-Martín & Walker, 2021). The material and biological conditions of an ecology include the human involvement in the institution whose languages, lives, and identities transcend static and territorialized notions of language. Indeed, each of us has experienced tensions when it comes to our positionality and identity as writing instructors, and self-reflexivity was a way of learning how to navigate these tensions. For instance, our narratives show that Mijan was well-aware of his language identity being different from those of his students and how this fact informed his teaching; Cristina was cautious about transferring her writing pedagogies into a new educational context that had a more homogenous student population where language diversity was not a clear learning objective; Demet refers to experiencing apprehensions before her first class; and Su Yin begins her narrative asking "what do our identities allow or prevent us from doing?" and stating that, in her case, other aspects of our identities that are more visible than language, e.g., skin color, shape the initial assumptions students make about our abilities to teach writing in English.

The impact of ISU's Writing Program philosophies, which encourage instructors to see language use as a translingual practice, were significant in helping us grow as teachers and as emerging scholars specializing in TESOL and applied linguistics at an interdisciplinary English program. While many universities promote inclusivity and all sorts of diversity, we argue that the key factor is that these philosophies were transformed into daily practices, which could be observed at the micro-level, i.e., activities in our department, the writing program, and academic programs. In other words, the material conditions of the graduate programs that we were enrolled in involved actual opportunities to learn about language related issues through specific graduate level courses—some of them taught by Lisya—addressing a range of topics, such as language ideologies, second language writing, and cross-cultural issues in TESOL. These courses provide a site for graduate students to reflect on the ways in which their identities are taken up across multiple settings or about their own language histories. In turn, these instructors contribute by developing resources for all writing instructors and students to use in their classes. As these collaborations were inherently crucial to professionalizing writing instruction in the ISU Writing Program, our roles moved beyond individual attempts in bringing up issues of language diversity in our writing courses. We all contributed to the ISU Writing Program philosophy and collectively engaged with the scholarship on L2 writing and translingualism with other writing instructors. For instance, Su Yin, Cristina, and Mijan all wrote articles about language issues in writing for the program's undergraduate research journal, the key resource used across FYW courses. An archive of externally created resources (such as articles and videos) and internally produced resources (such as podcasts and presentations) about language diversity were—and still are—being compiled by the writing program for instructors and students. In addition to offering graduate courses in applied linguistics, Lisya provided workshops for incoming writing instructors and faculty across disciplines on various issues, such as language transfer, negotiation of grammar, and systemic functional linguistics. She engaged students in discussions around translingualism, discussed second language writing pedagogies in her graduate courses and served as a graduate mentor for students from different branches of English Studies.

All the resources available to us and other instructors, we believe, made an impact on our teaching—and that of other instructors in the program—and informed our dispositions in the class as we dealt with issues of language difference. In our data, there are multiple references by all of us to activities and resources about language and writing, such as Demet's whole unit on linguistic identities, which aimed to raise students' awareness on issues regarding language varieties and predominant perspectives and attitudes about language. Close attention to language takes a central role in our teaching of writing and it has shown to be of importance in the way we present ourselves in the classrooms.

At the same time, the available resources did not only change us and our teaching, but our presence also changed the space, as ecologies consist of interconnected relationships. In other words, we shape the physical environment that we exist in, highlighting multidirectional transformations between those who exist in this particular ecology. The philosophy of the ISU Writing Program and the interdisciplinary nature of the department were translated into concrete actions that created room for us to enact on our linguistic identities. Developing a philosophy that supports diverse instructors is only the first step. The fact that the institutional ecology of the program enabled the construction of spaces in our writing pedagogies for bringing in our linguistic identities as a site of learning was possible because of a practiced philosophy, which involved intense laboring of bringing translingual approaches to writing into daily practice. Therefore, an important, but often missing, second step is transforming philosophies into actions that create an environment for diverse instructors to draw on their identities that transcend the classroom space, such as the creation of program-wide learning outcomes that address language diversity in writing. Outside the classroom, instructors were encouraged to participate in professional development activities, such as recording podcasts about writing diversity, exchanging teaching strategies at the ISU Writing Program summit, and writing articles for the program's own journal. As such, the philosophy was inherently linked to the practices and activities of the writing program, encouraging the visibility of multilingual instructors.

This strong connection between theory and practice inside and outside the classroom, then, created room for transnational writing teachers' identities. Our knowledge was constantly drawn on to inform the pedagogy and philosophy of the writing program, reflected in the nine program-wide learning outcomes that all course plans were based on. Initially, translingualism was part of the 8th learning outcome about differences in writing, within and across communities often associated with language in the US, but the active discussions of translingualism prompted the creation of a 9th learning outcome about translingual and transnational literacies to account for the diverse practices of *all* student writers. This demonstrates the impact of our presence, as well as the purposeful inclusion of and critical engagement with language issues in this space, highlighting the synergy between us and the writing program and the fluctuating and emergent natures of writing program ecologies (Reiff et al., 2015). Ultimately, to fully support transnational writing instructors, we must intentionally create an open space for this type of support, as theory is meaningless without sustainable practice.

We believe that our diverse writing instructor identities and our agentic positions in our specific programs cannot be placed in the NNEST/

NEST binary. Through our narratives on identity-as-pedagogy and institutional analysis, we see that multilingual writing instructors are aware of the sociohistorical connection between native speaker ideology and racialization. Through their pedagogical practices, they actively dismantle various monolingual ideologies by breaking linguistic hierarchies and perceiving identities from a multicompetent framework. As this chapter illustrates, recognizing and valuing writing pedagogies generated by multilingual instructors as productive sites of learning highly depends on the institution's language dispositions about legitimacy of language difference and literacy practices.

Recommendations and Conclusion

As our narratives illustrate, multilingual writing teachers can enrich and transform spaces that are commonly seen as homogenous. Our experiences highlight that "we must intentionally create contexts" (Donahue, 2018, p. 36) for effective writing instruction to account for language differences, diverse literate activities, and writing in the twenty-first century. Writing programs can be strengthened by these instructors' rich knowledge of non-English languages, expertise in writing/language studies, and a wide range of literacy practices, which have been overlooked for so long. Our strengths are also vital for broadening FYW students' understanding of what it means to participate in writing/literate activities in global communities and facilitating their developing understanding of literate practices across contexts and communities as *all* writers move in and out of different domains of writing. Although recognizing these assets is critical, we need to pay attention to the role of institutional structures and the ways NNESTs impact the curricula of writing-intensive courses.

In this context, we emphasize the need for writing programs and departments to critically engage with language ideologies to develop curricula that reflect our diverse ways of engaging with writing and literacy today. By extension, we underscore the importance of developing inclusive pedagogical practices, becoming more responsive to the needs of all student writers, creating opportunities for multilingual instructors to be involved in programmatic decisions, and validate their *identity-as-pedagogy* work. One possible venue for this is collaborative workshops offered by different units on campus to bring heightened awareness on various cross-cultural writing issues that emerge in classroom spaces. Inviting transnational writing instructors who specialize in TESOL and applied linguistics to give workshops on issues such as language difference or genres across communities could help all FYW teachers to become better equipped to understand and facilitate students' translingual dispositions and value linguistic resources of student writers.

While these workshops can help writing instructors and faculty become more aware of how language and culture influence students' reading and writing, some may continue to perceive language difference as a deviation from the norm rather than as an act to create space for agency and empowerment. To disrupt monolingual ideologies in our institutions and departments, we believe that these types of collaborations in the form of workshops or roundtable discussions should be part of the curriculum and offered as an ongoing professional opportunity for all instructors. Additionally, writing programs can work on making NNESTs' *identity-as-pedagogy work* visible and legitimate by having them overtly discuss cross-language issues they encounter in their courses with other writing instructors and administrators and by sharing course materials and assignments for incoming instructors as part of their socialization and training.

Moving forward, future studies could examine how instructors' pedagogical choices are shaped by their experiences as English as a foreign language (EFL) teachers, where high-stakes writing assessments, controlled composition, and large class sizes might have placed constraints on learning and teaching of L2 writing (Seloni & Henderson-Lee, 2020) and how knowledge about writing instruction evolves through time. Yet, as many of us have experienced, we constantly revise our pedagogies with the help of new institutional ecologies and the changing needs of students. Our languages, identities, and even educational backgrounds in writing programs are not fixed attributes, and thus, we cannot anticipate their trajectories. Therefore, we call for future research and praxis on writing programs, teacher education programs, and writing pedagogies to account for integrative approaches to language, writing, and identity as a dynamic, contextual, and co-constructed human activity.

References

Alvarez, S. P., Canagarajah, S., Lee, E., Lee, J. W. & Rabbi, S. (2017). Translingual practice, ethnic identities, and voice in writing. In B. Horner & L. Tetreault (Eds.), *Crossing divides: Exploring translingual writing pedagogies and programs* (pp. 31–48). Utah State University Press. https://10.7330/9781607326205.c002.

Aneja, G. A. (2016). Rethinking nativeness: Toward a dynamic paradigm of (non)native speakering. *Critical Inquiry in Language Studies, 13*(4), 351–379. https://doi.org/10.1080/15427587.2016.1185373.

Anzaldúa, G. E. (1987). *Borderlands/ La frontera: The new mestiza.* Aunt Lute Books.

Canagarajah, S. (2018). Translingual practice as spatial repertoires: Expanding the paradigm beyond structuralist orientations. *Applied Linguistics, 39*(1), 31–54. https://doi.org/10.1093/applin/amx041.

De Costa, P. & Norton, B. (2017). Introduction: Identity, transdisciplinarity, and the good language teacher. *The Modern Language Journal, 101*(Supplement 2017), 3–14. https://doi.org/10.1111/modl.12368.

de Oliveira, L. C. & Lan, S-W. (2012). Preparing nonnative English-speaking (NNES) graduate students for teaching in higher education: A mentoring case study. *Journal on Excellence in College Teaching, 23*(3), 59–76.

Donahue, C. (2009). "Internationalization" and composition studies: Reorienting the discourse. *College Composition and Communication, 61*(2), 212–243. https://www.jstor.org/stable/40593441.

Donahue, C. (2018). Rhetorical and linguistic flexibility: Valuing heterogeneity in academic writing education. In X. You (Ed.), *Transnational writing education: Theory, history, and practice* (pp. 21–40). Routledge. https://doi.org/10.4324/9781351205955-2.

Hatch, J. A. (2002). *Doing qualitative research in education settings.* State University of New York Press.

Horner, B., Lu, M.-Z., Royster, J. J. & Trimbur, J. (2011). Language difference in writing: Toward a translingual approach. *College English, 73*(3), 303–321.

Johnson, K. E. & Golombek, P. R. (Eds.). (2002). *Teacher's narrative inquiry as professional development.* Cambridge University Press.

Kamhi-Stein, L. (2004). *Learning and teaching from experience: Perspectives on nonnative English-speaking professionals.* University of Michigan Press. https://doi.org/10.3998/mpub.9648.

Kitalong, K. S. (2017). "Yep, yep. Got it": Establishing common ground between international teaching assistants and first-year composition students. In N. DeJoy & B. Q. Smith (Eds.), *Collaborations & innovations: Supporting multilingual writers across campus units* (pp. 77–94). University of Michigan Press.

Kubota, R., Corella, M., Lim, K. & Sah, P. K. (2021). "Your English is so good": Linguistic experiences of racialized students and instructors of a Canadian university. *Ethnicities, 23*(5), 758–778. https://doi.org/10.1177/14687968211055808.

Lantolf, J. P. (2012). Sociocultural theory: A dialectical approach to L2 research. In S. M. Gass & A. Mackey (Eds.), *The Routledge handbook of second language acquisition* (pp. 57–72). Routledge.

Martins, D. S. (Ed.). (2015). *Transnational writing program administration.* Utah State University Press. https://doi.org/10.7330/9780874219623.

Morgan, B. (2004). Teacher identity as pedagogy: Towards a field-internal conceptualisation in bilingual and second language education. *International Journal of Bilingual Education and Bilingualism, 7*, 172–188. https://doi.org/10.1080/13670050408667807.

Motha, S., Jain, R. & Tecle, T. (2012). Translinguistic identity-as-pedagogy: Implications for language teacher education. *International Journal of Innovation in English Language Teaching, 1*(1), 13–28.

Park, G. (2017). *Narratives of East Asian women teachers of English: Where privilege meets marginalization.* Multilingual Matters. https://doi.org/10.21832/9781783098736.

Pennycook, A. & Otsuji, E. (2015). *Metrolingualism: Language in the city*. Routledge. https://doi.org/10.4324/9781315724225.

Ramjattan, V. A. (2015). Lacking the right aesthetic: Everyday employment discrimination in Toronto private language schools. *Equality, Diversity and Inclusion: An International Journal, 34*(8), 692–704. https://doi.org/10.1108/EDI-03-2015-0018.

Reiff, M. J., Bawarshi, A., Ballif, M. & Weisser, C. (Eds.). (2015). *Ecologies of writing programs: Program profiles in context*. Parlor Press.

Reis, D. S. (2012). "Being underdog": Supporting nonnative English-speaking teachers (NNESTs) in claiming and asserting professional legitimacy. *Journal on Excellence in College Teaching, 23*(3), 33–58.

Rubin, D. L. (1992). Nonlanguage factors affecting undergraduates' judgments of nonnative English-speaking teaching assistants. *Research in Higher Education, 33*(4), 511–531. https://doi.org/10.1007/BF00973770.

Ruecker, T., Frazier, S. & Tseptsura, M. (2018). "Language difference can be an asset": Exploring the experiences of nonnative English speaking teachers of writing. *College Composition and Communication, 69*(4), 612–641. https://doi.org/10.58680/ccc201829694.

Sánchez-Martín, C. (2018). Teaching writing through transformation: Linguistically diverse writing teachers' enactments of linguistic diversity [Doctoral dissertation, Illinois State University]. ProQuest Theses and Dissertations. http://doi.org/10.30707/ETD2018.SanchezMartin.C.

Sánchez-Martín, C. & Walker, J. R. (2021). Grassroots professional development: Engaging multilingual identities and expansive literacies through pedagogical-cultural historical activity theory (PCHAT) and translingualism. In B. R. Schreiber, E. Lee, J. T. Johnson & N. Fahim (Eds.), *Linguistic justice on campus: Pedagogy and advocacy for multilingual students* (pp. 180–197). Multilingual Matters. https://doi.org/10.21832/9781788929509-012.

Seloni, L. (2012). Going beyond the native-nonnative English speaker divide in college courses: The role of nonnative English speaking educators in promoting critical multiculturalism. *Journal of Excellence in College Teaching, 23*(3), 120–155.

Seloni, L. & Henderson-Lee, S. (2020). *Second language writing instruction in global contexts: English language teacher preparation and development*. Multilingual Matters. https://doi.org/10.21832/9781788925877.

Selvi, A. F. (2010). All teachers are equal, but some teachers are more equal than others: Trend analysis of job advertisements in English language teaching. *WATESOL NNEST Caucus Annual Review, 1*, 156–181.

Widdowson, H. G. (1994). The ownership of English. *TESOL Quarterly, 28*(2), 377–389. https://doi.org/10.2307/3587438.

Zheng, X. (2017). Translingual identity as pedagogy: International teaching assistants of English in college composition classrooms. *The Modern Language Journal, 101*(S1), 29–44. https://doi.org/10.1111/modl.12373.

4　Dismantling Racial Microaggression: Translingual, Nonnative Identities as Pedagogical Resources

Nabila Hijazi
GEORGE WASHINGTON UNIVERSITY

As a nonnative English speaker who has taught first-year writing as both a graduate student and a professional track faculty member, I can attest to the multiple challenges nonnative English-speaking teachers of writing (NNESTs) constantly face on the ground of their nonnativeness. Resistance comes from not just native students but also nonnative students who expect to receive a "real American" learning experience from native English-speaking teachers (NESTSs), who are presumed to have the voice of authority. Witnessing first-hand students' weird looks and shrugs—even when they try to hide their reactions—when they meet me for the first time has intrigued me to examine the relatively nascent literature about the complex relationship between students and nonnative teachers of writing, particularly those who come from marginalized communities.

Scholars have asserted the need to understand the diversity of NNESTs (Huang, 2014; Moussu & Llurda, 2008; Park, 2012). Many explore the intersections of race and nonnativeness and challenge the normalized assumptions about teachers' identity (Amin, 2001; Pennycook, 2007; Romney, 2010; Yazan & Rudolph, 2018). Several have examined the intersection of teachers' racial and linguistic identities (Fan & de Jong, 2019; Huang & Varghese, 2015) and highlighted the issue of "linguistic racial profiling" NNESTs encounter due to their race (Romney, 2010). Some studies specifically address students' perceptions and reception of the distinction between native and nonnative English-speaking teachers, especially teachers of writing in first-year composition classes (Liu, 2005), while others discuss how nonnative English-speaking teachers of writing construct and negotiate their ethos and professional identity as they venture into teaching first-year writing (Ruecker et al., 2018). However, the experiences of NNESTs, whose composite, intersectional, and translingual identities are potential pedagogical resources, have been under-examined (Zheng, 2017). This chapter details the pedagogical practices, grounded in Brian Morgan's "teacher identity as pedagogy" (2004, p. 178), which I adopted in my first-year writing course, *English 101: Academic Writing*, to respond to the multiple layers of (dis)comfort and discrimination directed towards my NNEST identity. My teacher identity does not refer to only my linguistic identity (Zheng, 2017) but also to my multi-layered, intersectional minority identity, that of a nonnative, Arab, Muslim woman.

For some students, my intersectional positionality as a nonnative, female, Muslim faculty member may trigger overt resistance. For other students, resistance takes a more subtle form, that of microaggressions, a term defined as "commonplace verbal or behavioral indignities whether intentional or unintentional, which communicate hostile, derogatory, or negative racial slights and insults" (Sue et al. 2007, p. 273). In this chapter, I delineate my classroom practices that utilize teachers' identities as pedagogical resources. Instead of zeroing in on differences and inequalities, I deploy these differences as "substance and process of learning" (Morgan, 2004, p. 178) and make a case for a "pedagogy of discomfort" that challenges students to question their beliefs and assumptions about multiple identities and what it means to be a NNEST and prompts them to examine asymmetrical power relations (Prebel, 2016). These practices include text selections that center around the minority teacher's persona and identity that challenge students' level of comfort around a NNEST and their preconceived notions of what an effective teacher of writing should be, and an inquiry-based digital storytelling assignment that follows a translingual approach which corroborates and substantiates the proposition that NNESTs translinguistic identities as a strength, not a constraint. I manifest how my interventions shape students' thinking about marginal identities, more specifically my Muslim, female, and nonnative identity, and challenge the conviction of an appropriate *single story*. I provide tools to explore the very questions that my "axis of identities" raises in the classroom—and a call to reposition the role of nonnative English-speaking teachers of writing (NNESTs).

Intersectionality: Multiple Layers of Non-Nativity and Prejudice

The current political situation in the United States negatively stigmatizes minorities and fosters strong feelings of (dis)comfort, thus making it essential to consider the ideology of nativeness, an *Us-versus-Them division* (Shuck, 2006). A native speaker of English is *perceived* to be *White Anglo-Saxon*

(Matsuda, 2003; Norton, 1997) while nativism indicates a distrust of difference. The word *native* is also used to provoke a sense of nationalism (Higham, 1981). Thus, the dichotomy of native versus nonnative speakers of English (Faez, 2011; Mahboob, 2010) is a discourse "that is often used to justify exclusionary practices that perpetuate the normalization of Whiteness, American-ness, and nativeness in certain prestige varieties of English" (Shuck, 2006, p. 260). This discriminatory discourse validates students' perceptions of NNESTs as deficient and less competent while White NES teachers of writing as having perfect, authentic, and authoritative voice, due to their stark *White* accent (Amin, 2001; Baratta, 2018; Huang, 2018; Romney, 2010). It is a type of discourse that positions me, a nonnative speaker of English, as well as other minorities as *linguistic Other*: less visible, less trusted, and even feared—creating and solidifying discomfort around NNESTs. As Barbara Perry has noted, when we consider the intersection of gender with these other identities, the situation becomes more complicated, "murkier," and even "stormier" (2014, p. 79). Perceiving the native speaker as the standard automatically places me, a Muslim female NNEST, as, foreigner, and ultimately *Other* and *outside the nation*—nonnative to the nation, regardless of my education and competency in the English language. And, while Anglo-Saxon immigrants are accepted in the United States, other immigrants are frequently asked about their birthplace and origin, since they speak with an accent that is different from that constructed norm (Amin, 2001). While not all foreign accents are devalued, accents that are not linked to *white* skin or those that signal a *third-world* homeland accrue negative reactions and increase the level of discomfort students display towards NNESTs (Lippi-Green, 2012). With the term *White* being synonymous with *Western*, *Third-World-looking* refers to *non-Western* and automatically *subordinate—others* "to be feared, ridiculed, and loathed for their difference" (Perry, 2014, p. 75).

While race and accent already play roles in how I am perceived, my *hijab* (the veil or headscarf that Muslim women wear) is another pertinent marker, placing me in the "them" category, complicating my role as NNEST, especially because of the negative stigma attached to the veil (Macdonald, 2006). Sahar Amer in her book, *What Is Veiling?*, describes how veiling, when associated with Islam, is not a neutral term, but rather a judgmental term that evokes discomfort and "fear, anxiety, and a rising sense of threat" (2014, p. 2). Ultimately, as a *headscarfed* Muslim female NNES teacher, with non-Western, Islamic conservative attire, I am "caught at the intersection of discrimination against religion and discrimination against women" (Aziz, 2014, p. 5). I anticipate being viewed as less linguistically competent, nonnative, outsider, and by extension, *other*.

Multiple Forms of Racial Microaggressions Towards my NNEST Identity

I've occupied multiple positions—graduate student, contingent faculty—and it's not always possible to know how those positions are at issue when I experience multiple types of microaggression in the classroom[1] like many NNES teachers (see Tseptsura and Wang-Hiles, this volume, for examples). I teach a wide range of courses, including composition, writing center theory and practice, grammar, and women's studies, at a public East Coast Research I university where at least 50 percent of students identify as White. As a Muslim female NNEST, wearing a conservative all black hijab that covers my torso and a long sleeve maxi dress covering my full body, I am highly visible. That visibility puts my identity to the test from the first moment I walk into the classroom. Each semester, I encounter different forms of microaggression with my students' looks, questioning if they are or I am in the right classroom, occupying the rightful space, with some whispering, "Is this the teacher?" and others checking their phones to confirm the location of the classroom. As I introduce myself, I feel as if—like many NNEST, (e.g., Tseptsura, this volume)—I have to present a mini-version of my curriculum vitae, so students will know they are in trusted hands.

Students' reactions and concerns persist and even appear at the end of the semester. In course evaluations, a standard practice that invites students to critique instructors' teaching pedagogies, my English 101 students, for example, wrote about their initial reactions upon discovering I am their teacher:

> I'm not going to lie, I was kind of taken aback when I realized that I was going to be taught English by someone with an accent. But I realized later that she knew her stuff, and I can honestly say that I learned more from her than any teacher this semester and probably all the teachers I've had here at Maryland. Thanks for everything.

Another noted:

> She made sure that all students that attended were involved in every class. She truly cares and is extremely knowledgeable about the topic and wants us all to do well. But she talks really fast, sometimes it was hard to get everything down because of the accent.

---

[1] Microaggression in the classroom includes "interrogations of the teachers' nativeness, insinuations of their foreignness to English, and behavioral indications that they are 'invading' the classroom" (Ramjattan, 2019, p. 374).

Clearly, students have acknowledged my expertise and command of the materials but still acknowledged how my accent can be a barrier. Additionally, a student from my *English 101X: Academic Writing* class, which is designed for students for whom English is a second language, indicated in his end-of-semester course evaluation that "I learned so much about writing this semester and my writing improved but I expected the teacher for this class to be white and with no accent," confirming that even ESL students may exhibit more resistance to NNESTs. My students' end-of-semester comments further confirm the rampant misconception among students of what a teacher of writing should be or look like.

Moreover, in the end-of-semester course evaluation, students are asked about the qualities the instructor deserves special praise or needs special attention; one of my students wrote about how I "made sure everyone understood and went to great lengths to ensure that no one was confused," while another mentioned how they enjoyed that I was so full of energy: "She was very kind and took the time to read each student's papers." However, they wished I "talked a bit slower." Even though most of the comments have a positive aspect, they still insinuate that my accent, in combination with my speaking style, composes a stigma that is attached to my NNEST's persona. Nonetheless, students' evaluations of my teaching qualities present insights about my teacher identity, further confirming the value of teacher identity as pedagogy.

Feminist Composition Pedagogy: "Pedagogy of Discomfort"

To challenge these stereotypes and deconstruct the notion of the normative image of the ideal teacher, I have utilized feminist composition pedagogy, which is defined

> as a keen awareness of classroom dynamics, continuously striving to confront issues of power and authority as they play out between students and teachers; it is an attempt to move students to critical consciousness, especially in regards to racism, classism, sexism, homophobia, and other ideological forces that create hierarchies. (Siebler, 2008, p. 3)

Using feminist composition pedagogy has allowed me to create a high-energy learning environment to engage with my students in difficult conversations and to overcome the multiple barriers and levels of misjudgment that my female, Muslim, and nonnative body encounters. I developed a three-part pedagogical strategy: 1) recognizing and naming the discomfort and then teaching writing skills through that discomfort, 2) teaching the inquiry-based digital storytelling assignment that creates a space for translingual affordances, and 3) engaging in reflective teaching practices to ensure my growth and further solidify my competency as an NNEST.

Recognizing and Naming Discomfort: Teaching Controversial Texts and Unfamiliar Topics

The pedagogical strategies I have developed to respond to my unique situation and to my students' preconceived stereotypes is to bring materials that make the concerns of my students an object of discussion. I have designed writing assignments around difficult texts and unfamiliar topics, veiling for example, that reflect my own identity not just as a teacher but also as a person. I evoke and utilize a pedagogical notion of "teacher identity as pedagogy" (Morgan, 2004, p. 178), as I make the identity that is an issue for my students a subject of analysis for us to think about together. I use the tensions that arise in a text that reflects my identity as a resource of pedagogy and for engaging in critical dialogue. Such texts allow my students to see my intellect beyond my female body, the headscarf that represents my religious affiliation, and the speech pattern that marks my nonnativeness.

English 101: Academic Writing at my institution is rhetorical in its approach and is based on a common set of assignments, beginning with a summary assignment, moving to a rhetorical analysis, and then scaffolding a research paper that begins with an inquiry into a topic through a digital storytelling assignment. The goal is first to inquire and to determine what is known—and credible—about a topic or issue. Engaging in inquiry and responding to questions lead to rhetorical practice. Thus, inquiry and rhetoric rely on investigating, listening to, and reflecting upon the diverse thoughts and ideas of others. Reflection and revision are major parts of the curriculum. During the first week of classes, as I introduce the Summary assignment, I assign Naheed Mustafa's article, "My Body Is My Own Business," published by *The Globe & Mail* in 1993. Mustafa argues that women should not be judged by their bodies and that hijab is a form of strength and empowerment, contrary to the popular principle of the hijab representing male oppression. Summarizing the text and engaging in in-class discussions around the author's main points, purpose, and audience invite unsanctioned, critical conversations and open the space for my students and me to hone close reading practices and to think critically about identity. These conversations challenge the walls of rejection and the existing stereotypes and craft space for me to explain the multiple identities that exist in this country and to legitimize them as normative while challenging the idea that the *White, female body* constitutes the standard, and anything that is non-White is different, foreign, or in other words, *nonnative, other*. Through the naming of the discomfort and using the tension as a resource, I, with my students, navigate through layers of resistance and microaggressions and engage in critical discussions and learning.

As my students start to become comfortable around these difficult conversations, and as we transition to a rhetorical analysis assignment, I require my students to analyze TED Talks such as Dalia Mogahed's *What it's like to be Muslim in America* or Kimberley Crenshaw's *The Urgency of Intersectionality*. But, before they set out to analyze those texts, I encourage students to participate in a discussion of Chimamanda Ngozi Adichie's *The Danger of a Single Story*, encouraging students to see that too often we focus on a single story, excluding cultural influences, other perspectives, and the rich tapestry of different experiences in the world. I emphasize that the *single story* approach is limiting and makes us misinterpret people, their backgrounds, and their lives while leading to misjudgment, disconnection, and conflict. Students realize how Adichie addresses concerns of listening, reflection, and argument—key themes in the curriculum, especially as they move through their own inquiries and arguments. The discussions cultivate spaces that promote tolerance and acceptance while demystifying the idea of multiplicity and *othering*.

Discussions of identity and tolerance feel awkward in the beginning, but students eventually start to open up. One student praised the selection of these texts and the discussion around them in this way:

> The TED Talk, "What it's like to be Muslim in America," Mrs. Hijazi asked us to analyze, made me and other classmates engage in a critical and important discussion, especially since we live in a polarized and challenging sociopolitical environment. These discussions made us think capaciously about our identity and contest the concept of one American identity.

Another wrote: "I thought that the choice of the TED Talk was especially relevant in today's social climate, and it really made me think about the tragedy of 9/11 from a different perspective." While teaching around difficult conversations is an effective classroom strategy that can be used by all teachers, NESTs and NNESTs, it is particularly effectual for NNESTs as they confront the subjects that feed into the dominant stereotype of how a teacher of writing should look or sound. Avoiding these conversations perpetuates the same narratives that have dehumanized others who look different or whose beliefs are not part of the Western standard. By integrating discussions that intrigue students to explore their emotions around discomfort, I dismantle barriers that cloud and color my students' critical analysis and prevent them from solidifying their biases.

Digital Storytelling with a Translingual Approach: From Confrontation to Affirmation

As an academic invested in translingual writing, I design assignments to solicit students' reactions towards translingual practices and to challenge them to think critically about their own internalized monolingual bias. Adopting Suresh Canagarajah's conceptualization that "translingual addresses the synergy, treating languages as always in contact and mutually influencing each other, with emergent meanings and grammars . . . an understanding of the production, circulation, and reception of texts that are always mobile; that draw from diverse languages, symbol systems, and modalities of communication; and that involve inter-community negotiations" (2013, p. 41), I encourage my students to engage in translingual practices in multiple texts, written or digital. Digital storytelling brings students' interests and backgrounds into the pedagogical process, allowing everyone to have a voice while affording them the flexibility in finding forms of expression and making linguistic and content decisions.

The Digital Storytelling assignment, an open-ended narrative inquiry project, is the first step in the inquiry and research process in my writing class. At this stage in their writing process, students do not make an argument but rather engage in an exchange of ideas. The Digital Storytelling assignment, a combination of multimodal and translingual approaches, is an affordance for students to remix different forms of print and digital languages to create a translingual amalgam of literacies. By exploring these different forms of expression, my students challenge their conception of themselves as authors and their definition of acceptable academic genres. The assignment is a chance for them to invest in questioning their beliefs, opinions, interpretations, and assumptions—rather than using them as a foundation. It is a time when they may ask hard questions, even if those hard questions challenge their beliefs and viewpoints. And, of course, I add a disclaimer that after inquiry, many of them may still believe the same thing, but that belief will be honed, nuanced, tested, enriched, and supported with evidence rather than merely accepted.

In the Digital Storytelling assignment, students are asked to consider a personal experience and question and probe that experience, seeking an understanding of what is at issue in the experience. In this assignment, I ask them to do what academics do: begin with a topic of inquiry, formulating a set of questions to pursue and research. As they record their stories, they are encouraged to engage in different modes and translingual writing practices, mixing the languages they know. To give them an example, I show my own digital story, in which I share one of my experiences at the airport being scrutinized and questioned due to my religious, Middle Eastern identity, and the type of inquiry and academic topics I would be able to pursue based on my personal story—such as racial profiling. In my digital story, I show personal images of myself and my children and use short sentences in Arabic. I ask my students to reflect on my translingual practice, and the majority express their feelings of being curious and intrigued. As they watch my digital story, they focus on the sound and the flow of the narrative of the video. Some shared that the inclusion of Arabic made them experience "what Arabic to English speakers feel learning English," a student wrote in her reflection. She explained how they "felt a positive response to the formatting and inclusion of the Arabic" and saw the power of language others have that they may not have.

Translingual writing as an approach resists the monolingualist reification of language and nation and allows for "honoring the power of all language users to shape language to specific ends [and] recognizing the linguistic heterogeneity of all users of language both within the United States and globally" (Horner et al., 2011, p. 305). It invites students with diverse linguistic and cultural backgrounds to negotiate the various languages and rhetorical styles they bring into their writing (Lu & Horner, 2013). Digital stories, with their own set of affordances and pedagogy, map space for students to develop their unique voices and invite them to consider multiple stories, including those not their own. This helps deconstruct the negative stigma attached to accents that are not considered standard or *White*, including mine. Integrating digital stories in the writing classroom helps my students showcase their voices in a variety of ways—to express strong voices by telling their own stories in their own ways and their own accents, while expanding the audience for their work. Sharing their digital stories through multiple venues, such as YouTube, allows my students, with their multiple accents, to reach out to a broader audience, ultimately making both our composition classroom and the Digital Storytelling assignment "commitment[s] to creating connections between the external world and the classroom" (Siebler, 2008, p. 3). Through this assignment, students gain agency, regardless of what accent they have, whether considered native or nonnative, moving away from the imagined, native-nonnative binary.

In these pedagogical practices, my students and I question our personal positionalities and challenge our assumptions, allowing for nuanced understanding and acceptance, regardless of our different personal beliefs which shape our personalities. The composition classroom becomes a space for dialogues about contradictions, allowing students to engage in self-development.

However, this self-development is not unidirectional but multidirectional, as we educators recognize our own discomfort with students' resistance to our nonnative identity and place in the classroom. However, through text selections and inquiry-based assignments, my students are already thinking about identity, and my faculty identity is more fully recognized in the classroom. By making my students aware of the multilayered identity I occupy and perform in the classroom, I am able to challenge and change conventional educational practices that have solidified the *native speaker fallacy* (Phillipson, 1992).

My students learn how to approach and value a multiplicity of identities. This discomfort can provide opportunities for reflection on and examination of beliefs not only about writing but also about different identities and modes of writing. My classroom becomes a space where we challenge our assumptions about ourselves and others. I start with my students confronting their external biases towards different types of teacher identity and persona. Instead of just enhancing their understanding of composition principles, I help them think through their biases and prejudice first. I help students to become more aware of microaggressions, their own and those of others so that they can be ready to respond helpfully in a way that fosters understanding and learning.

An Extra Layer of Translingual Practices

While I use the same curriculum, assignments, and text selections in all of my *English 101: Academic Writing* classes, I tend to emphasize my speech patterns more overtly in *English 101X*, the course section designated for nonnative speakers. When I introduce myself on the first day of class, I make a declarative statement to my students: be prepared to engage in class discussion and to speak out in class. All of us have an accent, including me. Although this statement may put me at a disadvantage since I am not the presumed native English-speaking teacher (NEST), it encourages my students to open up and feel comfortable about valuing their own accents. I repeat the statement several times throughout the semester to encourage those who are reluctant to participate to be comfortable with their nonnative identities.

In addition to underscoring my accent to facilitate our discussions, I draw on my translingual identity and utilize my first language. A good number of international students who take *English 101X* come from Gulf countries where Arabic is the main language. When my students feel frustrated and do not understand a concept, I switch to Arabic to explain the concept. When choosing the correct vocabulary to use in their essays, they often struggle to find the best word to use. Through our conversation, I help them use the right one instead of relying on a thesaurus, which may not give the correct word, considering the context. Also, when engaging in literal translation, I explain why a linguistic form or rhetorical concept that works in Arabic composition does not necessarily translate to an English context. For many of them, including students who come from other countries and who speak languages other than Arabic, I became a familiar face; several expressed their appreciation of having a teacher who went through the same struggles they are facing and has come a long way. Many expressed feeling happy and empowered for being able to honor their first or second language as they had the chance to use it in combination with English in their digital stories to express their views and identities.

Engaging in Reflective Practices: Becoming Comfortable

Thinking introspectively about one's own teacher subjectivities in the classroom allows for self-reflection that informs our pedagogical approaches and practices. Assignments in my *English 101: Academic Writing* focus on identities and allow students to practice reflection, a mode of cognition and inquiry that allows writers to build on existing writing skills, question their attitudes towards writing, and evaluate the rhetorical choices they make (Taczak, 2015). Ultimately, for the last assignment, the "Reflective Memo," students reflect on all the writing they did throughout the semester. I ask them about the challenges they had in the course and how they addressed those challenges in their writings. I inquire about how their prior knowledge of writing expanded, confirmed, complicated, and or altered their writing practices and approaches. I ask students to reflect on the Digital Storytelling assignment and the choices of the TED Talks; to address how beneficial or helpful the digital story is to their initial inquiry or writing; and to answer if they would keep it as part of the curriculum. One student wrote:

> I was pleasantly surprised by how many different ways we were able to express ourselves in this course, beyond just writing papers. I do not think that I would have learned what I did if we did not use so many modes of communication, such as digital storytelling. This class has opened my eyes to how academic writing is not limited to a strict, formulaic paper, but rather a wide variety of methods for communicating with the audience. The class showed me the importance of different and multiple identities.

This type of response shows that my students are becoming comfortable with different texts and accepting the plurality of identities and accents. By stepping back to reflect on their writing, the assignments, and the assigned texts, students ponder on the diverse thoughts and ideas of others and engage in critical thinking. Since writers' identities are shaped and reshaped by their lives, including prior experiences, with reflection, they tap into and reevaluate these experiences as they become better writers (Taczak, 2015). While stepping back to think critically about their writing process and development (Yancey, 1998), they also reflect thoughtfully on perspectives that are different from their own. Ultimately, these reflections further confirm the purpose of my assignments: that students' beliefs are honed, enriched, and supported with evidence rather than merely accepted and allow for developing a better understanding of others. These reflections empower me as a NNEST and guide my pedagogical advancement. My pedagogical strategies for negotiating my teacher persona produce material effect, allowing me and my students to navigate and dismantle multiple layers of discrimination and misconception—moving away from resistance to acceptance.

Conclusion

In the past, academic discourse has been dominated by a monolingual orientation that defined the so-called native speaker, which renders the expertise of the NNEST, as less, deficient, or even illegitimate. Multiple subject positions, including accent, race, gender, and religion, intersect to position minority female composition faculty as vulnerable and expose to complex patterns of bias; we are perceived as *Other* and as outside the nation—*nonnative* to the nation and nonnative speakers of English. Therefore, it is important to challenge the dominant, normative view of language and adopt pedagogical and classroom practices which center around critical strategies that address microaggressions in the classroom and allow for understanding the value of translingual faculty and teaching practices. The academic writing program at the institution where I work has been supportive on a macro and micro level, promoting and adopting various pedagogical practices that honor diversity and multiplicity and support NNESTs. For instance, recently Chimamanda Adichie's TED Talk *The Danger of a Single Story* became part of the standard syllabus to teach the "Summary" and "Rhetorical Analysis" assignments. Students are asked to discuss how Adichie addresses concerns of social justice, civic deliberation, listening, reflection, and argument, key themes pertinent to their own inquiries and arguments. Adichie's TED talk is also used in "New Teacher Orientation," when academic writing program administrators (a role I had for two years) shape new faculty members' pedagogical practices by illustrating lessons on responding to students' writing, reactive versus responsive commentary, lesson planning, and dealing with classroom scenarios including classroom disruptions. For professional development day events, the academic writing program has been inviting speakers from various minority groups, including ones who identify as NNEST. These scholars encourage teaching practices that address microaggressions and invigorate antiracist pedagogy.

I have helped organize workshops for NNESTs titled "Coffee with Multilingual Teachers," in which I drew from my experience as a Muslim female NNEST and shared ways to deal with students' resistance. We discussed the challenges NNESTs face while teaching *English 101: Academic Writing* and how these challenges have changed in relation to becoming more experienced as teachers. During these workshops, NNESTs were encouraged to share their feelings of any kind of resistance or discrimination from students because of their NNEST identity and how they handled the situation. Some shared their experiences overcoming differences and achieving student engagement and acceptance. I raised the challenge of engaging with translingual teaching practices in an asynchronous online format in which students could not necessarily hear their own differing accents or my own. Unsurprisingly, my concerns were shared by other NNESTs. Together, we talked about lesson plans that we found to be successful and unsuccessful in an environment that facilitated collegiality and collaboration. We even signed up for a "teaching-partner" program, a peer pedagogical support program that provides writing instructors an opportunity to observe and be observed by another instructor and otherwise offers a source of peer support throughout the semester and mutual reflection where both teachers would grow. The analysis and discussions between teaching partners have provided contexts and conditions that affect future training and support of writing teachers.

In addition, unlike earlier studies on NNESTs that mainly address the discrimination that NNESTs face due to their nonnative identity, this chapter describes pedagogical practices centered around NNESTs' intersectional, multilayered identity, in relation to race, gender, nonnativeness, and translingual status, and denotes it as a strength instead of a deficiency. Throughout this chapter, which is a reflection on my own positionality and my classroom practices that utilize translingual writing in order to challenge the dominant, normative view of NNESTs as less competent, I call for a curriculum that helps students see past a single genre and mode of delivery—a single story of identity. I also call for more support from writing program administrators to assist NNESTs to honor and explore their identities as pedagogical practices in the classroom and facilitate a translingual identity, and to engage in reflective teaching practices (Khor et al., and Tseptsura, this volume).

Beyond offering statements of inclusion and diversity, institutions can expand their curriculums to include authors who identify as NNEST—something my institution started doing. Consistent attention to explicit anti-racist and social justice pedagogies, through readings, discussions, and campus-wide events, helps solidify everyone's knowledge of anti-racist and social justice pedagogical practices, which help eliminate "linguistic racial injustice." Honoring multiple identities helps administrators and students see beyond a standard identity construct and recognize that NNESTs are not a homogeneous group; with each having a different linguistic, translingual, or even multilayered identity, each contributes to the richness and multiplicity of identities that defeat the single story or native speaker fallacies or the imagined ideal status of a NEST.

References

Amer, S. (2014). *What is veiling?* Edinburgh University Press.

Amin, N. (2001). *Negotiating nativism: Minority immigrant women ESL teachers and the native speaker construct* [Doctoral dissertation, University of Toronto]. National Library of Canada = Bibliothèque nationale du Canada.

Aziz, S. F. (2014). Terror(izing) the "veil": American Muslim women caught in the crosshairs of intersectionality. In S. O. Ilesanmi, W. C. Lee, & J. W. Parker (Eds.), *The rule of law and the rule of God* (pp. 207–232). Palgrave Macmillan. https://doi.org/10.1057/9781137447760_10.

Baratta, A. (2018). "I speak how I speak:" A discussion of accent and identity within teachers of ELT. In B. Yazan & N. Rudolph (Eds.), *Criticality, teacher identity, and (in)equity in English language teaching* (pp. 163–178). Springer. https://doi.org/10.1007/978-3-319-72920-6_9.

Canagarajah, A. S. (2013). Negotiating translingual literacy: An enactment. *Research in the Teaching of English, 48*(1), 40–67. http://www.jstor.org/stable/24398646.

Crenshaw, K. (2016, October). *The urgency of intersectionality* [Video]. TED Conferences. https://www.ted.com/talks/kimberle_crenshaw_the_urgency_of_intersectionality?language=en.

Faez, F. (2011). Reconceptualizing the native/nonnative speaker dichotomy. *Journal of Language, Identity & Education, 10*(4), 231–249. https://doi.org/10.1080/15348458.2011.598127.

Fan, F. & de Jong, E. J. (2019). Exploring professional identities of nonnative-English-speaking teachers in the United States: A narrative case study. *TESOL Journal, 10*(4), 1–17. https://doi.org/10.1002/tesj.495.

Higham, J. (1981). *Strangers in the land: Patterns of American nativism, 1860–1925*. Greenwood Press.

Horner, B., Lu, M.-Z., Royster, J. J. & Trimbur, J. (2011). Language difference in writing: toward a translingual approach. *College English, 73*(3), 303–321. https://

kcccomp.commons.gc.cuny.edu/wp-content/blogs.dir/2708/files/2019/10/Horner-Lu-2011.pdf.

Huang, IC. (2014). Contextualizing teacher identity of non-native-English speakers in U.S. secondary ESL classrooms: A Bakhtinian perspective. *Linguistics and Education, 25*(1), 119–128. https://doi.org/10.1016/j.linged.2013.09.011.

Huang, IC. (2018). Power and ownership within the NS/NNS dichotomy. In B. Yazan & N. Rudolph (Eds.), *Criticality, teacher identity, and (In)equity in English language teaching* (pp. 41–56). Springer. https://doi.org/10.1007/978-3-319-72920-6_3.

Huang, IC. & Varghese, M. M. (2015). Toward a composite, personalized, and institutionalized teacher identity for non-native English speakers in U.S. secondary ESL programs. *Critical Inquiry in Language Studies, 12*(1), 51–76. https://doi.org/10.1080/15427587.2015.997651.

Lippi-Green, R. (2012). *English with an accent: language, ideology and discrimination in the United States* (2nd ed.). Routledge.

Liu, J. (2005). Chinese graduate teaching assistants teaching freshman composition to native English speaking students. In E. Llurda (Ed.), *Non-native language teachers. Educational Linguistics* (Vol 5) (pp. 155–177). Springer. https://doi.org/10.1007/0-387-24565-0_9.

Lu, M.-Z. & Horner, B. (2013). Translingual literacy, language difference, and matters of agency. *College English, 75*(6), 582–607. https://ir.library.louisville.edu/cgi/viewcontent.cgi?httpsredir=1&article=1064&context=faculty.

Macdonald, M. (2006). Muslim women and the veil: Problems of image and voice in media representations. *Feminist Media Studies, 6*(1), 7–23. https://doi.org/10.1080/14680770500471004.

Mahboob, A. (2010). *The NNEST lens: Non-native English speakers in TESOL*. Cambridge Scholars Publishing.

Matsuda, A. (2003). Incorporating world Englishes in teaching English as an international language. *TESOL Quarterly, 37*(4), 719–729. https://doi.org/10.2307/3588220.

Morgan, B. (2004). Teacher identity as pedagogy: Towards a field-internal conceptualisation in bilingual and second language education. *International Journal of Bilingual Education and Bilingualism, 7*(2), 172–188. https://doi.org/10.1080/13670050408667807.

Moussu, L. & Llurda, E. (2008). Non-native English-speaking English language teachers: History and research. *Language Teaching, 41*(3), 315–348. https://doi.org/10.1017/S0261444808005028.

Mustafa, N. (1993). *My body is my own business.* The Globe & Mail.

Norton, B. (1997). Language, identity, and the ownership of English. *TESOL Quarterly, 31*(3), 409–429. https://doi.org/10.2307/3587831.

Park, G. (2012). "I am never afraid of being recognized as an NNES": One teacher's journey in claiming and embracing her nonnative-speaker identity. *TESOL Quarterly, 46*(1), 127–151. https://doi.org/10.1002/tesq.4.

Pennycook, A. (2007). *Global Englishes and transcultural flows.* Routledge.

Perry, B. (2014). Gendered islamophobia: Hate crime against Muslim women. *Social Identities*, 20(1), 74–89. https://doi.org/10.1080/13504630.2013.864467.

Phillipson, R. (1992). *Linguistic imperialism*. Oxford University Press.

Prebel, J. (2016). Engaging a "pedagogy of discomfort": Emotion as critical inquiry in community-based writing courses. *Composition Forum*, 34. https://files.eric.ed.gov/fulltext/EJ1113429.pdf.

Ramjattan, V. A. (2019). Racist nativist microaggressions and the professional resistance of racialized English language teachers in Toronto. *Race Ethnicity and Education*, 22(3), 374–390. https://doi.org/10.1080/13613324.2017.1377171.

Romney, M. (2010). The colour of English. In A. Mahboob (Ed.), *The NNEST lens: Non-native English speakers in TESOL* (pp. 18–34). Cambridge Scholars Publishing.

Ruecker, T., Frazier, S. & Tseptsura, M. (2018). "Language difference can be an asset": Exploring the experiences of nonnative English-speaking teachers of writing. *College Composition and Communication*, 69(4), 612–641. http://www.jstor.org/stable/44870978.

Siebler, K. (2008). *Composing feminism(s): How feminists have shaped composition theories and practices*. Hampton Press.

Shuck, G. (2006). Racializing the nonnative English speaker. *Journal of Language, Identity & Education*, 5(4), 259–276. https://doi.org/10.1207/s15327701jlie0504_1.

Sue, D. W., Capodilupo, C. M., Torino, G. C., Bucceri, J. M., Holder, A. M. B., Nadal, K. L. & Esquilin, M. (2007). Racial microaggressions in everyday life: Implications for clinical practice. *The American Psychologist*, 62(4), 271–86. https://doi.org/10.1037/0003-066x.62.4.271.

Taczak, K. (2015). Reflection is critical for writers' development. In L. Adler-Kassner & E. Wardle (Eds.), *Naming what we know: Threshold concepts of writing studies* (pp. 78–81). Utah State University Press.

TED. (2009, October 7). *Chimamanda Adichie: The danger of a single story* [Video]. YouTube. https://www.youtube.com/watch?v=D9Ihs241zeg.

TED. (2016, March 15). *Dalia Mogahed: What it's like to be Muslim in America* [Video]. YouTube. https://www.youtube.com/watch?v=wzkFoetp-_M.

Yancey, K. B. (1998). *Reflection in the writing classroom*. Utah State University Press.

Zheng, X. (2017). Translingual identity as pedagogy: International teaching assistants of English in college composition classrooms. *The Modern Language Journal*, 101(S1), 29–44. https://doi.org/10.1111/modl.12373.

5

Cultural Adaptation and Building Authority As a NNES: A Reflective Study

Mariya Tseptsura
UNIVERSITY OF ARIZONA

In the fall 2014, I was teaching a first-year writing course to a mixed group of international and U.S. students at a large public research university in the Southwestern United States. As an international graduate teaching assistant at the time, I was still relatively new to composition as a field and a profession after earning my BA and MA degree in linguistics and translation studies in Russia and my second MA degree in TESOL in the US. The composition course I was teaching focused on improving students' knowledge of rhetorical conventions across a variety of genres with a special focus on intercultural communication and linguistic diversity. For one of four major units, students analyzed a literary text, a play by an American playwright David Henry Hwang titled *M. Butterfly*. For the most part, students reacted positively to the text and had many engaged discussions of its themes. However, at one point during a whole-class discussion, a NES White male student asked in a slightly accusatory way, "Did you choose it because you liked it?" He seemed to imply that the text had few merits on its own, an opinion voiced in a previous online discussion, and that my curricular decisions were based on my personal preferences rather than on my expertise or subject knowledge. At that moment, my body language showed great discomfort: I was standing when the student asked the question, but after hearing the question, I sat down, my arms and legs crossed, and my head lowered. It felt like an attack on my teaching skills and my authority in the classroom. My first reaction was to defend my teaching qualifications as well as the play's many virtues. However, I checked myself and instead re-directed the question to the whole class, asking the students, "Why do you think I chose this play?" One student commented that it was confusing, to which I replied with a joke, "Ah yes, I always like to make my students suffer." The class laughed, and another student offered a different suggestion: "because it's open to many interpretations." A few students also commented that the play was difficult to understand sometimes, at which point the first student repeated his question again (this time with even more emphasis): "Did you choose it because you *liked* it?" This time, I caved into the impulse to defend myself and laid out my reasons: the play was accessible and thought-provoking; it was multilayered and fit well with our cross-cultural class. To that, the student replied with, "So what you're saying is that you *did* choose it because you liked it." The class laughed, and I felt defeated. I proceeded to admit that I would not have chosen the play if I hadn't liked it, and that students were entitled to their own opinion whether they liked the play or not. At that point I moved on to the next item on the agenda.

After the class, I dwelled on the incident for a long time, wondering if there was a better way to handle the situation. Did the student persist in asking the question because he felt comfortable asking questions in our class or because he felt it within his right to question the authority of a NNES international TA? Would he still repeatedly ask these questions in the same tone if I were a male, U.S.-born NES instructor, or would he have more trust in such instructor's decisions? Or perhaps I would not feel my authority was questioned if I was a NES instructor? Do my students have any trust in my knowledge and expertise, or would I have to justify every pedagogical decision I make to them?

I was able to analyze in detail my reactions to this incident—and many others like it—because the class meeting was videotaped as part of a reflective autoethnographic study I conducted that semester. The study grew out of a desire to investigate my own teaching practices and how well they aligned, or not, with my evolving ideals and beliefs about education and teaching. I was particularly interested in exploring how, as an NNEST, I navigated challenges around building a confident teaching persona in a space where I was one of the few NES instructors in the writing program. In this chapter, I draw on the study to look beyond language differences and explore how the process of building confidence and authority as a NNEST is affected by cultural and ideological differences that often coexist with (and are complicated by) nonnative speaker status. I start with offering a more nuanced discussion of authority in teaching that takes into consideration cultural and disciplinary differences. I then describe the design of the present study, discuss its results, and offer implications for NNESs and writing program administrators.

Authority, Culture, and Teaching Writing As a NNEST

"Power" and "authority" in educational settings have been conceptualized in multiple ways. One of the better-known conceptualizations is Max Weber's classification of authority into three (later expanded into four) types. Weber (1957) divided authority into *legal* (or bureaucratic) authority that relies on laws and rules; *traditional* authority upheld by traditions and time, and *charismatic* authority whereby individuals garner support and following from people due to personal qualities and emotional appeal. Later, sociologists using Weber's classification added a fourth type called *professional* authority, supported by the person's expertise in a given area of knowledge or activity. Moreover, a crucial part of Weber's theory is that authority is a social relationship (Pace & Hemmings, 2007): authority figures are able to give commands because people obeying them see their authority as legitimate.

This point dovetails with Patricia Bizzell's (1991) description of authority as well; to exercise authority in the classroom, teachers must first persuade their students to trust their knowledge and good will: "Persuasion must precede authority" (p. 851). Bizzell stressed that students need to believe their teacher has their best interests at heart to follow along with a curriculum that they might resist or find difficult. Likewise, in their description of an exemplary writing instructor, Steven Vanderstaay et al. (2009) explained how the teacher they observed relied almost exclusively on his professional authority while eschewing his bureaucratic authority in order to create an engaged and productive learning community in his classroom. Notably, they identified an "internal authority" coming from a deep-seated "belief in himself" (p. 277). Thus, the most desirable type of teacher authority stems from confidence in one's own abilities and students' trust.

In composition studies, authority and power relations have been a frequent topic of investigation. As Bizzell (1991) put it, "one might read the history of modern composition studies as a series of attacks on classroom uses of power" (p. 847). Proponents of critical pedagogy in composition as well as theorists of social-constructivist approaches to writing and rhetoric have questioned the role of ideology in shaping the reality of its followers and urged writing instructors to use writing instruction, in Patricia Mayes' (2010) words, "as a vehicle for exploring and critiquing power relations, diversity, justice, oppression, and other social issues; . . . the ultimate goal is a transformative effect on power relations in the classroom and perhaps in society in general" (p. 190). Social-constructivist theorists in composition studies, including James Berlin, Bizzell, David Bartholomae, and John Trimbur, also advocated for critiquing the existing dominant ideologies and social injustices by decentralizing the classroom and sharing power with the students. However, as Robert Yagelski (1999) pointed out, decentralizing power in the classroom requires a balancing act between "using one's legitimate authority as a teacher on the one hand and, on the other, taking appropriate measures to undercut that same authority so that it does not inhibit the effort to foster critical consciousness in students" (p. 41). These decentralizing efforts also involve constant questioning of the writing instructor's own practices, which can be, in Yagelski's words, unsettling and uncomfortable. This process can be even more daunting for teachers coming from international backgrounds whose mindset is often shaped by a different set of internalized beliefs about education, teaching, and authority. While many, if not most, of NNES instructors in composition come from international backgrounds and represent a wide range of cultures, the effects of cultural background on understanding and enactment of authority are often missing from the discussions of authority in composition studies.

"Culture" often defies precise definitions; in this chapter, I adopt Geert Hofstede's (1980) definition of culture as "the collective programming of the mind that distinguishes the members of one group or category of people from another" (p. 9). In Hofstede's framework, cultures differ across five major dimensions: power distance, uncertainty avoidance, individualism versus collectivism, masculinity versus femininity, and long-term versus short-term orientation. For our discussion of power and authority, the first dimension is most important. Power distance is defined as "the extent to which the less powerful members of organizations and institutions (such as the family) accept and expect that power is distributed unequally" (Hofstede & NcCrae, 2004, p. 62). All societies exhibit varying degrees of inequality between those at the top of social hierarchy and those at the bottom, but in cultures with high power distance, the less powerful members of society are more likely to accept that distance as a given. The high-power distance is also evident throughout the education system where power balance is often skewed: the teacher possesses a large degree of authority by virtue of holding the position itself, and students rarely get a chance to negotiate power relations in the classroom or to question their teacher's decisions. Research into the experiences of students from more traditionally high-power distance cultures studying in a lower-power distance countries exemplifies these cultural differences; for instance, Yi Zhang (2013) found that compared to mainstream U.S. students, students from China, Taiwan, and Hong Kong commonly perceived learning as more instructor-centered and felt intimidated to reach out to their online instructors when issues occurred. Conversely, Huong Tran Nguyen (2008), exploring cultural influences on five Vietnamese American teachers' professional identity construction, demonstrated that these teachers expected "to command authority in the classroom and reverential respect from their students and parents" simply due to their status as teachers (p. 113). Furthermore, teachers coming from high-power distance cultural backgrounds might have difficulties adjusting to teaching practices shaped by lower-power distance cultural discourses such as higher value placed on students' active participation in class discussions or collaborative work such as peer reviews.

Instructors starting to teach in a different cultural setting are exposed to new cultural and disciplinary discourses that might change their understanding and beliefs about power and authority in the classroom. At the same time, adjusting their teaching practices to align with their changing beliefs might prove more challenging for NNES instructors. Even if NNES international instructors might desire to adopt more egalitarian teaching practices or follow a critical pedagogy framework, they are likely to discover that due to the challenges their NNES status creates for establishing credibility, they have limited resources when it comes to building authority in their classrooms. NNES instructors often face students' prejudice because of their language status (e.g., Liu, 2005; Reis, 2012; Shehi, 2017) that undermines their credibility as writing instructors. In addition, the deficit view of NNESs, when internalized, also negatively affects these instructors' faith in their own teaching abilities (e.g., Canagarajah, 1999; Llurda, 2009; Medgyes, 1994, among others). Such challenges can be further exacerbated for those NNES instructors who might be in a more precarious position due to factors beyond their language background, such as their status in the profession, gender, ethnicity, age, etc. Novice teachers who are international teaching assistants (ITAs) are in an especially vulnerable position: their authority is likely to be challenged by NES and NNES students alike, not only due to perceived differences or deficiencies in language use, but also as the result of possible gaps in their knowledge of cultural expectations for teaching and writing in U.S. higher education settings (Collins et al., 2021; Shehi, 2017; see also Kasztalska & Maune, this collection).

Considering that students' trust and the instructor's own confidence are the two crucial components for building professional authority, it is not surprising that many NNES instructors have to rely on traditional or institutional authority (in Weber's terminology). This falling back on teacher-centered pedagogy is more likely to happen if the ITA's home culture is characterized by high power distance orientation; after all, "teachers are most likely to teach the way their teachers taught while they were growing up in schools" (Fagan, 2022). This point was echoed by Michael Stancliff and Maureen Daly Goggin (2007), who also stressed that for novice teachers, "inexperience leads to rigidity and pedagogical 'frame-lock'" (p. 15). And while it is true for all novice teachers, international NNES instructors' challenges are more complicated due to cultural distance (compared to U.S.-born NESs) and lack of targeted resources and support for international NNES provided by graduate and writing programs.

Furthermore, novice instructors might not always realize that there is a disparity between their espoused beliefs about teaching and their actual teaching practices. For example, in Christopher Anderson's (2002) study of a group of ESOL teachers at a higher education institution in the UK, he observed that while teachers often claimed to be following "student-centered" (p. 202) teaching philosophy and pedagogy, in practice, the control they exercised over their lessons created an authoritarian, teacher-centered classroom. One tool that both NES and NNES novice instructors can utilize to make these conflicts between beliefs and practices more apparent is critical reflective practice. Stancliff and Goggin (2007) described a teacher training curriculum that used critical reflection in order to reconcile the rift between the functional ("nuts and bolts" of teaching) and conversion (rhetoric and composition theory) approaches in teacher training. Furthermore, they emphasized that there is no "atheoretical" approach to teaching as "every act of teaching arises from some set of assumptions about what teachers should teach and how students learn" (p. 15). While their work targeted mainstream NES teachers-in-training, for NNESTs, critical reflection can uncover other layers of conflicts or discrepancies rooted in different cultures, languages, and ideologies.

Study Design

Reflective teaching has been used in multiple disciplines in a variety of ways. John Dewey (1933) was the first prominent advocate of reflection, which he defined as an action characterized by "active, persistent, and careful consideration of any belief or supposed form of knowledge" (p. 9). Reflection-in-action became a staple in professional development in multiple fields due to the work of Donald Schön (1983), who described how professionals in different fields dealt with problems by reflecting on their past knowledge and current issues at hand. In TESOL studies, reflective practices have been the focus of Thomas Farrell's work (2004; 2013; 2015). Farrell suggested multiple ways teachers can reflect on their teaching: through peer and mentor observations, through teaching circles and observation groups, but also through self-directed reflective studies where teachers audio or video record themselves and/or keep a teaching journal. Farrell emphasized that for teachers, reflective practice entails examining "their beliefs and practices about teaching and learning so that they can better understand these" (2013, p. 22). Reflective practice is thus directed not only at the issue or task at hand (Schön's reflection-in-action) but also at the underlying beliefs and ideas at the foundation of teacher practices.

The present study followed Farrell's recommendations for reflective practice and used systematic self-observation techniques for collecting data (Chang, 2016). For two semesters of teaching first-year composition courses, fall 2014 and spring 2015, I collected all of my lesson plans and teaching materials, I recorded my immediate reflections on each class meeting in a teaching journal, and I video- or audio-taped most of the class meetings. The camera for video recording was set up to record only the front of the classroom, where I stayed most of the time. The students were not recorded on video, although their voices sometimes were; I explained the purpose for recording our meetings to my students and assured them they were not on camera and any conversations I might record would be kept confidential. The students' behavior did not appear to be affected by the presence of the recording device.

In collecting and analyzing the data, I used Jerry Gebhard's (2006) reflective questions:

- What are my beliefs about teaching? Are my practices consistent with these beliefs?
- What do I think I do in the classroom? What do I actually do?
- Are there any issues of self I need to address? Am I facing my teaching self?

I started my teaching journal with reflecting on my past educational experiences and my beliefs about education. I watched or listened to the class recordings and transcribed selected instances that seemed particularly important. I then read my journal entries, lesson plans, and the transcripts together in order to analyze and reflect on my experiences. In my analysis of journal entries and class meeting recordings, I paid particular attention to in-class discussions and activities, my reactions to student comments or questions, and my classroom management tactics.

In my analysis of the research data, I followed the framework exemplified in Lara Handsfield and colleagues' (2010) research: they examined how everyday interactions "illustrate the microscopic and everyday dimensions of power" (p. 405). In analyzing my teaching materials, journal records, and transcripts of video and audio recordings, I was looking for possible contradictions between my ideas about teaching and what I was actually doing in the classroom. I focused my attention on the pedagogical moments where power dynamics came to the forefront such as the way I organized class discussions, let students ask questions and the way I answered them, and the way I directed the students to engage with the different in-class activities. I also paid close attention to the physical aspects of my classroom, namely what space was typically occupied by students and what space was normally reserved for myself as well as my body language and tone of voice. While the events I analyzed were small-scale, it is these interactions that compose the entire class, including its atmosphere, power dynamics, the kind of dialogues that happen in it, and the quality of instruction and learning. Furthermore, these micro-level interactions, as Mayes (2010) pointed out, lay the foundation for the construction of power. In the following section, I describe my initial reflection on my past educational experiences in a different cultural setting and proceed to discuss some of the most prominent themes and instances that exemplify the issues of power dynamics in my attempts to build a more desirable professional authority.

Learning Through Reflection

Past Educational Experiences and Ideological Shifts

At the beginning of the research project, I reflected first on my past experiences with power and authority in the classroom in my teaching journal. Russian culture in general is marked by a high-power distance in Hofstede's framework of cultural dimensions. The Russian education system, despite in theory breaking up with the Soviet past, still bears the signs of its problematic history. As I went through primary and secondary school in the 1990s and completed my college degrees in the 2000s, the school systems still bore a distinct presence of Soviet ideologies. Delbert Long et al. (1999) provided a more critical description of Soviet education: "The Soviet school system was from its inception a vital instrument of state policy. It was used . . . to mold youth into adults who did not question the right of party leaders to control all property, all institutions, all forms of media—in essence, to control the thoughts, feelings, and actions of people" (p. 21). The influence of the Soviet system and ideologies was evident on multiple levels, from individual subjects' curricula to the ways lessons and exams were organized.[1] Most of the classes I took employed a very rigid top-down structure: lectures were the most common format; peer reviews, as well as syllabi or other forms of course contracts, were nonexistent, and more importantly, the instructor held almost infinite power over students because students' final grade was determined solely based on an oral or occasionally written end-of-semester exam. Even though I was fortunate enough to learn from some outstanding professors who evoked deep appreciation and curiosity for their subjects, the system as a whole was marked by high power distance dynamics and employed many practices that can be described as oppressive or authoritarian. In my experience at one small

---

1   I do not wish to represent the entire Russian educational culture as a monolith, nor do I equate culture with the nation-state. As Kubota (2004) pointed out, all cultures are discursively constructed and undergo constant change. The culture commonly present in public schools in my mid-size hometown in the 1990s was different from the culture of public schools in Moscow during the same time period; similarly, I found significant differences across different cultures at different institutions, states, and communities in the US.

college and three large universities, I was never able to make my own choices when it came to deciding which courses to take—the entire curriculum was set for me when I chose my major, and I was also not able to choose between different instructors who taught these courses. Students had very little power over the direction of their academic careers or in negotiating their grades. Finally, writing was not typically taught at the college level (either in Russian or in a foreign language), and writing support or coaching was rarely available for major projects such as term or thesis papers.

When I moved to the US, I noticed some significant differences in the educational culture as a whole and experienced a paradigm shift on multiple levels. First, I saw a drastic change in the way classroom and coursework was organized, how much accountability was built into the curriculum (e.g., course grades were formed by multiple components rather than only one exam), and how differently instructor-student power dynamics worked. Furthermore, many rhetoric, composition, and TESOL courses I took introduced me to new ideas about power, ideology, social justice, education, and literacy. As I read the work of scholars ranging from Paolo Freire and Henry Giroux to bell hooks and Ira Shor, I became interested in critical pedagogy, which was a radical departure from my previous educational experiences. As I recognized the value in the ideals of critical pedagogy, promoting students' active role in the classroom and creating a more democratic space became important parts of my teaching philosophy. I sought to implement critical pedagogy values in my teaching practices as well by, for instance, inviting students to participate in curricular decisions such as co-creating grading rubrics, choosing how to be divided into groups, or choosing and conducting mini-lessons on the topics in grammar and mechanics that they deemed important. However, I also sensed that I was not always able to practice my beliefs when it came to my own teaching; for instance, I suspected that I resorted to more direct lecturing than I would have liked. Analyzing my classroom interactions provided me with a more accurate insight into my teaching practices.

Points of Disconnect Between Beliefs and Practices

I looked for tensions between my beliefs and practices within the classroom interactions and the ways I organized and conducted classroom activities. At some points, I was able to stop myself from overexplaining or lecturing and allow my students to arrive at answers on their own. For instance, during a sequence focused on narrative writing, groups of students were assigned some fairly complex articles to read and summarize to the class. When one of these articles proved difficult for one group of NNES students, they asked me for guidance, and instead of spoon-feeding them the answers as most teachers in my past experiences would do, I was able to guide them to arrive at their own understanding through a series of questions. Similarly, at a few instances, I was able to push students to try to find their own answers even when they expressly asked for my opinion as the ultimate authority. For example, during a whole-class discussion of one act of the play, I asked students to summarize an important scene and describe its significance. As a student was struggling to explain the meaning of the scene, I kept asking probing questions to help students arrive at a clearer understanding on his own: "Do we get a sense of why this character wants to leave? Do we know what the author is trying to say here?" To these questions, the student replied that he did not know and instead asked me directly to "tell [them] what it means." Instead of providing my own answers though, I asked other students to offer their ideas, and at that point another student stepped in with an interpretation of the scene, prompting a third student to make another suggestion, and the discussion proceeded. In such instances, I saw examples of a conscious effort not to act on an impulse to tell students "what that means" and instead apply some of the teaching strategies I deemed more effective.

However, I also realized that when I was not consciously making an effort to act more as a facilitator or guide rather than "bank clerk" depositing knowledge into my students (following Freire's metaphor), my teaching behaviors did not align well with my intentions. For instance, an overview of class recordings showed that the time I spent talking to the class was a significant part of most class meetings. A typical lesson plan would start with whole-class announcements and updates with a short lecture on a pressing topic such as assignment expectations or commonly asked questions; the class would then shift gears into a small group task followed by a whole-class discussion; depending on the class, it would be two small group activities and discussions. Even though the lesson plans looked good on paper, in practice, I ended up not only making class announcements and delivering mini-lectures, but also summarizing group activities extensively, following up on points students made that I wanted to clarify or elaborate on, and overall maintaining a much more constant lecturing presence than was warranted by the lesson plans. In my teaching journal, an early entry described it as a problem: "One more influence of my educational background [is] my tendency to lecture or talk a lot. I really want to decrease the amount of lecturing I do in class." Still, a few later entries with reflections on class meetings and lesson plans showed that I was not satisfied with how well I was able to accomplish that goal: "I talked a lot when it came to analysis—I should have engaged students' voices more, but it is extremely easy to slip back into the familiar and comfortable lecture format." My planning notes showed that I tried to find ways to address the issue, but ultimately, I was not always successful: "I tried to put breaks in between the slides and between different points on the presentation so that I'll have space to ask students' opinion first, before launching into 'let me tell you what I think.' But I'm not sure how useful it's going to be."

Establishing Authority

Another prominent theme that emerged from my analysis of the video and audio recordings of classroom interactions was the struggle I seemed to be having with establishing a sense of authority. At that relatively early point in my teaching career, I, as many other international teaching assistants, was anxious about my NNES status and how it might affect my students' perceptions of me as a teacher of English and writing. The internalized native speaker fallacy was a large factor in my anxiety, combined with occasional remarks from past students about my accent or my NNES background. While this anxiety abated with each new semester of teaching I successfully concluded (and with reading more literature dismantling the native speaker myth), it was never completely eliminated. Like many other NNES teachers of writing (e.g., Hijazi, this volume, and Shehi, 2017), I felt compelled to present the class with an abstract of my CV at the beginning of the semester, using my credentials as a justification—if not an excuse—for being their instructor. A typical first class meeting would start with me welcoming the students and introducing myself with a summary of my CV (and occasionally pulling up the actual CV on the class screen), explaining what degrees I have earned and describing my past teaching experience. In Weber's terms (1957), I felt that not only my professional and charismatic authority were lacking due to my novice status, but that my institutional authority was likely to be questioned because of my NNES status; by disclosing my qualifying degrees and teaching experience, I was preemptively trying to answer the question of why a NNES foreigner was teaching an English class.

However, despite struggling with a sense of inadequate authority in the classroom, some classroom interactions betrayed instances where I would exercise too much control over the direction whole-class conversations were going (for instance, I would try to silence or overlook some ideas while promoting others). While this type of directing is largely inevitable, a closer look at how I was doing it showed me that too often, I did not let students' comments lead the conversation in another direction even if it was appropriate, either because I did not immediately see the point in students' comments or because I wanted to have enough time to discuss other issues that were more important in my opinion. For example, in one reflective entry in my teaching journal, I asked a student to summarize a passage before discussing it to refresh everyone's memory. A normally quiet student volunteered to do it; as I wrote down the main points of the summary on the board, I started going over the passage myself, providing other details. In the journal entry, I noted: "this was one of the first times [the student] said anything in class in this sequence. It almost looked like I did not like his summary and decided to offer a better one. This could make him even more silent if he sees that his comments are not appreciated. Also, I clearly have my own agenda in exploring this passage in more detail, and I am pushing for a certain view."

Such instances betrayed my discomfort with letting go of the control over class interactions. Looking back at the incident described at the beginning of this chapter, I was eager to step back into my role as someone who sets the agenda and directs the class interactions when I sensed that my teacher authority was questioned. The incident described at the beginning of this chapter serves as another example of how my sense of authority influenced my teaching tactics. When the student first uttered the question ("Did you choose this play because you liked it?"), I tried to use it as an opportunity to have an open discussion of the course curriculum and offered my rationale for choosing the play after hearing other students' opinions on it. However, the student's persistent rejection of my explanation and repetition of the question made me extremely uncomfortable, and feeling like my teacher authority and credibility were under direct attack, I chose to exercise said authority and change the topic of conversation.

I noticed, however, that these instances of trying to retain control over the classroom were happening mostly unplanned and for the most part, unconsciously. My conscious efforts pointed in the opposite direction and sometimes made me avoid exercising my teacher authority in cases where it would have been warranted. In one such instance, I sought to use students' explicit permission to act on their behalf in order to enact a classroom policy instead of exercising my authority directly. Midway through the semester, I sought students' feedback on the course through an informal survey. A few students noted in their comments that other students checking their phones or laptops was distracting. Our syllabus stated that students were allowed to use computers for class work but not for personal purposes. I mentioned the survey responses in class and asked everyone to respect our class time and put away their devices when not using them for class work. Tellingly, I used the phrase, "now you've invested me with the authority to be more strict about it" as I was still concerned about directly commanding students. After that discussion, I proceeded to make a remark: "So, I just talked about a stricter cell phone use policy, *people in the back*." Instead of enforcing the policy directly, I chose to use students' own comments and humor as a way to make myself appear less authoritarian.

This incident illustrates another dilemma for me as an instructor: clearly, enforcing the no-cell phones policy would not have constituted an abuse of power on my part; nonetheless, I hesitated to enforce it because I was overly cautious about being perceived as an authoritarian teacher even as I still exercised traditional or legal authority in other, less obvious cases. My lack of assertiveness also led me to fall back into lecturing mode more than I wanted to when, for example, students were reluctant to participate in class discussions or when they did not complete a required reading assignment. By being overly conscious about being perceived as an overbearing teacher, I still ended up employing practices that I considered undesirable and overbearing.

Discussion and Conclusion

A question that surfaced at multiple points throughout my analysis of the data concerned the types of authority available to NNESTs of writing. For many international NNESTs just starting their teaching career, professional authority might seem out of reach. Charismatic authority is highly subjective and depends on a range of personal characteristics, from one's accent and command of English to race and gender. For an introverted, soft-spoken female instructor like me, it was not an option either. Traditional and bureaucratic authority seem to be the two kinds that are available to NNESTs as these types are independent of the personal characteristics of the teacher. When I tried to act based on other, more desirable types of authority (as when I attempted to have a more open dialogue about my decision to use the play as part of our class curriculum), I felt that my students did not accept that authority, which made me fall back on more traditional institutional authority. However, when teachers rely on these less desirable types of authority, it becomes little short of coercion, as Bizzell (1991) also warns. Some studies have demonstrated that over-relying on institutional authority can lead to "extensive student resistance" (Oral, 2013, p. 113), which further questions teacher authority and impacts classroom interactions. Nonetheless, when no other types of authority are available, novice NNES instructors are left with no other recourse.

Through this study, I realized that my teaching practices were deeply shaped by a desire to implement critical pedagogy that was undercut by constant feelings of insecurity. On one hand, I adopted the ideas of critical pedagogy and was eager to follow them in my own classroom. On the other hand, I felt my authority was always at question, never completely safe from scrutiny, and so I was not comfortable releasing whatever authority I could master. That conviction stemmed in part from my relatively novice status as a writing instructor and being new to the region, but also from my status as a NNES and my worry that my students would always question my pedagogical decisions simply because I am not a native speaker of English and not a native to the U.S. culture. Monika Shehi (2017) described a similar issue with NNESTs adopting translingual approaches in their classroom: if a NNEST follows a curriculum that actively questions the privileged position of standardized American English, their students might become "frustrated" if they believe "that the reason the privilege of SAE is challenged is to accommodate 'foreign' instructors whose language skills they believe to be inferior to their own" (p. 267). Thus, the path towards professional development and growth that many novice international NNESTs have to take is complicated by their cultural and linguistic backgrounds. To a large extent, the solution seems to lie in programmatic and institutional investment in NNES teachers' self-confidence and improving students' attitudes towards NNES instructors.

I learned from my experience that reflective practice holds great potential for NES and NNES teachers alike. All novice teachers regardless of their linguistic background are likely to fall back on more familiar teaching practices. Many NES novice instructors come to teach writing from a variety of backgrounds, and exposure to scholarship on the teaching of writing might create a rift between their previous beliefs about teaching and their current roles and expectations. Utilizing critical reflection tools can help these instructors, whether NES or NNES, to formulate their current stance on questions of teaching and pedagogy and absorb new information. In Icy Lee's (2015) words, "focus on critical reflection in teacher education can facilitate the integration of new knowledge and challenge the deep-seated beliefs" (p. 33). It can be especially beneficial for international NNES teachers who come from cultures that differ significantly from mainstream U.S. culture.

In the project described in this chapter, I used a variety of reflective practices such as keeping a teaching journal or video and audiotaping class meetings. However, there are multiple other practices that can be used in combination or individually, by NNES and NES alike. Julian Edge (2011) provided a helpful overview of different strands of reflective practice commonly used in TESOL teacher development; Lee (2008) described a number of ways to use reflective teaching journals, and Farrell's (e.g. 2004; 2013; particularly 2015) extensive list of publications on reflective practices provides a comprehensive guide to a variety of reflective strategies, including peer support groups and mentor observations, which can be implemented in a teaching practicum course or professional development program. Using reflective practices in a group setting that includes NES and NNES teachers is especially beneficial as it builds collaboration between instructors and allows NNESs to grow their confidence and all instructors—to share their strengths and challenges. Melinda Reichelt (this volume), for instance, described a "reading-writing autobiography" assignment in a pedagogy course that allowed NES and NNES instructors to learn about each other's experiences.

In my own project, I used a similar autobiography as a starting point to investigate my beliefs about teaching and education. Reflecting on my past experiences with learning and teaching helped me formulate the main differences I perceived between the U.S. and Russian education systems and allowed me to see points of disconnect between my teaching philosophy and what was actually taking place in my classroom. Examining these points of disconnect, in turn, made me investigate issues of power and authority in the classroom. NNES teachers who often face microaggressions, biases, and direct confrontations with their students (e.g., see Hijazi and Wang-Hiles, this collection) experience significant challenges in building their professional authority. I found myself oscillating between relying on my bureaucratic or traditional authority (using my institutional position of an authority figure rather than professional authority built on students' and my own belief in my teaching abilities) and eschewing exercising any power whatsoever. Neither of those scenarios left me satisfied with my teaching. It took me a few more years to gain enough expertise and teaching experience to feel confident in my professional authority. That timeline would likely have been shorter had I been able to articulate these conceptualizations of authority from the beginning.

There are ways to facilitate professional authority development for NNESTs. An important component of such training should address deficit-oriented perspectives towards NNESs and their legitimacy as language teachers. It is crucial that NNESTs get acquainted with literature that debunks the native speaker myth and points to the distinct advantages of NNESs as language and/or writing teachers. I was fortunate enough to have taken coursework in rhetoric, writing, and TESOL where I read the important works of Cook (1999), Kramsch (1997), Phillipson (1992), and Widdowson (1994), among others, who demonstrated the imperialist roots of the native speaker myth and advocated for NNES to be recognized as legitimate language users in their own right without being compared against the NES standard. However, composition teacher training programs rarely dedicate enough time to exploring the ideas of native speakerism, linguistic pluralism, and translingualism. Exploring these ideas in teaching practicums and other professional development trainings can not only help NNESTs find confidence in their language and teaching abilities but also help NES and NNES instructors alike find ways to introduce some of these concepts to their students in order to challenge negative biases and stereotypes (for more specific strategies, see Hijazi and Reichelt, in this volume), thus fostering more diverse and accepting classroom communities.

While many scholars recognize the importance of building authority for NNESTs (e.g., Shehi, 2017; Kasztalska & Maune, this volume), authority itself is often left undefined. Conceptualizing authority as stemming from different sources (institution, traditions, professional expertise) can benefit NNES instructors who seek to find a better balance of power in their classrooms and grow their confidence as instructors as well. Finally, an important source of authority, instructors' confidence, can be fostered at the programmatic and institutional levels, and many chapters in this volume offer strategies to promote collaboration between NNES and NES instructors and ensure NNESTs have the necessary support of their writing program administrators. Too often, NNESTs are left to face the challenges stemming from their nonnative status on their own. More robust institutional and programmatic support will allow NNESTs to build their professional expertise, confidence, and teacher authority.

References

Anderson, C. (2002). *Deconstructing teaching English to speakers of other languages: Problematizing a professional discourse* [Unpublished doctoral dissertation]. Canterbury Christ Church College.

Berlin, J. (1987). *Rhetoric and reality: Writing instruction in American colleges, 1900–1985*. Southern Illinois University Press.

Berlin, J. (1988). Rhetoric and ideology in the writing class. *College English, 50*(5), 477–494. https://doi.org/10.2307/377477.

Bizzell, P. (1991). Classroom authority and critical pedagogy. *American Literary History 3*, 847–863. https://doi.org/10.1093/alh/3.4.847.

Chang, H. 2016. *Autoethnography as method*. Routledge, Taylor & Francis Group.

Collins, J., Brown, N. & Leigh, J. (2021). Making sense of cultural bumps: Supporting international graduate teaching assistants with their teaching. *Innovations in Education and Teaching International, 59*(5), 511–521. https://doi.org/10.1080/14703297.2021.1919175.

Cook, V. (1999). Going beyond the native speaker in language teaching. *TESOL Quarterly, 33*(2), 185–209. https://doi.org/10.2307/3587717.

Dewey, J. (1933). *How we think: A restatement of the relation of reflective thinking to the educative process*. Henry Regnery.

Edge, J. (2011). *The reflexive teacher educator in TESOL: Roots and wings*. Routledge.

Fagan, K. (2022). The cultural practices and communicative teaching intent of Chinese student teachers in an American TESOL practicum. *Journal of Language, Identity & Education*. https://doi.org/10.1080/15348458.2022.2091573.

Farrell, T. (2004). *Reflective practice in action: 80 reflection breaks for busy teachers*. Corwin Press.

Farrell, T. (2013). *Reflective practice in ESL teacher development groups*. Palgrave Macmillan.

Farrell, T. (2015). *Promoting teacher reflection in second language education: A framework for TESOL professionals*. Routledge.

Freire, P. (1984). *Pedagogy of the oppressed* (M. Ramos, Trans.). Continuum.

Gebhard, J. G. (2006). *Teaching English as a foreign or second language: A teacher self-development and methodology guide*. University of Michigan Press.

Handsfield, L. J., Crumpler, T. P. & Dean, T. R. (2010). Tactical negotiations and creative adaptations: The discursive production of literacy curriculum and teacher identities across space-times. *Reading Research Quarterly, 45*(4), 405–431. https://doi.org/10.1598/RRQ.45.4.3.

Hofstede, G. (1980). *Culture's consequences: International differences in work-related values*. Sage Publication.

Hofstede, G. & McCrae, R. R. (2004). Personality and culture revisited: Linking traits and dimensions of culture. *Cross-Cultural Research, 38*(1), 52–88. https://doi.org/10.1177/1069397103259443.

hooks, b. (1994). *Teaching to transgress: Education as the practice of freedom*. Routledge.

Hwang, D. H. (1993). *M. Butterfly*. Penguin Publishing Group.

Kramsch, C. (1997). The privilege of the nonnative speaker. *PMLA, 112*(3), 359–369. http://www.jstor.org/stable/462945.

Kubota, R. (2004). The politics of cultural difference in second language education. *Critical Inquiry in Language Studies, 1*(1), 21–39. https://doi.org/10.1207/s15427595cils0101_2.

Lee, I. (2008). Fostering preservice reflection through response journals. *Teacher Education Quarterly, 35*(1), 117–139.

Lee, I. (2015). Student teachers' changing beliefs on a pre-service teacher education course in Hong Kong. In T. Wright & M. Beaumont (Eds.), *Experiences of second language teacher education* (pp. 15–41). Palgrave Macmillan.

Liu, J. (2005). Chinese graduate teaching assistants teaching freshman composition to native English-speaking students. In E. Llurda (Ed.), *Non-native language teachers: Perceptions, challenges, and contributions to the profession* (pp. 155–177). Springer.

Llurda, E. (2009). The decline and fall of the native speaker. In V. Cook & L. Wei (Eds.), *Contemporary applied linguistics Volume 1: Language teaching and learning* (pp. 37–53). Bloomsbury Publishing. https://doi.org/10.5040/9781474211789.ch-002.

Long, D., Bordovskii, G. & Long, R. (1999). *Education of teachers in Russia*. Greenwood Publishing Group.

Mayes, P. (2010). The discursive construction of identity and power in the critical classroom: Implications for applied critical theories. *Discourse & Society, 21*(2), 189–210.

Medgyes, P. (1994). *The non-native teacher.* Macmillan.

Nguyen, H. T. (2008) Conceptions of teaching by five Vietnamese American pre-service teachers. *Journal of Language, Identity, and Education, 7*(2), 113–136. https://doi.org:10.1080/15348450801970654.

Oral, Y. (2013). "The right things are what I expect them to do": Negotiation of power relations in an English classroom. *Journal of Language, Identity, and Education, 12*(2), 96–115. https://doi.org/10.1080/15348458.2013.775877.

Pace, J. L. & Hemmings, A. (2007). Understanding authority in classrooms: A review of theory, ideology, and research. *Review of Educational Research, 77*, 4–27.

Phillipson, R. (1992). *Linguistic imperialism.* Oxford University Press.

Reis, R. S. (2012). "Being underdog": Supporting nonnative English-speaking teachers (NNESTs) in claiming and asserting professional legitimacy. *Journal on Excellence in College Teaching, 23*(3), 33–58.

Shehi, M. (2017). "Why is my English teacher a foreigner?" Re-authoring the story of international composition teachers. *Teaching English in the Two-Year College, 44*(3), 260–275.

Shor, I. (1996). *When students have power: Negotiating authority in a critical pedagogy.* University of Chicago Press.

Stancliff, M. & Goggin, M. D. (2007). What's theorizing got to do with it? Teaching theory as resourceful conflict and reflection in TA preparation. *WPA: Writing Program Administration, 30*(3), 11–29.

Vanderstaay, S. L., Faxon, B. A., Meischen, J. E., Kolesnikov, K. T. & Ruppel, A. D. (2009). Close to the heart: Teacher authority in a classroom community. *College Composition and Communication, 61*(2), 262–282. https://www.jstor.org/stable/40593459.

Weber, M. (1957). *Theory of social and economic organization* (A. R. Anderson & T. Parsons, Trans.). Oxford University Press.

Widdowson, H. G. (1994). The ownership of English. *TESOL Quarterly, 28*(2), 377–389. https://doi.org/10.2307/3587438.

Yagelski, R. P. (1999). The ambivalence of reflection: Critical pedagogies, identity, and the writing teacher. *College Composition and Communication, 51*(1), 32–50. https://doi.org/10.2307/358958.

Zhang, Y. (2013). Power distance in online learning: Experience of Chinese learners in U.S. higher education. *International Review of Research in Open and Distributed Learning, 14*(4), 238–254. https://doi.org/10.19173/irrodl.v14i4.1557.

6

"What Authority I Have?": Analyzing Legitimation Codes of English Composition ITAs

Aleksandra Kasztalska
BOSTON UNIVERSITY

Michael Maune
MASSACHUSETTS INSTITUTE OF TECHNOLOGY

The native English speaker (NES) has traditionally been regarded as the judge of what is correct in language and as a language model for nonnative English speakers (NNESs) to emulate. Because of their presumably innate and superior linguistic competence, native English-speaking teachers (NESTs) may benefit from native-speakerism, or the belief that NESs make better language teachers than their NNES colleagues (Holliday, 2006; Kachru, 1990; Swan et al., 2015). Some research has suggested that native-speakerism in English language teaching (ELT) may limit nonnative English-speaking teachers' (NNESTs') access to employment (Fithriani, 2018; Mahboob & Golden, 2013; Rivers, 2016; Ruecker & Ives, 2015; Selvi, 2014) and that NNESTs may be challenged by students who prefer NESTs (Amin, 1999; Crandall, 2003; Thomas, 1999).

Recent scholarship has further suggested that, beyond language teaching, native-speakerism can also impact NNESTs of writing (e.g., Liu, 2005; Ruecker et al., 2018; Shehi, 2017). Writing classes invariably bring forth issues of language use and interrogate both teachers' and students' assumptions about language in general and, specifically, the language in which one is writing. Because writing and language assumptions are deeply interconnected, NNESTs of writing can be affected by native-speakerism as they negotiate their identities as teachers and experts on writing, as well as nonnative users of English.

One of the most robust contexts where the aforementioned issues arise are FYW courses. These writing seminars are the cornerstone of higher education in the US, as universities typically require that incoming freshmen take at least one, and sometimes more, of these writing-intensive classes. Due to the common practice of hiring international graduate students to teach lower-level courses, many of these introductory courses are taught by

DOI: https://doi.org/10.37514/INT-B.2024.2142.2.06   97 international teaching assistants (ITAs). While exact data on ITAs of composition is unavailable, April Ginther (2003) noted that ITAs and international research assistants make up about half of all "advanced-level research and teaching assistant activity being carried out by students" (as cited in Cassell, 2007, p. 1) at higher education institutions in the US. Consequently, a large number of writing courses are taught by ITAs, whose responsibility it is to introduce students to the expectations of academic writing and language conventions. It is therefore important to understand the experiences and challenges that these instructors may face in their work as teachers of writing.

Research on ITAs across disciplines has seemed to confirm that these instructors—like other NNESTs—may encounter issues with their students, who at times challenge their authority as legitimate teachers and criticize their use of English. For example, in their small-scale study of graduate teaching assistants (GTAs) who taught undergraduate ESL education courses, Barcu Ates and Zohreh R. Eslami (2012) found that the three NNES GTAs were directly challenged by their students, who claimed that they could not understand their instructors. The participants also believed that their language was "being monitored by [their] students" (Ates & Eslami, 2012, p. 108), as did the 25 ITAs surveyed by Aparna Hebbani and Katherine C. Hendrix (2014). On the other hand, while the six ITAs interviewed by Ekaterina Arshavskaya (2015) did not report being challenged in the classroom due to their NNES status, they admitted to sometimes struggling to keep up with their students' informal and fast speech, and cited anecdotal evidence of students dropping a course as soon as they learned that the teacher was an ITA. This anecdotal evidence is somewhat supported by Julie Damron's (2000) dissertation study. Having conducted focus groups with 26 NES freshmen, Damron concluded that these students were often dissatisfied with their ITAs' use of English and that some preferred to enroll in an American teacher's class rather than take a course led by an ITA. Some of the participants also seemed uninterested and unwilling to develop a better relationship with their ITAs, suggesting that it was the ITA's responsibility to adapt and adjust linguistically, culturally, and pedagogically to the local students.

The limited research on ITAs of composition has suggested that these instructors may also face challenges in their professional work. For example, George Braine (1999) recalled his "traumatic first semester" (p. 21) of teaching FYW in the US and having to adjust to new cultural, pedagogical, and linguistic standards while having to project authority. Moreover, Davi S. Reis (2011, 2012) reported on the experiences of two ITAs of ESL writing, whose professional self-identities seemed to be shaped by their status as a NNES and who consequently experienced self-doubt and feelings of inadequacy as writing teachers. In this chapter, we shed more light on the experiences of these diverse and multilingual teachers, who play such a key role in U.S. higher education.

The data we analyzed in this chapter were collected as part of a larger study (Kasztalska, 2015) that used interviews, focus groups, and questionnaires to examine the professional practices and identities of ITAs of composition at a large public university in the Midwest. In this chapter, we used legitimation code theory (LCT), a model of how knowledge and people become legitimate in a social field, to re-examine the published data in Aleksandra Kasztalska (2015) and shed more light on how native-speakerism works. LCT allowed us to synthesize a variety of analyses of this problem by revealing that the claims about an inherent difference between NESs and NNESs and the claims that NESs are better teachers of English or writing are rooted in a common basis of legitimation. In particular, our analysis suggests that these claims are made because of certain underlying assumptions about knowers and knowledge in ELT and composition. These assumptions, which operate as rules to (de)legitimate NNESTs, place emphasis on social group attributes rather than knowledge and abilities, which creates tensions between different stakeholders in the field. Informed by the LCT analysis, we argue that as a general rule writing programs should emphasize knowledge about writing rather than social attributes, namely native-speaker status, when making administrative, curricular, and personnel decisions.

Legitimation Code Theory

In analyzing the structure, types, and range of knowledge construed in the data, we drew on LCT. LCT is a sociological theory of knowledge that aims to be empirical in its methods and practical in its effects (Maton, 2014). Knowledge is modeled in LCT as a structure with different dimensions, and the most salient for this study is specialization. Specialization describes the "basis of knowledge claims to legitimacy" (Maton, 2014, p. 31) and reveals to what degree knowledge or types of knowers are being emphasized as necessary to make legitimate claims in a given field. When a claim is deemed legitimate because of the speaker's choice of object to study or their method of studying that object, then the relationship between the claim and the object of study—or the epistemic relations (ER)—is stronger. For example, when a scientist makes a claim in a research article, the claim can be deemed legitimate based on their choice to use the scientific method to arrive at and to justify the claim, which indicates that ER are relatively strong.

In contrast, when a claim is considered legitimate because of some attribute or disposition of the speaker, then the relationship between the claim and the speaker—or the social relations (SR)—is stronger. For example, a teacher may make a claim about teaching, and their claim may be deemed legitimate primarily because of some attribute or disposition of the teacher, such as extensive experience or native speaker status. This legitimation process shows stronger SR compared to ER. In short, specialization can show what serves as the basis for making legitimate claims in a field—knowledge (ER) and/or knowers (SR).

LCT posits that in any particular knowledge practice, such as teaching or writing, emphasis may be placed more or less on ER or SR along a cline. In other words, when trying to make a legitimate claim in a field, sometimes it matters more that one knows something and sometimes it matters more that one has a particular attribute as a practitioner in that field. Some knowledge practices emphasize ER over SR. These represent *knowledge codes* because legitimate knowledge is based more on "possession of specialized knowledge of specific objects of study" (Maton, 2014, p. 30) than on "attributes of actors" (p. 30). Conversely, some practices represent *knower codes* because they are legitimized by placing more emphasis on the knower and their attributes, such as their "dispositions" (Maton, 2014, p. 32), "natural talent," or "taste" (p. 31). Finally, practices that rely on both ER and SR equally are *élite codes*, while *relativist codes* rely on neither.

LCT has been useful in examining legitimation codes and knowledge structures of various educational fields. For example, Hanelie Adendorff and Margaret A. L. Blackie's (2020) LCT analysis of decolonizing science curriculum in South African universities has shown a productive way forward to addressing issues of equality and discourse. However, LCT has not yet been applied to examine native-speakerism and the experiences of ITAs in composition.

In our study, we used the dimension of specialization to reveal the basis of legitimation in the fields of composition pedagogy and ELT. In particular, we examined the degree to which these fields emphasize ER (knowledge) and SR (knowers). Because authority and legitimacy were key themes in the foundational study (Kasztalska, 2015), specialization provided a different analytical lens to classify and refine the interpretation and potential implications of knowledge practices in teaching composition.

Methods

In this chapter, we reanalyze the published results of questionnaires, interviews, and focus groups from a previous study conducted by one of the authors (Kasztalska, 2015), which examined the developing professional identities and practices of ITAs of composition and the role of world Englishes in this process. In this chapter, the term world Englishes refers to the framework, first proposed by Braj Kachru, for describing the global spread of English as well as the growing field of research on the emerging English varieties and their uses.

The participants in Kasztalska (2015) were 15 international graduate students pursuing Ph.D. degrees in English-related fields and working as ITAs at a large Midwestern university in the US. The majority of the participants were teaching composition, and a few taught or tutored oral English communication. The ITAs represented diverse linguistic and cultural backgrounds and had generally lived in the US for several years prior to the start of the study.

Due to scheduling conflicts, only 12 of the 15 ITAs in the study were able to participate in semi-structured focus groups, and four of these ITAs also took part in a follow-up interview that used Steinar Kvale and Svend Brinkmann's (2009) life world interview model to further explore the issues raised during focus groups. In addition, the three ITAs who were unable to take part in focus groups agreed to one-on-one semi-structured interviews. The focus groups and interviews centered on how the ITAs negotiated their identities as writing teachers and NNESs. In particular, the participants were invited to share their reasons for becoming teachers, their positive and negative experiences in the classroom, and the challenges they faced as writing instructors more generally and as NNESTs in particular. Additionally, the participants were asked to share how, if at all, they applied their knowledge of world Englishes to their teaching practice and how, if at all, the world Englishes framework influenced their own identities or helped them navigate native-speakerism in their professional lives. The researcher focused on world Englishes because this university offered courses specifically on world Englishes, and the majority of the participants had been exposed to this field in their graduate coursework.

All focus groups and interviews were audio-recorded and transcribed, and all participants were given female pseudonyms, even though some participants identified as male. The researcher decided to use female pseudonyms because at the time of the study there were so few male ITAs teaching composition that revealing this information about them might have made it easier for someone familiar with the university to infer the identity of the participants. All participants were asked to fill out an anonymous written questionnaire, which collected demographic, educational, and professional aggregate data.

In Kasztalska (2015), the first author followed John W. Creswell's (2013) guidelines to identify a number of themes emerging from the data. These were then subdivided into more specific codes, using John Lofland's (1971) classification. The major themes identified through this method included pedagogical, cultural, and linguistic challenges faced by the participants in their teaching. Another key theme was the influence and interaction of two discourses—that of world Englishes and native speakerism—on the ITAs' professional practice and identity. The researcher wanted to understand how, if at all, the ITAs' exposure to the world Englishes framework and research, which problematizes the concept of the native speaker and of the ideal English user, might challenge the participants' native-speakerist assumptions in ELT and in composition.

In the analysis presented in this chapter, both researchers used Karl Maton's (2014) legitimation code theory (LCT) to examine the participants' framing of the native speaker construct and the NES/NNES dichotomy. The LCT analysis drew on procedures from Maton and Rainbow Tsai-Hung Chen (2015) for LCT qualitative research design. Our goal was to provide a typological classification of the knowledge practices described by the participants, especially those related to native-speakerism. To this end, we built on the themes developed in Kasztalska (2015).

We initially coded each theme according to its ER and SR emphasis. We then grouped themes by their specialization code and conducted further analysis via research memos outlining the potential indicators of the code and representative participant quotes for those themes. We consolidated like themes in the same code to achieve parsimony. This process resulted in a translation device[1] (Maton, 2014; Figure 6.1, Tables 6.1 and 6.2) that serves as a set of systematic empirical indicators for classifying and describing the data according to their ER and SR and which serves to justify the conclusions from the data.

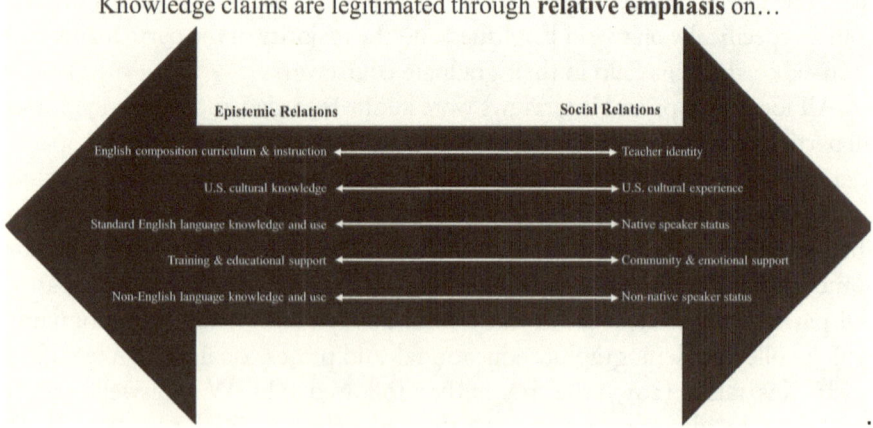

Figure 6.1. Overview of translation device for ITA dataset.

---

1   The authors wish to thank the LCT North American roundtable for their help in developing the translation device.

"What Authority I Have?"

In Figure 6.1, we provide an overview of the main ways the knowledge claims were legitimated in the data. Knowledge claims can be legitimated by emphasizing ER more or SR more, and the ER and SR are manifested through different concepts, as described in Figure 6.1. In Table 6.1, we expand on the ER concepts and provide empirical indicators and examples of each of the concepts. In Table 6.2, we expand on the SR concepts and provide empirical indicators and examples of each of the concepts.

Table 6.1. Epistemic Relations Translation Device for Coding ITA Dataset

Epistemic Relations Concept	Empirical Indicator	Example
English composition curriculum & instruction	Knowledge of teaching methods (ESL, rhet/comp), course structure, and/or content knowledge (texts, genres, academic conventions) is emphasized.	"It's completely different here in the context of U.S. . . . That we need to emphasize those three things [logos, pathos, and ethos] when you make an argument? . . . That was something that I don't know."
U.S. cultural knowledge	Knowledge of specific cultural artifacts and/or practices from US is emphasized.	"[The] approach that I was getting training was a . . . digital rhetorics approach? And we had to do . . . movie reviews, writing . . . narratives with . . . the pictures or something? . . . That was all kind of new to me? So I kind of struggled how to exactly teach them. . . . I'd never written that kind of thing . . . in my life. Before."
Standard English language knowledge and use	Knowledge of English academic/specialized vocabulary, grammar, and standard pronunciation is emphasized.	"Even in the textbook sometimes I would . . . read the text and I would see the words that I don't know. I was like, wow. What is this? . . . What does this word even mean? You know, I had to . . . look it up in the dictionary."
Training & educational support	Having previous teaching experiences, training in local pedagogies, and sharing of materials, strategies, and knowledge are emphasized.	"Because it's . . . a really tough transition for me because that was the first time I actually taught in the classroom setting ever. Before that I was only a tutor."
Non-English language knowledge and use	Knowledge of non-English vocabulary, grammar, and pronunciation is emphasized.	"At the end of the day, I feel more competent as an English teacher to teach writing and grammar and all kinds of other skills. Because I'm a nonnative speaker, I have been taught all these things in the past, so I know where students make mistakes and how I can help them basically with all those areas, a lot better."

Table 6.2. Social Relations Translation Device for Coding ITA Dataset

Social Relations Concept	Empirical Indicators	Examples
Teacher identity	Identifying as a good writer and/or an authoritative and knowledgeable teacher is emphasized.	"Sometimes I feel like . . . To be the teacher? . . . Especially in Asian culture? . . . Teachers tend to appear to be knowledgeable? And know everything . . . So I feel like, should I be your teacher?"
U.S. cultural experience	Past experience in U.S. culture and relating to that culture is emphasized.	"I don't know what kinds of classes that they take in high school? And what kinds of things that they learn? . . . So whenever they talk about, like, high hool experience in their essays . . . I couldn't really, you know, share the same feelings."
Native speaker status	Being a native speaker is emphasized as the basis for being a legitimate teacher and/or writer.	"Because they are native speakers, their writing will be good."
Community & emotional support	Emotional support, sense of community, and validation from peers, students, and faculty are emphasized.	"I feel like if you do kind of have this rapport with the students and they do trust you and you trust them, so they're actually willing to help you. Like, if you don't know something . . . Can you tell me more? And . . . they feel like they can actually help you."
Nonnative speaker status	Being an international student and/or nonnative speaker is emphasized as the basis for being a legitimate teacher.	"I think we have similar education. We share this common language. And so I think it's actually [an] advantage for me to teach these group of students. Cause I can relate [to] their difficulties?"

Results and Analysis

The Native Speaker is a Knower Code

The native speaker construct was often framed by the ITAs as a knower code, meaning that whether one can claim to be a NES or not depends more on their attributes than on their knowledge of the language. One of the more significant attributes that defined the NES is identifying as or being identified as a NES. For example, one participant drew an analogy between NES status and a person's skin color—both of which she framed as innate, immutable characteristics. She likened a NNES's desire to sound like a native to something as unrealistic as wanting to change one's skin color: "And then I think you are, for example, you are an Asian? And then you wanna be like a Caucasian . . . How can you change your skin color? It's just like that." In using racial terms to discuss the NES/NNES dichotomy, the participant likened NES status to belonging to a social group that one is generally born into, thus suggesting that NES status is based primarily on who a person is, instead of what they know. This finding supports Alan Davies' (2004) observation that the NES/NNES distinction reveals more about one's "autobiography" (p. 438) and their social membership than their language abilities. The participant's response also points to a possible racial dimension of the NES/NNES dichotomy (Butcher, 2005; Hackert, 2009; Mahboob, 2009). Further evidence is offered by another ITA who received "weird reactions" from her students, which she attributed to the fact that she is not White and speaks with a nonstandard accent: "I had surprises on their faces when they saw me. I'm this girl with black hair, dark eyes, I don't look American at all, I have this accent, where did I come from?" In sum, the basis of legitimation for being a NES rested largely on identifying with or being identified as part of that particular social group—which gives credence to Davies' (2004) argument concerning the circular reasoning of native-speakerism.

Another significant form of evidence supporting knower code classification of NES status was the ITAs' emphasis on a certain kind of *knowing*—a feel for the language or an innate intuition that differs from explicit principles and procedures of knowledge. As one participant suggested, NES competence extends beyond knowledge of grammar or the ability to produce grammatically "correct" sentences, and includes something less tangible yet "native-sounding":

> I could write correct sentences but the correct sentence does not mean the best sentence or the perfect sentence or the native-sounding, or it would sound native to the native speaker. So they would tell . . . this is written by the international student. Because the way they write, even though it is correct, even though it is grammatically correct . . . There is something different there.

As this excerpt suggests, only a NES can write a "perfect" sentence, and it is the NES who judges whether a sentence sounds perfect, based on how native-sounding it is. In other words, the language produced by a NES differs from that of a NNES precisely *because* it possesses some ineffable quality or characteristic that marks it as native-like. This further supports our claim that the NES construct is a knower code, which legitimizes those with an intuitive, tacit *knowing* over a more clearly defined, principled *knowledge*, such as grammatical knowledge.

Writing and Writing Pedagogy Emphasize Native Speaker Status

In discussing writing and writing pedagogy, the ITAs suggested that these fields place some emphasis on a particular type of knower as a basis for legitimation. For example, several participants admitted that they used to subscribe to the "good writer fallacy" (Kasztalska, 2018), or the belief that NESs are innately good writers. This belief places the basis of legitimation for being a good writer on the kind of knower that a person is—that is, a NES. As one ITA put it, as a novice teacher she assumed that even her first-year U.S. students would produce strong papers: "Because they are native speakers, their writing will be good." Moreover, she experienced a "writing crisis that came from thinking of [herself] as a bad writer because [she's] not a . . . native writer." In essence then, the good writer fallacy conflates NES status and writing skills, thus framing writing as an inherent attribute rather than a learned ability, which prevents some ITAs from seeing themselves as strong writers in English or as legitimate teachers of English writing. Thus, the good writer fallacy as an extension of native-speakerism may contribute to the feelings expressed by ITAs and other NNESTs who see themselves as subpar teachers and English users (Braine, 2004; Reis, 2012; Tang, 1997; Wolff, 2015).

In emphasizing NES status, the good writer fallacy also relies on the writer relating to U.S. cultural artifacts and practices as a basis for being a legitimate writer. This may lead to a perceived imbalance between the NNEST and NES student, in which the student is framed as being more competent in writing because of their experience with U.S. culture. One ITA reported that she recognized this imbalance as based on the lack of a shared past experience: "I don't know what kinds of classes that they take in high school? And what kinds of things that they learn? . . . So whenever they talk about, like, high school experience in their essays . . . I couldn't really, you know, share the same feelings." This past experience of acculturation into U.S. culture also played a role in teaching writing, as another ITA explained:

> I also had difficulty with understanding . . . cultural issues? Like, when we discuss something . . . related to politics I really didn't have anything to say because I didn't have any background in that area. So I couldn't really bring that into discussion in my class . . . And it was not just about politics. It was about many different topics that I didn't feel comfortable having students discuss about . . . because I don't know anything about it. And writing always includes something about culture, I think.

Thus, along with the emphasis on the NES identity, the ITAs seemed to also recognize an emphasis on becoming legitimate through experience with NESs' dominant culture. Both of these place the basis of being a legitimate teacher of writing on social identities and/or experiences (SR) rather than discrete knowledge (ER).

This lack of shared cultural experience compounds the already challenging situation many ITAs face in their "traumatic first semester" (Braine, 1999, p. 21) as novice writing instructors. According to another ITA:

> [NES student background] is something that is very difficult for me to relate to when I taught [mainstream composition] in the beginning. Because it's . . . a really tough transition for me because that was the first time I actually taught in the classroom setting ever. Before that I was only a tutor . . . I was teaching American students. I have zero international students in my class, unfortunately.

These statements echo those made by ITAs in other studies, whose authors called for more intercultural training for ITAs to help them relate to and teach domestic students (Ates & Eslami, 2012; LeGros & Faez, 2012), as well others who argue that students should receive similar training (e.g., Corbett, 2003). At the same time, while the emphasis on shared experience in composition can be a challenge for ITAs working with NES writers, our research also suggests that it can help ITAs work with NNES writers. This sentiment was echoed by several participants, who stated that because they can "relate to the experiences [international students] are going through," ITAs understand their students' needs and offer meaningful feedback. In sum, the evidence suggests that writing instructors are legitimated by NES identity and the acculturation that comes with that status; on the other hand, when teaching NNES students, the ITAs' NNES status can grant them some legitimation.

Because NES status appears to be a knower code and because writing and writing instruction seem to emphasize a particular kind of knower—the NES—the ITAs' experiences suggest a code clash. In other words, the code that the participants use to legitimize themselves clashes in some ways with the one expected in the field they are working in. Specifically, the ITAs see their potential legitimacy as based on their knowledge of English and writing pedagogy, but the code they experience also includes the expectation that one must be a particular kind of knower or person—NES—with particular experiences—shared cultural knowledge.

One of the consequences of this code clash is that the ITAs, like other NNESTs in prior research (e.g., Crandall, 2003; Thomas, 1999), are not regarded as legitimate writers or teachers of writing by their students. This was suggested by a participant who felt that she had to "prove" to her students that she is "qualified even though [she's] not [a] native speaker." This code clash led her to feel anxious in teaching writing to NESs, who she feared may question her authority. While this ITA did not report any overt resistance from her students or outward prejudice, a few others felt they were challenged by students, at least in part due to their status as NNESs. For example, one ITA thought that some of her students were "testing [her] vocabulary" in an attempt to discredit her as a teacher, while another admitted that in their final course evaluations some students wrote that they wanted an "ENGLISH teacher," in all capital letters. This suggests that at least some NES students also subscribe to the good writer fallacy and rely on NES status in evaluating their writing teacher's legitimacy. As a result, the prevalent discourses on writing present a seemingly insurmountable obstacle for ITAs of composition, who are denied professional legitimacy on the basis of being NNESTs. This finding brings to our minds Suresh A. Canagarajah's (1999) observation about the "absurdity" of a field that "prepares one for a profession it disqualifies the person at the same time" (p. 77).

While the NES seems to be the "ideal knower" (Maton, 2014, p. 32) for being a writer and writing instructor, there is also a great deal of data in the study that challenges this form of legitimation. As also suggested by the ITAs, NNESTs were generally quick to discover that NES students were not always as skilled in their writing as one might assume. Several participants were surprised when they found some "terrible writing styles" or "grammatical mistakes" in papers produced by their NES students. The realization that NESs were not in fact innately talented at writing in their mother tongue seemed to have helped some ITAs see themselves as more legitimate teachers and recognize the importance of their knowledge and training in composition, which many of their students lacked. In other words, emphasizing knowledge in the practice and teaching of writing allowed NNESTs to recognize that they really "can help some students" and to claim authority as writing teachers.

Implications

Our LCT analysis of the data reveals two key findings. Firstly, the NES tends to be discursively constructed as a knower code rather than a knowledge code. In other words, what distinguishes NESs from NNESs is not primarily their use of language, but rather their identification or perceived status as a NES. This finding supports Davies' (2004) assertion that the NES/NNES distinction is not a matter of linguistics or language abilities, but instead marks an individual's perceived social membership in the NES group, which is often contingent upon nonlinguistic factors, such as place of birth or race (Mahboob, 2009; Moussu & Llurda, 2008). Secondly, teachers perceived as NNESs, including ITAs, may experience a code clash when attempting to claim legitimacy as teachers of English writing. This is because the "good writer fallacy" (Kasztalska, 2018) frames writing competence as an innate attribute of NESs, rather than a learnable skill, and thus delegitimizes NNESs as English writers. The code clash also stems from the framing of successful teaching of writing as contingent upon the teacher and student sharing some cultural background and knowledge, which many NNESTs do not share with NES students. As a result of the code clash, many ITAs in this study and in other studies (e.g., Ates & Eslami, 2012; Liu, 2005; Ruecker et al., 2018) may struggle to see themselves as legitimate writing teachers or as an authority in the classroom.

This study largely supports earlier assertions that the "native speaker fallacy" (Phillipson, 1992, p. 182) can impede NNESTs' attempts to claim legitimacy as English teachers (Varghese et al., 2005). In addition, our LCT analysis also reveals the underlying assumptions about knowledge and knowers in ELT and composition. There are several key implications of our research for writing program administration (WPA) and for ITA training, but our overarching recommendation is that WPAs recognize native-speakerism as a knower code and strengthen their ER, emphasizing knowledge more in teaching writing. Emphasis on knowledge as the basis of legitimation should not only inform how writing and the teaching of writing are discursively framed, but should also inform course instructor assignments, teacher training, and writing curriculum.

WPAs Should Emphasize Knowledge in Course Instructor Assignment.

Firstly, course instructor assignment decisions should not be based on the teacher's NES status, but instead on their knowledge and overall readiness. To this end, we recommend that WPAs work more closely with ITAs and other TAs to assess their readiness for teaching specific courses. Moreover, writing programs should not assume that an ITA is inherently better suited to working with international students or that local TAs should work with NESs. Instead, WPAs should follow the example set by the institution in this study, which regularly assigns ITAs to both ESL and mainstream writing courses. Above all, writing programs should understand the educational and professional backgrounds, as well as teaching abilities of all incoming TAs, thus placing a stronger emphasis on knowledge—as opposed to internal attributes—for course instructor assignment.

WPAs Should Emphasize Knowledge in Training ITAs.

We suggest that writing programs re-evaluate their ITA training to emphasize knowledge. Since many ITAs in this and other studies (Liu, 2005; Reis, 2012) report anxiety over teaching composition, especially to NESs, they may benefit from more explicit training. First, ITAs can benefit from learning about the local cultural and educational context and about the local student population, as this information should inform every teacher's instruction. Second, ITAs may need more extensive training in composition theory and pedagogy, which can help them make sound pedagogical choices and follow best teaching practices. Additionally, a stronger foundation in composition may allow ITAs to more readily see themselves as experts on writing and as authorities in their classrooms.

Moreover, we argue that to prepare ITAs for working with NESs and to challenge the "good writer fallacy," ITA training programs should expose these teachers to texts produced by both experienced and inexperienced NES and NNES writers. In concurrence with the emerging studies on ITAs of composition (Liu, 2005; Ruecker et al., 2018), our research suggests that exposure to different types of writing can remind NNESTs of composition that one's status as a NES or NNES does not reflect or limit their writing abilities. ITAs are often surprised to find that many of their NES students cannot produce strong academic texts, which leads ITAs to embrace more of a knowledge orientation to writing and realize that writing is ultimately learned. When reminded of their own training and experience with academic writing, ITAs can more easily claim legitimacy as English writers and as teachers of writing.

While we argue that there needs to be more emphasis on knowledge in the training of prospective writing teachers, we are *not* arguing against an emphasis on social relations in general. We critique certain knower codes in this chapter, but we also recognize the need for preparing and supporting ITAs through certain practices that emphasize knowers. Specifically, we agree that writing programs need to familiarize ITAs with local cultures and student populations, build stronger peer support systems for ITAs, as well as foster a feeling of community and emphasize diversity (Liu, 2005; Nemtchinova et al., 2010; Ruecker et al., 2018). ITAs may also benefit from working with or shadowing a more experienced instructor before they teach their own class (see Reichelt, this volume). In sum, while a certain knower emphasis is important in ITA training, we argue that WPAs should place more emphasis than they currently do on knowledge in their training of prospective teachers.

"What Authority I Have?"

WPAs and Writing Teachers Should Make Writing Expectations More Explicit.

Finally, our LCT analysis suggests that for students to benefit from ITAs' and NESs' instruction, the bases of legitimation for successful writing and being a successful writer should be made as explicit as possible. In order to reveal the "hidden curriculum" (Cortazzi & Jin, 1996, p. 169), students need to know the "rules of the game" (Maton, 2014, p. 11) for writing in terms of specialized knowledge, principles, and procedures, as well as knower attributes and dispositions. Neither of these should be hidden or implicit. When knowledge and knowers are not discussed, students are left to make inferences that often lead to misconceptions like the "good writer fallacy" (Kasztalska, 2018). As we have shown, this misconception can lead to a code clash between ITAs and some NES students' image of a legitimate writing teacher. In effect, ITAs may not be regarded as legitimate teachers of English writing because they are not NESs and they do not share cultural experiences with their students.

To challenge or avert the development of these misconceptions, writing must be explicitly framed as a knowledge code that can be learned, rather than an internal attribute like NES status or having a specific cultural background. To this end, following Mary Macken-Horarik (2011), we advocate for writing programs to *foreground* explicit teaching of writing knowledge and to *background* the reliance on internal attributes and shared cultural experience. However, we also recognize that sometimes knowledge is not enough; students need to be *taught* to develop some internal attributes to head off misconceptions about NNESTs. In particular, we advocate—alongside Todd Ruecker and colleagues (2018)—for explicit teaching of the value of linguistic and cultural diversity in order for students to develop a more just disposition towards teachers and writers from diverse backgrounds. Only through emphasizing knowledge and developing knowers can we help shape effective educational contexts for students to learn writing from NNESTs and to see these teachers of writing as legitimate.

References

Adendorff, H. & Blackie, M. A. (2020). Decolonizing the science curriculum: When good intentions are not enough. In C. Winberg (Ed.), *Building knowledge in higher education* (pp. 237–254). Routledge. https://doi.org/10.4324/9781003028215-14.

Amin, N. (1999). Minority women teachers of ESL: Negotiating White English. In G. Braine (Ed.), *Non-Native Educators in English Language Teaching* (pp. 93–104). Lawrence Erlbaum Associates. https://doi.org/10.4324/9781315045368.

Arshavskaya, E. (2015). International teaching assistants' experiences in the U.S. classrooms: Implications for practice. *Journal of the Scholarship of Teaching and Learning, 15*(2), 56–69. https://doi.org/10.14434/josotl.v15i2.12947.

Ates, B. & Eslami, Z. R. (2012). Teaching experiences of native and nonnative English-speaking graduate teaching assistants and their perceptions of preservice teachers. *Journal on Excellence in College Teaching, 23*(3), 99–112.

Braine, G. (1999). From the periphery to the center: One teacher's journey. In G. Braine (Ed.), *Non-Native educators in English language teaching* (pp. 15–27). Lawrence Erlbaum Associates. https://doi.org/10.4324/9781315045368.

Braine, G. (2004). The nonnative English-speaking professionals' movement and its research foundations. In L. D. Kamhi-Stein (Ed.), *Learning and teaching from experience: Perspectives on nonnative English-speaking professionals* (pp. 9–24). University of Michigan Press. https://doi.org/10.3998/mpub.9648.

Butcher, C. A. (2005). The case against the "native speaker." *English Today, 21*(2), 13–24.

Canagarajah, S. A. (1999). Interrogating the "native speaker fallacy": Non-linguistic roots, non-pedagogical results. In G. Braine (Ed.), *Non-native educators in English language teaching* (pp. 77–92). Lawrence Erlbaum Associates. https://doi.org/10.4324/9781315045368.

Cassell, E. C. (2007). *Understanding community linguistic diversity: An ecological approach to examining language use patterns of international graduate students* [Doctoral dissertation, Purdue University]. Purdue e-Pubs. https://docs.lib.purdue.edu/dissertations/AAI3287301/.

Corbett, J. (2003). *An intercultural approach to English language teaching*. Multilingual Matters.

Cortazzi, M. & Jin, L. (1996). Cultures of learning: Language classrooms in China. In H. Coleman (Ed.), *Society and the language classroom* (pp. 169–206). Cambridge University Press.

Crandall, J. (2003). They DO speak English: World Englishes in U.S. schools. *ERIC/CLL News Bulletin, 26*(3), 1–3.

Creswell, J. W. (2013). *Qualitative inquiry and research design: Choosing among five approaches*. Sage.

Damron, J. A. (2000). *Chinese 101, a prerequisite to math 100? A look at undergraduate students' beliefs about their role in communication with international teaching assistants* [Doctoral dissertation, Purdue University]. Purdue e-Pubs. https://docs.lib.purdue.edu/dissertations/AAI3018186/.

Davies, A. (2004). The native speaker in applied linguistics. N A. Davies & C. Elder (Eds.), *The Handbook of Applied Linguistics* (pp. 431–450). Blackwell Publishing Ltd. https://doi.org/10.1002/9780470757000.ch17.

Fithriani, R. (2018). Discrimination behind NEST and NNEST dichotomy in ELT professionalism. *KnE Social Sciences, 3*(4), 741–755. https://doi.org/10.18502/kss.v3i4.1982.

Hackert, S. (2009). Linguistic nationalism and the emergence of the English native speaker. *European Journal of English Studies, 13*(3), 305–317. https://doi.org/10.1080/13825570903223541.

Hebbani, A. & Hendrix, K. G. (2014). Capturing the experiences of international teaching assistants in the US American classroom. *New Directions for Teaching and Learning, 138*, 61–72. https://doi.org/10.1002/tl.20097.

Holliday, A. (2006). Native-speakerism. *ELT Journal, 60*(4), 385–387. https://doi.org/10.1093/elt/ccl030.

Kachru, B. B. (1990). *The alchemy of English: The spread, functions, and models of non-native Englishes.* University of Illinois Press.

Kasztalska, A. (2015). *The role of world Englishes in supporting international teaching assistants' professional identity and development* [Doctoral dissertation, Purdue University]. Purdue e-Pubs. https://docs.lib.purdue.edu/dissertations/AAI3736165/.

Kasztalska, A. (2018). International teaching assistants in the composition classroom: From world Englishes to translingualism and beyond. *Journal of Language, Identity & Education, 18*(3), 161–175. https://doi.org/10.1080/15348458.2018.1545584.

Kvale, S. & Brinkmann, S. (2009). *InterViews: Learning the craft of qualitative research interviewing.* Sage.

LeGros, N. & Faez, F. (2012). The intersection between intercultural competence and teaching behaviors: A case of international teaching assistants. *Journal on Excellence in College Teaching, 23*(3), 7–31.

Liu, J. (2005). Chinese graduate teaching assistants teaching freshman composition to native English speaking students. In E. Llurda (Ed.), *Nonnative Language Teachers: Perceptions, Challenges and Contributions to the Profession* (pp. 155–177). Springer. https:/.doi.org/10.1007/0-387-24565-0_9.

Lofland, J. (1971). *Analyzing social settings: A guide to qualitative observation and analysis.* Wadsworth.

Macken-Horarik, M. (2011). Building a knowledge structure for English: Reflections on the challenges of coherence, cumulative learning, portability and face validity. *Australian Journal of Education, 55*(3), 197–213. https://doi.org/10.1177/000494411105500303.

Mahboob, A. (2009). Racism in the English language teaching industry. In A. Mahboob & C. Lipovsky (Eds.), *Studies in Applied Linguistics and Language Learning* (pp. 29–40). Cambridge Scholars Press.

Mahboob, A. & Golden, R. (2013). Looking for native speakers of English: Discrimination in English language teaching job advertisements. *Voices in Asia Journal, 1*(1), 72–81.

Maton, K. (2014). *Knowledge and knowers: Towards a realist sociology of education.* Routledge. https://doi.org/10.4324/9780203885734.

Maton, K. & Chen, R. T.-H. (2015). LCT in qualitative research: Creating a translation device for studying constructivist pedagogy. In K. Maton, S. Hood & S. Shay (Eds.), *Knowledge-building: Educational studies in legitimation code theory* (pp. 27–48). Routledge. https://doi.org/10.4324/9781315672342.

Moussu, L. & Llurda, E. (2008). Non-native English-speaking English language teachers: History and research. *Language Teaching, 41*(3), 315–348. https://doi.org/10.1017/S0261444808005028.

Nemtchinova, E., Mahboob, A., Eslami, Z. & Dogancay-Aktuna, S. (2010). Training non-native English speaking TESOL professionals. In A. Mahboob (Ed.), *The NNEST lens: Non-native English speakers in TESOL* (pp. 222–238). Cambridge Scholars Publishing.

Phillipson, R. (1992). *Linguistic imperialism*. Oxford University Press.

Reis, D. S. (2011). Non-native English-speaking teachers (NNESTs) and professional legitimacy: A sociocultural theoretical perspective on identity transformation. *International Journal of the Sociology of Language, 2011*(208), 139–160. https://doi.org/10.1515/ijsl.2011.016.

Reis, D. S. (2012). "Being underdog": Supporting nonnative English-speaking teachers (NNESTs) in claiming and asserting professional legitimacy. *Journal on Excellence in College Teaching, 23*(3), 33–58.

Rivers, D. J. (2016). Employment advertisements and native-speakerism in Japanese higher education. In F. Copland, S. Garton & S. Mann (Eds.), *LETs and NESTs: Voices, views and vignettes* (pp. 79–100). British Council.

Ruecker, T., Frazier, S. & Tseptsura, M. (2018). "Language difference can be an asset": Exploring the experiences of nonnative English-speaking teachers of writing. *College Composition and Communication, 69*(4), 612–641. https://www.jstor.org/stable/44870978.

Ruecker, T. & Ives, L. (2015). White native English speakers needed: The rhetorical construction of privilege in online teacher recruitment spaces. *TESOL Quarterly, 49*(4), 733–756. https://doi.org/10.1002/tesq.195.

Selvi, A. F. (2014). Myths and misconceptions about nonnative English speakers in the TESOL (NNEST) movement. *TESOL Journal, 5*(3), 573–611. https://doi.org/10.1002/tesj.158.

Shehi, M. (2017). Why is my English teacher a foreigner? Re-authoring the story of international composition teachers. *Teaching English in the Two-Year College, 44*(3), 260.

Swan, A., Aboshiha, P. & Holliday, A (2015). Introduction. In A. Swan, P. Aboshiha & A. Holliday (Eds.), *(En)countering native-speakerism: Global perspectives* (pp. 1–8). Palgrave MacMillan. https://doi.org/10.1080/15348458.2017.1344103.

Tang, C. (1997). The identity of the nonnative ESL teacher: On the power and status of nonnative ESL teachers. *TESOL Quarterly, 31*(3), 577–580. https://doi.org/10.2307/3587840.

Thomas, J. (1999). Voices from the periphery: Non-native teachers and issues of credibility. In G. Braine (Ed.), *Non-native educators in English language teaching* (pp. 5–14). Lawrence Erlbaum Associates. https://doi.org/10.4324/9781315045368.

Varghese, M., Morgan, B., Johnston, B. & Johnson, K. A. (2005). Theorizing language teacher identity: Three perspectives and beyond. *Journal of Language, Identity, and Education, 4*(1), 21–44. https://doi.org/10.1207/s15327701jlie0401_2.

Wolff, D. (2015). *All in the same boat? Native and non-native English speaking teachers' emerging selves in a US MATESOL program*. Michigan State University.

7　Native English-Speaking Students' Perceptions of a Nonnative English-Speaking Writing Teacher, Teaching Effectiveness, and Language Performance

Lan Wang-Hiles
WEST VIRGINIA STATE UNIVERSITY

My experience as a writing instructor at my current institute began with challenges due to taking over two writing courses in the midst of a semester already five weeks into the session when the original instructor quit. After meeting with the instructor to learn about the course objectives, expected outcomes, the students, the class dynamics, and observing two class periods, I revised the initial syllabi, adding what I believed to be necessary, then entered classrooms, full of native English-speaking students (NESSs). The classes did not go as smoothly as I had desired, and the students' evaluations were not as high as I expected. While I appreciated students' positive comments and ratings regarding my teaching, I was taken aback by several comments that were not on my teaching, but on my nonnative English-speaking teacher (NNEST) status and language. Comments such as "A good teacher, but too bad she is Chinese" and "She does not speak English well" I perceived as racially and linguistically discriminatory.

 I understood that the sudden change of instructors, teaching style, and content would cause anxiety to students as they strove to adapt. Also, for most students, I might be the first NNEST of their entire academic experiences. These reasons alone could lower the evaluation scores; however, some students' negative comments about my NNEST status and linguistic competence made me intellectually and emotionally restless. As an introduction to my background, I am a female native speaker of Chinese, born and raised in China. I earned my BA in English literature and a master's certification of English pedagogy in China, and instructed English at a Chinese university for eight years. Then I earned my master's in applied linguistics and ESL and doctorate in composition and TESOL in the US. I am experienced in composition instruction at universities in the US. I began to teach writing as a doctoral student in the US. At the previous U.S. universities where I instructed, I taught research writing courses for graduate students, focusing on teaching thesis writing development. With almost twenty years of university-level English teaching experience in the US and China, my educational background and teaching experience should more than qualify me as a writing instructor. While my current university is a small public HBCU, more than 85% of the students are white. The majority of the students are only first-generation college students, and I am the only NNEST in the English department.

Truly, students' evaluations are valuable; yet, their linguistic and racial bias against NNESTs is damaging. It undermines NNESTs' teaching authority in the classroom, creates an unhealthy teaching-learning environment, and accordingly, negatively affects students' learning. Perceived bias against NNESTs also sways NNESTs' self-esteem and academic reputation, particularly if student evaluations are a key measurement on faculty retention, promotion, and tenure. My experience intensified my interest in exploring whether the mediocre evaluations I received were simply an isolated incident due to the abrupt change of instructors, my NNEST status cause students' dissatisfaction, or did I not teach well. Further, since language performance is closely related to teaching effectiveness, student evaluations of my teaching are likely based on my language performance and their acceptance of a NNEST. Hence, this study investigated NESSs' perceptions of having a NNEST teach writing and their evaluations of the NNEST's teaching effectiveness and language performance.

Research on Nonnative English-Speaking Teaching Professionals

Numerous studies have discussed NNESTs, including international faculty (Aneja, 2016; Braine, 1999; Kamhi-Stein, 2004; Llurda, 2004; Reves & Medgyes, 1994) and international teaching assistants (Bresnahan & Kim, 1993; Fox & Gay, 1994). Topics of linguistic bias, racial and gender discrimination are the foci (Bresnahan et al., 2002; Canagarajah, 1999; Kaur & Raman, 2014; Lazos, 2012; Lippi-Green, 2012; Vargas, 2002). Among them, the notion of native speakers being ideal English instructors (Chun, 2014; Lasagabaster & Sierra, 2010; Saraceni, 2015; Saunders, 2001) and learners favoring native speakers' accent (Kaur & Raman, 2014; Kumaravadivelu, 2008) are discussed most. NNESTs' linguistic proficiency and teaching credibility are constantly questioned by students, native English-speaking colleagues, even NNESTs themselves (Crystal, 1997; Thomas, 1999).

Gail Shuck's (2009) study addressed the existence of the native-nonnative dichotomy, pointing out the fact that people often perceive native speakers as English experts with no accent and understandable in comparison with nonnative speakers. Rosina Lippi-Green (2012) also disclosed a phenomenon in educational settings that when native speakers are confronted with an accent, particularly Asian accents, either unfamiliar or foreign to them, they can decide whether to participate in the communication or not even "reject their responsibility" and "demand that a person with an accent carry the majority of the burden in the communication" (p. 72). Due to ethnocentrism (Bailey, 1984), failure in native-nonnative communications is often blamed on nonnative speakers' proficiency or accent, but rarely on native speakers' willingness and ability to understand (Kang et al., 2015). Accordingly, native speakers are habitually ranked higher than nonnative speakers in terms of correctness, pleasantness, familiarity, and acceptability for communication (Kaur & Raman, 2014).

While we cannot deny that nonnative speakers' language may make communication harder; yet intelligibility is a joint constructive effort by both speaker and listener in communication (Rajadurai, 2007). According to Stephanie Lindemann (2002), natives speakers' lack of willingness to understand nonnative speakers can impede the interaction. Consequently, even though NESSs may understand their NNESTs well, some still rate the communication as dissatisfactory. Dan Villarreal's (2013) model of the communication gap between undergraduates and their international faculty also disclosed the linguistic bias against NNESTs. As he introduced, "accent misunderstanding" and "accent bias" are two separate terms, the former relates to "linguistic, cognitive, and cultural factors; both instructor and students create the misunderstanding gap," the latter however, relates to "social and cognitive factors; students only create the gap in communication" (p. 10). Therefore, NNESTs receive lower ratings even though students learn as much from them as from their NESTs (Finegan & Siegfried, 2000).

Kent Saunders (2001) once pointed out that an instructor's native language does not affect student learning; rather, the instructor's native language not being English caused them receiving "significantly lower ratings compared to the instructors whose native language is English" (p. 352). Sadly, Asian instructors' race and language are particularly perceived as a disadvantage, being rated more negatively than their colleagues who have common U.S. names (Lippi-Green, 2012; Subtirelu, 2015). Back in 1999, William Becker and Michael Watts already criticized that instead of rating instructors' teaching effectiveness, some students rated based on their "expected grades, instructor's popularity, even teacher's age, sex, or ethnic background" (p. 344). While two decades have passed, racial and linguistic discrimination against

NNESTs still seems to exist; NNESTs are rated nonobjectively, their races and accents are blamed. A foreign name, appearance, accent, even gender may still trigger a skeptical attitude toward NNESTs' teaching credibility. This situation is largely influenced by a Western monolingual and mono-cultural perception of English instruction (Kachru, 2009) and the observation that English teaching jobs favor native speakers (Saraceni, 2015).

Thankfully, the focus has shifted discussing from native-nonnative dichotomy to the importance of being professional. In 1992, Robert Phillipson criticized discrimination against NNESTs, lamenting the native-speaker fallacy. Peter Medgyes (1994) argues that nonnatives may have more fully developed skills, such as explicit knowledge about the linguistic structure of English. Likewise, Suresh Canagarajah (1999) asserts "multilingual speakers' proficiency in more than one language system develops a deep metalinguistic knowledge and complex language awareness" (p. 80). NNESTs also prove themselves skilled in teaching methods, identifying and solving students' problems, explaining rules, and delivering knowledge as they have gone through the learning process themselves (Lipovsky & Mahboob, 2010; Ma, 2012; Mahboob, 2004; Moussu & Llurda, 2008).

With the increasing numbers of NNESTs teaching rhetoric and composition in higher education, studies regarding nonnative-speaking composition instructors have begun to emerge. Priti Kumar (2002) revealed experiencing her NES students' apprehensions about her teaching credibility after seeing her appearance and hearing her Indian accent. Over years, student evaluations of her composition classes still reflect their "apprehensions and preconceived notions about [her] ethnicity" (2002, p. 286). Even though students' attitude changed from apprehension to acceptance and praise after taking her writing courses, some students admitted being biased against her because she did not grow up speaking English but was teaching English. Kumar asserted the importance of self-confidence and improvement, but also affirmed the significance of colleagues' support while empowering her professional authority. Similarly, Xue-Lan Rong (2002) reflected on the misunderstanding, ignorance, and racial bias from her colleagues and students when first hired, pinpointing that students' attitude is also influenced by her colleagues' attitude and the ethos of the institution. Hence, she stressed the importance of new instructors rapidly learning about the students and the undercurrents of school academic, administrative, and political culture. She also proposed the need for addressing colleague and school attitudes toward minority faculty, believing that their positive outlook can have a positive impact on students' attitude toward NNESTs. Monika Shehi (2017) revealed the social and academic barriers she encountered in composition classrooms and the difficulty facing linguistically privileged NES students. Thus, she advocated for linguistic diversity. Similarly, Todd Ruecker and colleagues (2018) introduced the intertwined bias NNESTs often encounter, endorsing NNESTs' needs for linguistic diversity and pedagogy support. These studies, from the viewpoint of NNESTs, discussed the experiences most nonnative-speaking composition instructors have encountered. My study, from NES students' perspectives, explored their perceptions of a nonnative-speaking composition instructor and their evaluations of a NNEST's teaching effectiveness and language performance.

Design and Methodology

This study consists of two surveys followed by interviews (see Appendices). Survey I, entailing two parts, attempted to discover NES students' perceptions of having a NNEST teach them writing and their evaluations of my teaching effectiveness in multiple aspects. Part I has eight open-ended questions, asking about NES Students' opinions and experiences of having a NNEST; Part II contains close-ended Likert-scale questions, asking about NES students' evaluations of my instruction in 17 aspects. Based on the preliminary results of Survey I collected over three semesters, I designed Survey II as a complement to Survey I. Survey II, with five multiple-choice questions and two open-ended questions, investigated NESSs' perceptions of my language performance, as it determines my teaching effectiveness and NESSs' opinions of a NNEST. At the concluding portion of Survey II, I requested additional volunteers to participate in a follow-up interview in order to further explore students' insights on my linguistic capability. Five volunteers responded and participated. Both surveys and the interviews with unstructured questions helped me gain thorough and in-depth opinions of NESSs' perceptions of a NNEST.

Participants for the surveys and interviews were undergraduate NESSs who took my research writing course from different departments and programs in five semesters. Research writing is a required course for all undergraduates to take with college writing as a prerequisite. Both surveys were anonymous; students received a copy two weeks before the end of the semester, and then voluntarily turned them in at the end of each semester. That way students would experience my teaching performance holistically throughout the semester, and still have the time to carefully form their reflective evaluations. Participants for Survey I were students from five research writing classes over three semesters. Excluding incomplete submissions, 84 surveys were valid for further analysis. Participants for Survey II and follow-up interviews were students from three subsequent research writing classes over two semesters. Among the collected surveys, 63 were completed for analysis, with five participants interviewed one-on-one after the semester was completed and all the students' grades were turned in.

As described, my data sources were two surveys and follow-up interviews. I employed a modification of Steven Terrell's (2011) sequential explanatory strategy for data collection: surveys including both quantitative and qualitative data were collected followed by qualitative data refinement through interviews. The quantitative data provided a basic and broad understanding of NESSs' perceptions of me as a NNEST, my teaching effectiveness, and language performance. The qualitative data included in the surveys and interviews allowed me to learn their opinions better and in more depth. I utilized descriptive analyses and percentage of responses to analyze the quantitative data and employed inductive interpretation to analyze the qualitative data.

One limitation is that even though I conducted the interviews after submitting the participants' grades, more objective data might have been obtained if someone else conducted the interviews. Also, the interview results could only represent the five participants' opinions. Yet, as an instructor and researcher, the advantage was that I was able to identify specific aspects and moments of the course that an outsider would not have been privy to.

Findings

The results of the two surveys and interviews indicated that overall, most NESSs accepted my NNEST status and were satisfied with my teaching and language performance. Survey I revealed that despite some initial skeptical attitudes when first seeing me and hearing my accent, the vast majority of NESSs experienced improvement in their writing and research skills, including the very few who disliked my NNEST status. The majority of NESSs believed that they had made a correct decision to stay in my classes. The ones who disliked my NNEST status but stayed due to their schedules, intellectually admitted that staying in my class was a correct decision; yet emotionally, they felt uncomfortable due to my NNEST status. These implied that although NESSs were overall satisfied with my teaching, racial discrimination against my NNEST status might still be a factor with those who preferred only NES teachers. Further, students' evaluation results indicated that my language performance and NNEST status were not rated as highly as other aspects in terms of teaching effectiveness. Survey II indicated that while NESSs comprehended my English and accepted my language performance, slightly less than one third responded that occasionally my accent, sentence structure, and vocabulary use occasionally caused minimal distractions in comprehension. Nevertheless, they did not perceive any observed language flaws affected my teaching effectiveness. NESSs were satisfied with my language performance, and there was no miscommunication.

Survey I Results: NES Students' Perception of My NNEST Status and Teaching Effectiveness

In responding to whether they knew I am a NNEST or not (Question1), 66 of 84 participants (78.57%) stated that prior to meeting me, they did not know, nor did they care. The other 18 (12.43%) knew my NNEST status because either they had taken my other courses before or when their friends recommended my course. Regarding students' concerns of having a NNEST teach them writing (Question 2), most of the participants demonstrated an open and accepting attitude without concerns. A few examples are "I don't judge professors on their native languages; realizing you had to learn English and earn your doctorate, you would know what to teach"; "I picked you specifically because someone recommended you." And "I admired the fact that you are able to teach English to Americans." Yet, some confessed to an initial skeptical attitude, being unsure about my teaching and linguistic capability. However, they stayed after taking my first class. A few admitted hesitations but stayed due to their restricted schedules or thought I "deserved an opportunity." Two of them, however, were greatly concerned about my NNEST status. As one wrote, "It bothered me greatly that you are a nonnative."

When answering whether the right decision was made to stay in my class (Question 3), almost all participants responded positively; very few however, reported both "yes" and "no" including the two who disliked my NNEST status. One wrote "yes because my English writing has improved, but no because sometimes you expected too much." The other wrote, "Yes I learned new things from you, but I found it [is] hard to take the grammatical criticism from someone who is not a native to the language."

Regarding my strengths as a NNEST in teaching (Question 4), all except one observed my strengths as clear instruction, knowledge of writing, constructive and detailed feedback on assignments, and good communication with students. To my surprise, quite a number of participants praised my spoken English in particular; they also expressed their enjoyment of learning the differences between Chinese and American rhetoric. The two who complained about my NNEST status also listed some of my strengths, such as I gave "specific and to the point directions," my feedback "was always thorough and detailed throughout," and I "cared for students, which is rare among faculty and it's a good quality to have."

Regarding my weaknesses (Question 5), the majority reported no weaknesses being found; however, a few stated that my occasional awkward sentence structures and uncommon vocabulary use were distracting. One of the two students who disliked my NNEST status wrote a complaint: "You don't *speak* English well." A unique comment, which drew my attention, was "sometimes you take the American meaning of something too literally because you lack cultural understanding." To some extent, I admit that not being raised in the US, I lack some culture-specific understanding. Regarding suggestions on my teaching improvement (Question 6), in addition to suggesting that I fix the issues mentioned in Question 5, students expressed their appreciation of having me as their writing instructor.

When asked whether NNEST status would influence their course selection for English-department courses (Question 7) and non-English department courses (Question 8), almost all participants demonstrated a high acceptability of NNESTs, answering "No" to both questions. Language intelligibility, nonetheless, is a decisive factor for four participants. For them, a NNEST status would not sway their decisions on choosing English courses offered by English faculty; but it would be one criterion in choosing non-English courses offered by other departments or programs such as math, computer science, etc. due to NNESTs' heavy accents. Their answers implied that NNESTs who teach English courses are exposed to concentrating more on accent compensation. A couple of other participants held an opposing opinion however, preferring NESTs to teach English, but not caring if NNESTs teach non-English courses. One participant expressed a changed attitude regarding courses offered by NNESTs and wrote, "Before taking your class, I cared whether my professor is an American or not, but not anymore." Not surprisingly, the two participants who had zero tolerance toward NNESTs only wanted courses to be taught by NESTs regardless of the subject-matter being English or non-English classes.

Part II of Survey I contains 17 Likert-scale questions with a scale of 1 to 5: 1=Poor, 2=Average, 3=Good, 4=Excellent, and 5=N/A, yielding a mixed evaluation of my teaching. Figure 7.1 shows the most relevant questions about my teaching with students' evaluations of the following aspects: 1) feedback/comments on written assignments, 2) interaction, handouts, email communication, and individual conferences with students, and 3) instructor's accessibility/flexibility, which earned me over 90% of "Excellent" and 100% positive rate, if including both "Excellent" and "Good". In addition, I received a positive rate of 96.4% (n=81) on my knowledge of rhetoric, 92.8% (n=78) on research skill instruction, and 95.2% (n=80) on my overall course instruction.

However, evaluation results (see Figure 7.2) also indicated that two aspects regarding my language performance included a handful of "Average" ratings although no "Poor" ratings. For example, 15.48% (n=13) participants rated my language use in speech as "Average," even though 66.66% (n=56) rated "Excellent" and 17.86% (n=15) rated "Good." Likewise, 22.61% (n=19) rated my grammar use as "Average," although 64.29% (n=54) rated "Excellent" and 13.10% (n=11) rated "Good." These results matched the perceived weaknesses addressing my language performance in Part I.

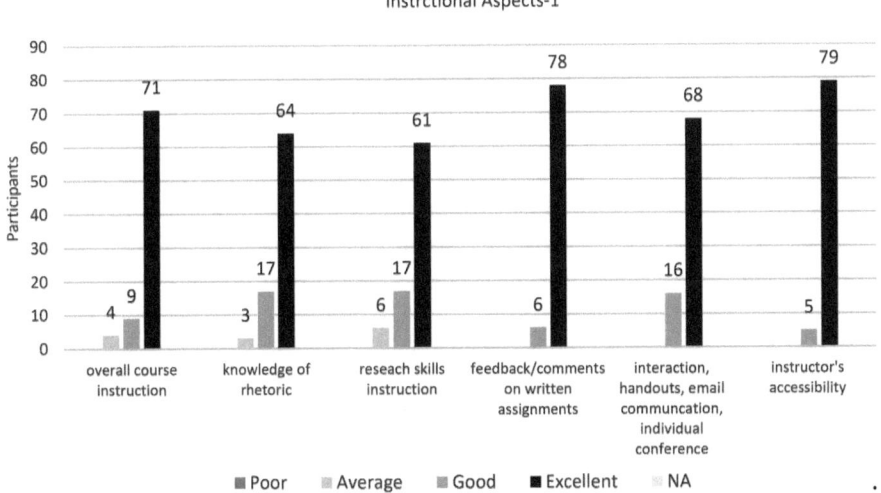

Figure 7.1. Selected evaluation of NNEST's instructional aspects-1.

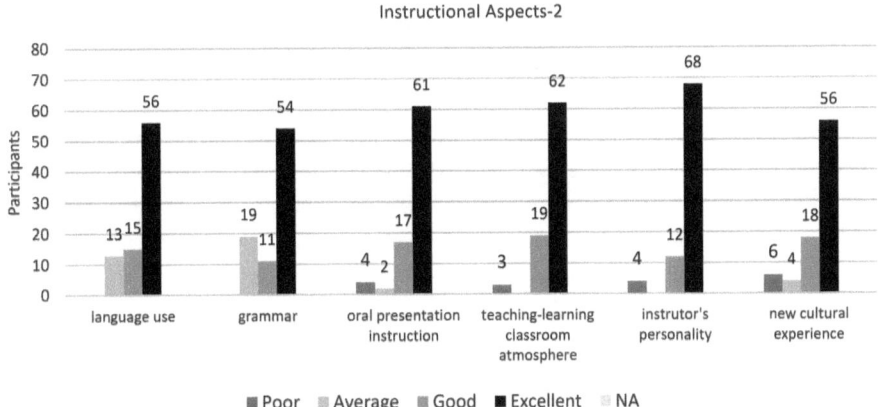

Figure 7.2. Selected evaluation of NNEST's instructional aspects-2.

Moreover, I received "Poor" ratings in oral presentation instruction (4.76%, n=4), teaching-learning classroom atmosphere (3.57%, n=3), and instructor's personality (4.76%, n=4). These "Poor" evaluations drew my attention because these items directly relate to my NNEST status and language performance, which motivated me to conduct Survey II and interviews to further investigate my language performance as a NNEST. Regarding new cultural experience, the rhetorical references and analogies from Chinese culture incorporated in the course, earned the most "Poor" ratings (7.14%, n=6). This result may entail students' ignorance or lack of interest in other cultures.

Survey II and Interview Results: Students' Perceptions of My Language Performance

Language performance is pivotal in instruction. Imparting knowledge, expressing and negotiating ideas, and interacting with students is all done via language. Being a NNEST, learning about students' opinion of my language performance is vital especially given NESSs' evaluations of my teaching effectiveness in Survey I.

Survey II Results

The results of NESSs' understanding of my English (Question 1) indicated that 80% (n=51) of them had "No difficulty" understanding me, while 20% (n=12) "Somewhat" did. Among these 12 participants, they chose the following reasons: sentence structure (n=5), vocabulary use (n=5), grammar (n=2), accent/pronunciation (n=2), and a mix of all above (n=4). Regarding my language performance (Question 2), no "Poor" ratings were selected; two participants (3.17%) rated "Acceptable, but not ideal"; 40 participants (63.50%) rated "Good," and 21 participants (33.33%) rated "Excellent."

Since study findings indicate that although students comprehend NNESTs fully, they may still not accept NNESTs' accents/pronunciations (e.g., Lindemann, 2002), I asked about NESSs' comprehension level (Question 3) and acceptance level (Question 4) of my accent/pronunciation. The results suggest that 44.5% (n=28) of the participants comprehended my accent/pronunciation, yet 19% (n=12) of them had to listen carefully and 36.5% (n=23) comprehended me with minimal distraction (see Table 7.1). In comparison, participants' acceptance level of my accent/pronunciation was extremely high. However, one participant expressed discomfort.

Regarding whether my speech errors hindered students' comprehension or not (Question 5), 16 participants (25.4%) were not aware of any errors in my speech, nor did they have issues comprehending me, 22 (34.92%) fully understood me without meaningful distractions, another 22 (34.92%) felt that my errors caused only minimal distractions, and three (4.76%) believed they were occasionally confused, such as by my unfamiliar vocabulary usage.

When asked to list other difficulties with my language performance (Question 6), one wrote, "You talked a mile a minute!" In terms of providing suggestions on my language improvement (Question 7), positive and rewarding comments such as "I don't think you have any language issues. You speak as clear as American professors"; "I love the way you speak; it's very clear and specific!"; "You speak much clearer than lots of Americans, and your English is better than many professors." I was encouraged by comments such as "Teaching in a new language is hard, but you have done a beyond excellent job" and "I honestly don't see any issues. I was highly impressed with how well you could speak English. It's hard to teach a class in another language."

For appraisals and constructive comments, participants identified my accent, but did not believe it was heavy or disruptive. As one wrote, "I don't know how to fix your minimal accent. I have a southern accent, and I don't fix it. So it's not your fault." Another wrote, "Your accent is just unique, it's easy to comprehend and causes no trouble." One participant even suggested that students take more responsibility and commented, "Having an accent isn't a bad thing, nor is your fault. If people have trouble with your accent, it's their fault for being so close-minded."

Participants also observed that I frequently use "full stop" to refer to a "period." In this regard, my early English learning experience in China might be a reason. In late 1970s to 1980s, British English was dominant and prevalent in China. The most popular English TV program was *Follow Me*, produced by BBC; the most widely used English textbook was the *New Concept* series, teaching British English. My first English dictionary was *The Oxford English Dictionary*. Many courses I took at university were about British literature.

Table 7.1. NNEST's Accent/Pronunciation Comprehension and Acceptance Level

Comprehension Level		*Acceptance* Level	
hard to comprehend	0 (0%)	not acceptable	0 (0%)
comprehensible, but have to listen carefully	12 (19%)	acceptable, but uncomfortable	1 (1.58%)
comprehensible with minimal distractions only	23 (36.5%)	acceptable, mostly comfortable	24 (38.1%)
fully comprehensible without difficulty	28 (44.5%)	totally acceptable and comfortable without issues	38 (60.3%)

Due to my British English learning background, I may habitually utilize British English vocabulary. Just as one participant described, "Your English is always easy to understand. Occasionally there might be a few words I don't use. But I still could understand what you meant." Obviously, my vocabulary repertoire differs from my NESSs' vocabulary, which could confuse some students. Additionally, several students suggested that I slow down while talking. This comment also appeared in their answers to Question 6, which reinforced the idea of slowing my pace in speech for clarity purposes.

Interview Results

I conducted five individual interviews with three male and two female undergraduates in my office after the semester was completed and grades submitted. Each unstructured interview lasted approximately 20 minutes. When interviewing, I took notes and asked follow-up questions for them to elaborate more. All interviewees were NESSs with pseudonyms, except for Liz, a bilingual in English and French. Among them, three were first time taking a NNEST's class (see Table 7.2).

As mentioned previously, linguistic issues revealed in both surveys targeted my awkward sentence structure, uncommon vocabulary use, grammatical use, and accent. Thus, I asked interviewees purposefully about their experiences and opinions regarding these issues and my language performance as well as their suggestions for improvement. None of the five noted issues with my sentence structure. As Rich claimed, "I never thought about it, nor as I was aware of [it]." For my vocabulary use, Liz could tell that some of my words were British English, but she understood them. Abbey said that she learned "full stop" means "period." Similarly, Mark had heard of "full stop," but did not really understand it until he was in my class. In terms of grammatical errors, Mark recalled my tense use was wrong few times, although he understood what I meant.

Table 7.2. Interviewees' Demographics

Name (gender)	Native Language	Major/Program	School Year	1st NNEST Experience
Liz (f)	English & French	Chemistry	Sophomore	Yes
Abbey (f)	English	Education	Sophomore	No
Rich (m)	English	Biology	Freshman	Yes
Mark (m)	English	Music	Senior	No
Jack (m)	English	Computer Science	Freshman	Yes

When asked about my accent, participants could identify it, but did not feel it was heavy. As Liz said, "I was already surrounded by many international students, so I had no issues with your accent." Rich did not recall any moments that he could not understand me. For Jack, my accent was not "obvious" and I spoke "clear enough" so he had no difficulty understanding me. Mark argued that "compared with other nonnative English-speaking professors, your accent is much easier to understand." However, according to Abby, my accent required her "a little more effort to listen." According to her, my intonation was different, not my pronunciation.

In responding to my language performance and teaching effectiveness, none observed any negative consequences; rather, they commented positively on my teaching. Abby contended, "I don't think your teaching effectiveness is negatively affected by your language. I think you do both well," even though she was the one who had to listen to me closely. Similarly, Liz, Rich, and Jack expressed their enjoyment taking my class; they disagreed that my language flaws affected my teaching. Mark revealed that this was his second attempt to take the same course, because he had failed it once with a different instructor. As Mark shared, taking my class in the beginning, he just "wanted to get it done" because he had already taken the class once and did not expect to learn anything new. According to him, he did not hold a serious attitude in the beginning. However, my class made him "put effort" into each assignment. In Mark's eyes, I was "the best English professor" he had ever had, even though I am a NNEST. His observations also showed in his improved attitude and grades.

Regarding language performance improvement, Liz and Rich did not make any specific suggestions; they encouraged me to continue my way of speaking and teaching. Abby, Mark, and Jack confirmed my language performance. They also suggested that students listen carefully and keep focused. As Jack stated, "teaching and learning are joint efforts. We can't depend on the instructor's effort only; we should involve in the learning more active and stay focused in class." Since the survey results suggested that I speak too quickly, I particularly asked about their opinions of it. None of the five respondents thought I spoke too fast; rather, they believed my speed was about right. Yet, Abby pointed out that due to my intonation, students might expect me to slow down.

The interviews revealed that students were satisfied with my accent/pronunciation even though it required them to pay closer attention when I spoke. My linguistic use and errors in speech could occasionally cause minimal interference with comprehension, which required my further explanations and their greater concentration. Regardless, my teaching effectiveness was not negatively affected by my language performance.

Conclusion

Overall, NESSs perceived me as a competent NNEST, holding a favorable attitude toward my instruction. They comprehended my language and accepted my accent. NESSs were generally confident with my language performance and teaching effectiveness. The study results indicated that receiving unsatisfactory evaluations in my initial writing instruction was likely influenced by my unexpected substitution as their instructor. However, that a small number of students continued to express limited confidence in my credibility could explain more than why I initially had received biased comments; it suggested that linguistic and racial bias existed toward me as a NNEST. The study results indicate that NNESTs' races, linguistic backgrounds, genders, experiences, personalities, and teaching contexts are all variables that can determine students' perception of NNESTs with aggravating or mitigating biases.

This study disclosed my linguistic and cultural deficiencies, which require continued refinement of my linguistic competence and cultural understanding. It also suggests that NESSs reflect upon their biases against NNESTs and build awareness of cultural and linguistic diversity in academia.

The study results together with my teaching experience indicate that some NESSs, especially first-generation and freshman students, may not be familiar with NNESTs' teaching methods, language use, and accent. Thus in classroom, NNESTs may need to shift their teaching method from an authoritative lecturing to interactive discussion. Complementing verbal communication instruction with written forms via visual aids (e.g., handouts, emails) is also an effective strategy in amplifying linguistic intelligibility. One-on-one assistance works extraordinarily well in my classes because students seem more attentive when getting direct help. Moreover, consistent communication with students helps students understand NNESTs' expectations for them and assess NNESTs' strengths. Further, NNESTs should be willing to employ culturally appropriate management strategies (Weinstein et al., 2003) to promote mutual sociocultural understanding and respect between NNESTs and NESSs. Once students realize that instructors care for them on both instructional and personal levels (Meyers, 2009), they tend to be more accepting and appreciative of their instructors, no matter native or nonnative; in turn, reinforcing both their and their instructor's performances.

Being a NNEST, I suggest that in the classroom, we keep our identity, authenticity, and authority by introducing our backgrounds and credentials to reduce students' skepticism, and be professional, competent, and confident to demonstrate our intellectual strength and knowledge. On the other hand,

NESSs should also realize that language is not the only factor determining NNESTs' teaching quality (Kim, 2002). Rather, their ability to deliver well-prepared classes and a caring and willing-to-help personality are crucial. NNESTs are expected to educate students the value of inclusiveness, empowering students through encouraging and accepting their intellectual challenges, but also offering them new and meaningful cultural experience. That way, students may gradually change from resistance to appreciation of NNESTs.

This study advocates that NNESTs negotiate racial, linguistic, and cultural difference throughout their professional lives (Hune, 2011) and that students realize the equality of language variety and racial diversity in classrooms. This study calls for a joint effort by all writing instructors, native and nonnative, writing programs, and institutions to understand that English is not the sole domain of or a privilege for native English speakers; rather, it belongs to all English users. The increasing adoption of English as the language of education, business, and culture demonstrates that we live in a multicultural and world Englishes environment of plurality. This reality requires academia to abandon any pre-conceived attitudes toward NNESTs and experience a transformation of their mindset. Teachers, therefore, should encourage students to step outside of their comfort zones and expose themselves to understanding that NNESTs can be and many are subject-matter experts in numerous fields, including English. NNESTs in particular, should work to inspire students to see the value of racial and linguistic differences, and promote equality and plurality in the classroom. My study may resonate with some NNESTs who experience similar challenges. But the main purpose is to seek greater understanding and support from writing programs. More importantly, we NNESTs can display our indispensability in Western academia, earn NNESTs the respect of students, colleagues, institutions, and build confidence in ourselves, by demonstrating our qualifications as knowledge informants and promoting the value of linguistic, racial, and cultural diversity.

References

Aneja, G. (2016). (Non)native speaker: Rethinking (non)nativeness and teacher identity in TESOL teacher education. *TESOL Quarterly, 50*(3), 572–596. https://doi.org/10.1002/tesq.315.

Bailey, K. M. (1984). The foreign TA problem. In K. Bailey, F. Pialorsi & J. Zukowski-Faust (Eds), *Foreign teaching assistants in U.S. universities* (pp. 3–15). NAFSA.

Becker, W. E. Jr. & Watts, M. (1999). How departments of economics evaluate teaching. *American Economic Review, 89*(2), 344–349. https://doi.org/10.1257/aer.89.2.344.

Braine, G. (Ed.). (1999). *Non-native educators in English language teaching*. Lawrence ErlbaumAssociates. https://doi.org/10.4324/9781315045368.

Bresnahan, M. I. & Kim, M. (1993). Factors of receptivity and resistance toward international teaching assistants. *Journal of Asian Pacific Communication, 4*, 1–12.

Bresnahan, M. I., Ohasih, R., Nebashi, R., Liu, W. & Shaerman, S. M. (2002). Attitudinal and affective response toward accented English. *Language and Communication, 22*(2), 171–185. https://doi.org/10.1016/S0271-5309(01)00025-8.

Canagarajah, S. (1999). Interrogating the "Native speaker fallacy": Non-Linguistic roots, non-pedagogical results. In G. Braine (Ed.), *Non-native educators in English language teaching* (pp. 77–92). Lawrence Erlbaum Associates. https://doi.org/10.4324/9781315045368.

Chun, S. (2014). EFL learners' beliefs about native and nonnative English-speaking teachers: Perceived strengths, weaknesses, and preferences. *Journal of Multilingual and Multicultural Development, 35*(6), 536–579. https://doi.org/10.1080/01434632.2014.889141.

Crystal, D. (1997). *English as a global language*. Cambridge University Press.

Finegan, A. & Siegfried, J. (2000). Are students rating of teaching effectiveness influenced by instructors' English language proficiency? *American Economist, 44*(2), 17–29.

Fox, W. S. & Gay, G. (1994). Functions and effects of international teaching assistants. *Review of Higher Education, 18*, 1–24.

Hune, S. (2011). Asian American women faculty and the contested space of the classroom: Navigating student resistance and (re)claiming authority and their rightful place. *Diversity in Higher Education, 9*, 307–335. https://doi.org/10.1108/S1479-3644(2011)0000009019.

Kachru, B. B. (2009). Asian Englishes in the Asian age: Contexts and challenges. In K. Murata & Jenkins, J. (Eds.), *Global Englishes in Asian contexts: Current and future debates* (pp. 175–193). Palgrave. https://doi.org/10.1057/9780230239531_11.

Kamhi-Stein, L. D. (Ed.). (2004). *Learning and teaching from experience: Perception on nonnative English-speaking professionals*. University of Michigan Press.

Kang, O., Rubin, D. & Lindeman, S. (2015). Mitigating U.S. undergraduates' attitudes toward international teaching assistants. *TESOL Quarterly, 49*(4), 681–706. https://doi.org/10.1002/tesq.192.

Kaur, P. & Raman. A. (2014). Exploring native speaker and non-native speaker accents: The English as a lingua franca perspective. *Procedia Social and Behavior Sciences, 155*, 253–259. https://doi.org/10.1016/j.sbspro.2014.10.288.

Kim, S. (Ed.). (2002). *Teaching in the U.S.: Handbook for international faculty and TAs*. The Ohio State University.

Kumar, P. (2002). Yellow lotus in white lily pond: An Asian American woman teaching in Utah. In L. Vargas (Ed.), *Women faculty of color in the white classroom* (pp. 227–291). Lang.

Kumaravadivelu, B. (2008). *Accent on the wrong issue when it comes to speaking English*. Education Post.

Lasagabaster, D. & Sierra, J. M. (2010). University students' perceptions of native and non-native speaker teachers of English. *Language Awareness, 11*(2), 132–142. https://doi.org/10.1080/09658410208667051.

Lazos, S. (2012). Are student teaching evaluations holding back women and minorities? In G. G. Muhs, Y. F. Niemann, C. G. González & Harris, A. P. (Eds.), *Presumed incompetent: The intersections of race and class for women in academia* (pp. 164–185). Utah State University Press. https://doi.org/10.2307/j.ctt4cgr3k.19.

Lindemann, S. (2002). Listening with an attitude: A model of native-speaker comprehension of non-native speakers in the United States. *Language and Society, 31*, 419–441. https://doi.org/10.1017/S0047404502020286.

Lippi-Green, R. (2012). *English with an accent: Language, ideology, and discrimination in the United States* (2nd ed.). Routledge.

Lipovsky, C. & Mahboob, A. (2010). Students' appraisal of their native and nonnative English-speaking teachers. *WA TESOL NNEST Caucus Annual Review, 1*, 119–154.

LIurda, E. (2004). Non-native-speaker teachers and English as an international language. *International Journal of Applied Linguistics, 14*(3), 314–323. https://doi.org/10.1111/j.1473-4192.2004.00068.x.

Ma, L. F. (2012). Strengths and weaknesses of NESTs and NNESTs: Perceptions of NNESTs in Hong Kong. *Linguistics and Education, 23*, 1–15. https://doi.org/10.1016/j.linged.2011.09.005.

Mahboob, A. (2004). Native and nonnative: What do the students think? In L. D. Kamhi-Stein (Ed.), *Learning and teaching from experience* (pp. 121–148). University of Michigan Press.

Medgyes, P. (1994). *The non-native teacher.* Macmillan.

Meyers, S. (2009). Do your students care whether you care about them? *College Teaching, 57*(4), 205–210.

Moussu, L. & Llurda, E. (2008). Nonnative English-speaking English language teachers: History and research. *Language Teaching, 41*(3), 315–348. https://doi.org/10.1017/S0261444808005028.

Phillipson, R. (1992). *Linguistic imperialism.* Oxford University Press. https://doi.org/10.1002/9781405198431.wbeal0718.pub2.

Rajadurai, J. (2007). Intelligibility studies: A consideration of empirical and ideological issues. *World Englishes, 26*, 87–98. https://doi.org/10.1111/j.1467-971X.2007.00490.x.

Reves, T. & Medgyes, P. (1994). The nonnative English speaking EFL/ESL teacher's self-image: An international survey. *System, 22*(3), 353–367. https://doi.org/10.1016/0346-251X(94)90021-3.

Rong, X-L. (2002). Teaching with differences and for differences: Reflections of a Chinese American teacher educator. In L. Vargas (Ed.), *Women faculty of color in the White Classroom* (pp. 125–144). Lang.

Ruecker, T., Stefan, F. & Tseptsura, M. (2018). Language difference can be an asset: Exploring the experiences of nonnative English-speaking teachers of writing. *College Composition & Communication, 69*(4), 612–641. https://www.jstor.org/stable/44870978.

Saraceni, M. (2015). *World Englishes: A critical Analysis.* Bloomsbury.

Saunders, K. (2001). The influence of instructor native language on student learning and instructor rating. *Eastern Economic Journal, 27*(3), 345–353.

Shehi, M. (2017). Why is my English teacher a foreigner? Re-authoring the story of international composition teachers. *TETYC, 44*(3), 260–275.

Shuck, G. (2009). Racializing the native English speaker. *Journal of Language, Identity, and Education, 5*(4), 259–276. https://doi.org/10.1207/s15327701jlie0504_1.

Subtirelu, N. C. (2015). "She does have an accent but . . .": Race and language ideology in students' evaluations of mathematics instructors on RateMyProfessors.com. *Language in Society, 44*, 35–62. https://doi.org/10.1017/S0047404514000736.

Terrell, S. (2011). Mixed-methods research methodologies. *The Qualitative Report, 17*(1), 254–280. https://doi.org/10.46743/2160-3715/2012.1819.

Thomas, J. (1999). Voices from periphery: Nonnative teachers and issues of credibility. In G. Braine (Ed.), *Non-native educators in English language teaching* (pp. 5–15). Lawrence Erlbaum Associates.

Vargas, L. (Ed.). (2002). *Women faculty of color in the white classroom*. Lang.

Villarreal, D. (2013). Closing the communication gap between undergraduates and international faculty. *The CATESOL Journal, 24*(1), 8–28.

Weinstein, C., Curran, M. & Tomlinson-Clarke, S. (2003). Culturally responsive classroom management: Awareness into action. *Theory into Practice, 42*(4), 269–276. https://doi.org/10.1207/s15430421tip4204_2.

Appendix 1: Survey I

You are invited to complete this survey about having a nonnative English-speaking writing instructor teach native English-speaking students writing. Your insight is highly valued as it will help me better work for writing students. Please be aware completing this survey involves no risk to you, your relationship with me, and your course grade. Your answers will be kept strictly confidential, even the instructor will not be able to identify your answers because it is anonymous. If you are interested in completing this survey, please return this survey face down the last day of the class of this semester into a designated box. Thank you for your time and insight.

Please answer the following open-ended questions based on your true opinions:

1. Before registering for this course or meeting me, did you know that I am a nonnative-English speaker teaching you this writing course? Put a check mark "√" at the suitable places.

    Yes _____   No _____   I don't care _____

2. After meeting me for the first time and/or when you realized that English is not my native language, did you have any concerns regarding

whether or not you would stay in this class due to my nonnative English speaker status? If "yes", please explain whether you wanted to drop or switch to a different instructor who is a native English speaker? Or did you decide to stay simply because it fit your schedule, or since this course is required, you had no better choices. Please be specific.

3. Since you stayed in this class, do you think your choice is a right one? Please explain.
4. What are some *strengths* you have observed in me as your writing instructor? Please explain.
5. What are some *weaknesses* you have observed in me as your writing instructor? Please explain.
6. In what ways, do you think I could have done better? Please be specific.
7. In general, does a "nonnative English-speaking instructor" status affect your choosing any *English courses* if you know your instructor is a nonnative English speaker? Please explain.
8. In general, does a "nonnative English-speaking instructor" status affect your choosing *any other courses* if you know your instructor is a nonnative English speaker? Please explain.

Please choose the number that can best represent your experience taking this writing course in each aspect by putting a check mark "√".

	1=Poor 2=Average 3=Good 4=Excellent 5=N/A				
Instructional Aspects	1	2	3	4	5
Overall, course instruction					
Course syllabus, e.g., policies, assignment requirements					
Knowledge of rhetoric, e.g., genre, organization, structure, etc.					
Research skills instruction, e.g., method and application, data collection, analysis, presentation, etc.					
Instructional language use, e.g., sentence structure, vocabulary, etc.					
English grammar					
Academic format and citation skills					
Composing research proposal, outline, questions for participants					

	1=Poor 2=Average 3=Good 4=Excellent 5=N/A				
Instructional Aspects	1	2	3	4	5
Searching and selecting scholarly reliable and relevant sources					
Documentation: literature review/annotated bibliographies					
Interaction, handouts, emails, and individual conferences					
Feedback/comments on assignments					
Oral presentation skills					
Teaching-Learning atmosphere, e.g., inviting, low-anxiety					
Instructor's accessibility/flexibility					
Instructor's personality					
New culture/knowledge experience					

Appendix 2: Survey II

1. Do you have difficulty understanding my English?
   Yes ____ Somewhat ____ No ____ If your answer is "*Yes*" or "*Somewhat*", please circle the cause that applies to you.)
   Accent/pronunciation
   Grammar use
   Sentence structures
   Vocabulary use
   A mix of all the above
2. Thinking of comprehension, how would you rate my language performance? Mark the one that best indicates your comprehension level of my language.
   Poor ____ Acceptable, but not ideal ____ Good ____ Excellent ____
3. What is your level of comprehension in regards to my accent? Mark the one that best indicates your comprehension level.

Hard to comprehend___

Comprehensible, but have to listen carefully___

Comprehensible with minimal distraction only___

Fully comprehensible without difficulty___

4. Regarding my level of accent what level did you experience? Mark the one that best indicates your acceptance level.

    Not acceptable at all___

    Acceptable, but uncomfortable___

    Acceptable, mostly comfortable___

    Totally acceptable, comfortable without issues___

5. I might have errors in my speech while teaching. Did any errors hinder your comprehension? If so, to what extent? Mark the one that best indicates your answer.

    Totally blocked my comprehension___

    To some degree, they confused me___

    Only occasional minimal distractions___

    Fully understand without meaningful distractions___

    None of the above I am aware of, nor did I realize or catch any errors___

6. In your opinion, what are some other issues in my language performance that you have identified? Please list them below and explain specifically.

7. In your opinion, what should I do to improve my language performance?

8 A Corpus Study on Written Comments by Nonnative English-Speaking and Native English-Speaking Teachers of First-Year Writing

Wen Xin
UNIVERSITY OF KANSAS

Language diversity has received tremendous attention in writing studies since the early 2000s (e.g., Canagarajah, 2006; Guerra, 2016; Horner et al., 2011; Lu & Horner, 2013; Young, 2009), which Paul Matsuda (2013) calls "a linguistic turn" (p. 129). Surprisingly, within the linguistic turn, research on language-related topics seems to have mostly addressed the diverse language use and backgrounds of students, whereas the linguistic diversity of writing teachers has received little attention, although the number of writing teachers who speak English as a second or additional language keeps increasing in writing classrooms. Todd Ruecker and colleagues (2018) therefore in a recent article called for more research on writing teachers who are nonnative English speakers (NNES) in order to better understand the challenges they face in teaching and to provide them with more supportive working environments.[1]

While the authors throughout this collection are responding to that call, this chapter focuses particularly on NNES teachers of first-year writing (FYW) because there have been, so far, only very few studies that focus on this group (e.g., Liu, 2005; Ruecker et al., 2018; Shehi, 2017; Zheng, 2017). Although those previous studies have provided valuable insights into NNES teachers' general experiences in teaching FYW, such as challenges they have encountered, identities they bring to writing classrooms, and the level of

---

[1] Research has problematized the dichotomy between nonnative English-speaking (NNES) and native English-speaking (NES) because it is often hard to define what counts as a native speaker of English and the dichotomy privileges NES and stigmatizes NNES (e.g., Braine, 1999; Canagarajah, 2006; Cook, 1999). The main reason this chapter draws upon the NNES-NES terms, as noted by Mariya Tseptsura and Todd Ruecker (this volume), is to connect and expand on the previous literature.

confidence and potential advantages they have in teaching, little research has explored how NNES teachers of FYW respond to students' papers through written comments.

However, examining written responses to students' writing is crucial to further our understanding of NNES teachers' experiences in teaching FYW for at least two reasons. First, Dana Ferris (1995) points out that responding to students' writing has always remained a crucial part of writing instruction. Therefore, the picture of NNES teachers' experiences in teaching FYW is incomplete without looking into how NNES teachers provide written feedback on students' writing. Second, according to Lynn Goldstein (2004) and Ken Hyland and Fiona Hyland (2006), how teachers respond to students' writing is affected by teachers' sociopolitical status and teacher-student relationship. Looking into NNES teachers' written comments on students' writing therefore can also provide some insights into NNES teachers' perceptions of their own authority and assumptions about their relationship with students.

To have a more comprehensive picture of NNES teachers' experiences in FYW classrooms, this study looks at written comments on students' graded papers by NNES teachers of FYW and compares them to those by their native English-speaking (NES) counterparts.[2] In addition, unlike previous research on NNES teachers of FYW that was conducted through self-reflection, case studies, questionnaires, and interviews (e.g., Chen, this volume; Hijazi, this volume; Liu, 2005; Ruecker et al., 2018; Shehi, 2017; Zheng, 2017), this study takes a different approach, exploring written comments on students' graded papers given by both NNES and NES teachers of FYW through a self-built, specialized corpus, with a goal of methodologically complementing the previous literature as well. Specifically, the overarching research question in this study is "Do written comments on students' graded papers by NNES teachers of FYW look different from those by their NES counterparts? If so, how and why?"

To carry out a productive comparison, this study focuses exclusively on linguistic elements that index teachers' sense of own authority and certainty and their relationship with students in written comments because it is partially through these elements that teachers position themselves as members of particular social groups and that potential differences between NNES teachers and NES teachers of FYW may be observed. These interpersonal elements, according to Ken Hyland (2005), can be systematically explored

---

2   The main reason why graded papers were collected for this study as opposed to rough drafts was that some participants did not provide written comments on rough drafts.

through a metadiscourse model. For example, through the interpersonal model of metadiscourse developed by Hyland (2005), Polly Tse and Hyland (2008) have uncovered how male and female writers represent and position themselves in biology and philosophy book reviews.

A Metadiscourse Model

Metadiscourse comprises the linguistic resources used by language users to organize texts or project their attitudes towards the texts or audiences (Hyland, 2005). For example, let us consider this sentence: "It is difficult to see, however, how metadiscourse can constitute a different level of meaning" (Hyland, 2005, p. 21). Here, *however* shows the logical connection between the clause shown and the previous information that the writer wants the audience to perceive in order to help the audience better interpret the text. *Difficult* indicates the writer's attitude towards the clause—*to see how metadiscourse can constitute a different level of meaning*. The writer attempts to have their audience share the same attitude with them or at least find their attitude valid.

Instead of simply being a stylistic choice, metadiscourse is a crucial part of communication. It is used based on writers' predictions of their audiences' knowledge in interpreting the text and audiences' potential reaction to the text. Such an audience prediction reveals something of how writers see themselves and their orientations towards their text and their audiences. As Tse and Hyland (2008) put it, "metadiscourse allows writers to use language to acknowledge, construct and negotiate social relations, representing themselves, their views and their audience" (p. 1236). Studying metadiscourse, therefore, can provide some insights into how writers understand themselves and position themselves in relation to their audiences.

In spite of its usefulness and productivity, metadiscourse is also a fuzzy concept mainly because there are different conceptions of what counts as metadiscourse, which in turn have led to different frameworks of metadiscourse. For example, Annelie Ädel's (2006) reflexive model of metadiscourse sees metadiscourse as linguistic elements used to not only refer to the text itself but the writer and the audience in the text as well, whereas Hyland's (2005) interpersonal model views metadiscourse as interpersonal linguistic resources used by writers to organize the text itself or project their attitudes towards the text or audiences. However, instead of considering different conceptions of metadiscourse as opposed views, as Ken Hyland (2017) suggested, we can see those conceptions on a continuum, contributing different aspects to our understanding of discourse. In this study, Hyland's (2005) interpersonal model of metadiscourse is used because this model enables us to explore how writers understand themselves and position themselves as members of particular social groups in relation to audiences (Hyland, 2005).

Hyland (2005), in his interpersonal model, divided metadiscourse into two categories— *interactive* resources and *interactional* resources. Interactive resources allow writers to make their texts more cohesive and coherent by anticipating audiences' expectations in order to make audiences reach writers' preferred interpretations. These resources include five sub-categories (Hyland, 2005, p. 49):

- **Transitions:** express the logical connection between two clauses (e.g., in addition, but, thus, and)
- **Frame markers:** refer to discourse acts, sequences, or text stages (e.g., finally, to conclude, in this section, my purpose is)
- **Endophoric makers:** help readers locate information in other parts of the text (e.g., noted above, see Fig., here)
- **Evidentials:** refer to sources from other texts (e.g., According to X, (Y, 2005), Z mentions)
- **Code glosses:** help readers better understand meanings of ideational material[3] (e.g., namely, e.g., such as, in other words)

Interactional resources focus on writer-audience interactions in a text, helping writers project themselves and signal their attitudes towards their texts and audiences. These resources also include five sub-categories (Hyland, 2005, p. 49):

- **Hedges:** withhold writers' full commitment to a proposition (e.g., might, perhaps, possible, about, suggest)
- **Boosters:** emphasize force or writers' certainty in a proposition (e.g., in fact, definitely, it is clear that, demonstrate)
- **Attitude:** express writers' attitudes towards a proposition (e.g., unfortunately, I agree, surprisingly)
- **Engagement:** explicitly refer to or build a relationship with readers (e.g., consider, note that, you can see that)
- **Self-mentions:** explicit reference to author(s) (e.g., I, we, my, our)

In short, metadiscourse is an important means writers use to facilitate communication and position themselves in relation to their audiences. In

---

3   In systemic functional linguistics (SFL), language is viewed to simultaneously carry three metafunctions, including *the ideational function*, *the interpersonal function*, and *the textual function* (Halliday, 1994). *The ideational function* refers to the use of language to represent experience and ideas.

comparing the metadiscoursal features used in written comments on students' graded papers by NNES teachers of FYW to those by NES teachers, this study has the potential to reveal whether (and how) NNES and NES teachers understand and position themselves differently in their written comments.

Corpus and Method

The corpus in this study consists of 56 samples of written comments on students' graded papers of different projects in FYW courses from eight teachers, with seven samples of written comments from each individual teacher (see a detailed description of the teachers' background information below).[4] One sample of written comments includes both marginal and end comments on students' papers because both types of comments work holistically to help students improve their writing. The total word count of the corpus is 17,318. Despite being a small corpus, the data was sufficient for the study because previous research that explored metadiscourse in teachers' written comments indicates that the frequency of metadiscourse is exceptionally high (Ädel, 2017).

The study was carried out in fall 2018 at a Midwestern research university where most teachers and students in FYW classrooms were NESs. After seeking IRB approval, I sent a recruitment email to all teachers of FYW in the English department through the First-and-Second-Year English listserv. I was able to recruit 12 teachers, three NNESs and nine NESs, and all of them were graduate teaching assistants. Considering all the three NNES teachers are females, I decided to exclude four NES teachers who are males in this study in order to minimize the potential influence of gender on the results. The remaining eight teachers (three NNESs and five NESs) all had taught FYW at least once before contributing their written comments to the study. In addition, all the teachers had taken a one-semester mandatory composition theory course at the same time as they were teaching FYW for the first time. The goals of the theory course included supporting teachers of FYW by offering structured opportunities to reflect on their teaching practices in dialogue with other teachers and familiarizing teachers of

---

4   The corpus of the present study is a sub-corpus of a larger corpus project that examined how the use of metadiscourse in FYW teachers' written comments varies according to various extralinguistic factors, including location of comments (marginal or end), course context (ENGL 101 or ENGL 102), gender, race/ethnicity, disciplinary background (rhetoric and composition, literature, or creative writing), native language, and years of teaching experience. The representativeness of the larger corpus was met by following the criteria of building a specialized corpus (e.g., Biber, 1990, 1993; Flowerdew, 2004; Reppen, 2010).

FYW with the scholarship in the field of composition studies and composition pedagogy, providing an overview of the theories and practices of composition instruction.

As for years of teaching experience, one of the NNES teachers (Iva) had had two years of teaching experience, with the rest of the two NNES teachers (Augie and AW) more than six years of teaching experience. On the other hand, only one NES teacher (Lillie) had had more than six years of teaching experience. Three of the NES teachers (Ann, Merc, Myers) had had three years of teaching experience, and the rest one (Fia) only one year of teaching experience.[5] In terms of disciplinary background, One NNES teacher (Iva) was pursuing a degree in creative writing, and the rest of the two (AW and Augie) in literature. Three of the NES teachers (Ann, Myers, and Merc) were also pursuing a degree in creative writing, the other two (Lillie and Fia) in rhetoric and composition. All the teachers were also asked to self-identify their race/ethnicity. One NNES teacher (Iva) self-identified as Asian, and the other two teachers (Augie and AW) self-identified as Black or African American and Arabic/Middle Eastern, respectively. Three NES teachers (Lillie, Fia, and Myers) self-identified as White, and the other two (Ann and Merc) self-identified as Asian and Black or African American and Hispanic or Latino, respectively. Table 8.1 summarizes the participants' background information.[6]

The method of the study involves a combination of quantitative and qualitative analysis of the corpus data. One difficulty in studying metadiscourse is that metadiscourse is an open category and can be realized in a variety of ways by units of varied length from individual words to whole clauses or sentences. Many previous studies did not cover all the metadiscoursal features (e.g., Hyland & Jiang, 2018; Tse & Hyland, 2008). Instead, they focused on some particular features that can be easily searched for through concordance software. Then the researchers manually excluded irrelevant instances. However, in the present study, all metadiscoursal features were manually searched for and coded in order to cover the full range of the use of metadiscourse in teachers' written comments.

---

5   All the names are pseudonyms.

6   While this study focuses only on the impact of native language on feedback practices, some research has found that other socio-cultural factors, such as gender, teaching experience, and disciplinary background may also affect how teachers comment on students' writing (e.g., Johnson & Roen, 1992; Lang, 2018; Xin, 2021). Also, because the corpus is relatively small in size, the results of this study will be only suggestive.

A Corpus Study on Written Comments

Table 8.1. Teacher Background Information

Teacher	First Language	Gender	Teaching Experience	Disciplinary Background	Race/Ethnicity
Iva	Other	Female	2 years	Creative Writing	Asian
Augie	Other	Female	6 years	Literature	Black or African American
AW	Other	Female	6+ years	Literature	Arabic/Middle Eastern
Lillie	English	Female	6 years	Rhetoric and Composition	White
Ann	English	Female	3 years	Creative Writing	Asian
Fia	English	Female	1 year	Rhetoric and Composition	White
Merc	English	Female	3 years	Creative Writing	Black or African American and Hispanic or Latino
Myers	English	Female	3 years	Creative Writing	White

The coding includes the metadiscoursal element identified, its pragmatic function in the text based on the taxonomy of the interpersonal model, and the participant who used the element observed. The process of spotting metadiscoursal features followed three key principles for identifying metadiscourse developed by Ken Hyland and Polly Tse (2004). The key principles include (p. 159):

- Metadiscourse is distinct from propositional aspects of discourse.
- The term "metadiscourse" refers to those aspects of the text that embody writer-reader interactions.
- Metadiscourse distinguishes relations which are external to the text from those that are internal.

(1) I wish you had spoken about your first-hand experiences with coaches in high school. (Lillie, NES)

For example, in (1), *your first-hand experiences with coaches in high school* refers to experiences that happened in real-life and thus are propositional. As a result, the entire phrase does not count as metadiscourse. The phrase *I wish you had spoken about* refers to an explicit expectation or attitude the teacher has for the student, and *you* represents the student being commented on in the text. Because the entire phrase *I wish you had spoken about* shows an interaction between the teacher and the student, the phrase counts as metadiscourse. As mentioned above, while the second person pronoun *you* counts as metadiscourse, the determiner *your* does not count mainly because *you* refers to someone in the world of discourse, whereas *your* refers to someone in the real world.

Results and Discussion

Do NNES Teachers Comment Differently than NES Teachers?

Table 8.2 shows the overall distributions of metadiscourse used by the NNES and NES teachers of FYW in the corpus.

Table 8.2. Normalized Distributions (per 10,000 words) of Metadiscourse across NNESs and NESs

Categories	Raw Frequency (rf)	Frequency(f)/10,000
NNES	1097	1664
NES	2134	1989
Sig (p-value)	LL=23.40, P<0.01	

Overall, the results indicate the prevalence of metadiscourse in both NNES and NES teachers' written comments, which is in line with Ädel's (2017) finding. It is also evident, from the results, that the NNES teachers use metadiscourse differently than their NES counterparts, with the NNES teachers using less metadiscourse than the NES teachers, and the Log-likelihood test shows that the difference is statistically significant.

Table 8.3 shows the overall distributions of both interactional and interactive met adiscourse in the corpus.

Table 8.3. Normalized Distributions (per 10,000 words) of Interactional and Interactive Metadiscourse across NNESs and NESs

Categories	Interactive		Interactional	
	rf	f/10,000	rf	f/10,000
NNES	427	648	670	1,016
NES	638	594	1,496	1,395
Sig (p-value)	LL=1.87, P>0.05		LL=47.93, P<0.0001	

In Table 8.3, we can see that the NNES teachers in this study use more interactive metadiscourse than the NES teachers, whereas the NES teachers prefer to use more interactional metadiscourse than the NNES teachers. However, a statistically significant difference is only observed in the use of interactional metadiscourse. Such findings, on the one hand, suggest that written comments by the NNES teachers are not statistically different from those by their NES counterparts in terms of the amount of guidance both groups of the teachers provide to help students better understand their written comments because interactive metadiscourse is mainly used to make the text more "reader-friendly" in order for the audience to reach the writer's intended interpretations, as I mentioned earlier. For example, in (2), the teacher, by using *the last page*, aims to make sure that the student knows where exactly the teacher is pointing to in the paper so that the student will have a better understanding of where some potential exists in the paper. In (3), the phrase *especially about what your journal looks like* in the parenthesis helps the student have a better sense of what is expected to be discussed more by the teacher.

> (2) *The last page* had potential as it started to inquire into the issue of racial tensions in the US. (Iva, NNES)
>
> (3) I would like to see some more descriptive language in your writing (*especially about what your journal look like*), but I was still able to mostly "see" your story. (Fia, NES)

On the other hand, the findings seem to suggest that the NES teachers, who use more interactional metadiscourse, focus more on engaging students in their written comments or offering evaluations on either students themselves or their papers, for interactional metadiscourse is essentially evaluative and engaging, as I discussed earlier. For example, in (4), by asking the student a question, the teacher attempts to explicitly engage the student into a conversation as if the question is being asked by an audience for the student while the audience is reading through the paper. In (5), using the word, *good*, the teacher gives a clear assessment on a particular point the student makes so that the student knows the point made has met the audience's expectation.

> (4) How is liberalism being defined here? (Lillie, NES)
>
> (5) Good point! (Fia, NES)

Turning to the sub-categories, it is found that within interactive elements, the NNES teachers use more code glosses, endophoric markers, and evidentials than the NES teachers, whereas the NES teachers use more frame markers and transitions than the NNES teachers, as shown in Figure 8.1. However, once the Log likelihood tests were applied to the difference in each sub-category, it turned out, as shown in Table 8.4, that only the divergence in the use of endophoric markers is statistically significant.[7]

As is shown earlier, endophoric markers point audiences' attention to particular parts of the text through which audiences will have a better understanding of what writers are currently discussing. For instance, in (6), the phrase *here between this intro and the second paragraph* helps the student have a clear sense of which sentence is *this sentence*. In (7), by employing the phrase *in the introduction paragraph*, the student knows where to look at in order to better understand the comment. Because endophoric markers are used more by the NNES than the NES teachers, the finding suggests that the NNES teachers in this study seem to be more concerned about the accuracy and readability of their written comments for students.

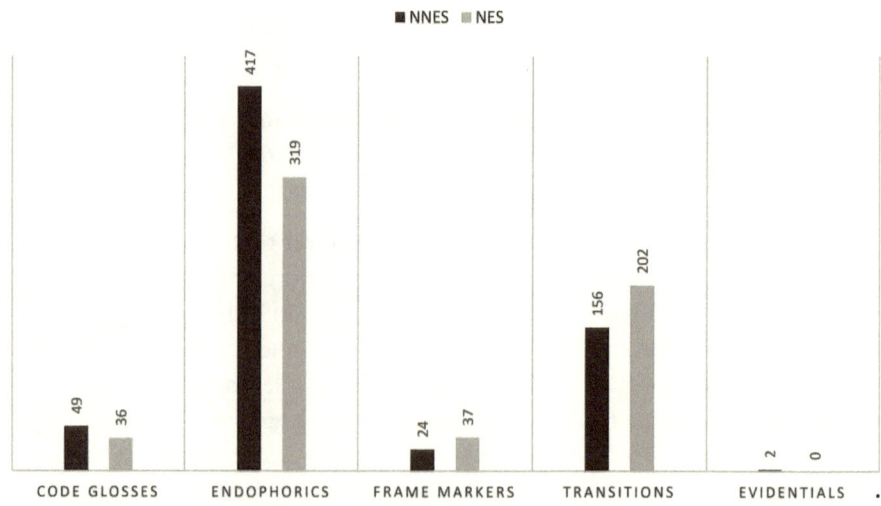

Figure 8.1. Normalized categorical distributions (per 10,000 words) of interactive metadiscourse across NNESTs and NESs.

---

7   In applied linguistic research, where most studies of metadiscourse have emerged, Aek Phakiti (2015) indicates that $p<0.05$ (5 in 100 chances of being wrong) or $p<0.01$ (1 in 100 chances of being wrong) are commonly found or used. In my study, considering the size of my corpus, I set the p-value to be less than 0.01 in order to be statistically significant.

Table 8.4. Normalized Categorical Distributions (per 10,000 words) of Interactive Metadiscourse across NNESs and NESs

Categories	NNES	NES	Sig (p-value)
Code Glosses	49	36	LL=1.45, P>0.05
Endophorics	417	319	LL=10.91, P<0.01
Frame Markers	24	37	LL=2.22, P>0.05
Transitions	156	202	LL=4.78, 0.01<P<0.05
Evidentials	2	0	LL=1.93, P>0.05
Total	648	594	LL=1.87, P>0.05

(6) *This sentence* causes an abrupt transition here *between this intro and the second paragraph.* (AW, NNES)

(7) As a reader, I think there is not enough grounding in your "negative" experiences *in the introduction paragraph. (Ann, NES)*

Unlike the categorical distributions of interactive metadiscourse where several sub-categories are used more by the NNES but several more by the NES teachers, the categorical distributions of interactional metadiscourse look more straightforward, as shown in Figure 8.2.

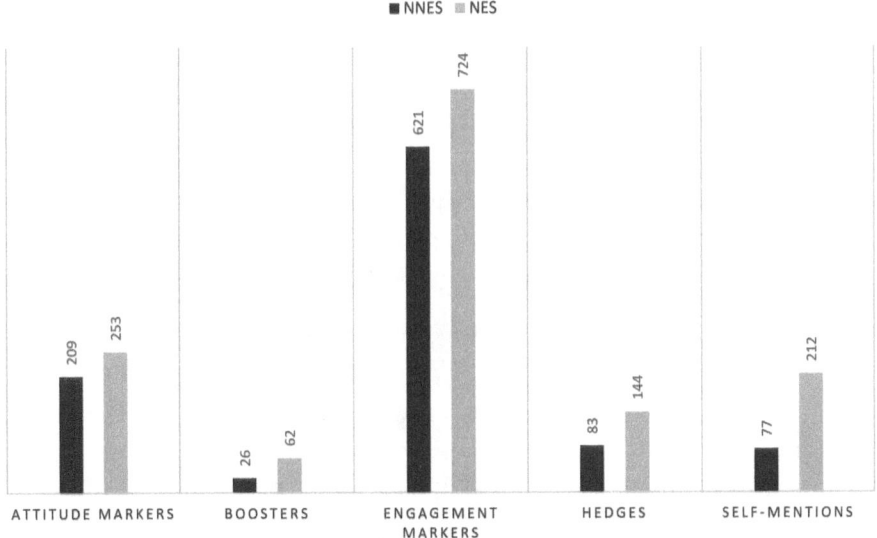

Figure 8.2. Normalized categorical distributions (per 10,000 words) of interactional metadiscourse across NNESTs and NESs.

The results show that each sub-category of interactional metadiscourse is used more by the NES than NNES teachers in their written comments. Again, the Log likelihood tests showed that only the differences in the use of boosters, hedges, and self-mentions are statistically significant, as shown in Table 8.5.

The pragmatic function of boosters, as is shown earlier, is to emphasize force or writers' certainty. In written comments, boosters often serve to reinforce teachers' evaluations on students' writing, as *do* in (8) and *very* in (9).

Table 8.5. Normalized Categorical Distributions (per 10,000 words) of Interactional Metadiscourse across NNESTs and NESs

Categories	NNES	NES	Sig (p-value)
Attitude Markers	209	253	LL=3.28, P>0.05
Boosters	26	62	LL=11.90, P<0.001
Engagement Markers	621	724	LL=6.49, 0.01<P<0.05
Hedges	83	144	LL=13.22, P<0.001
Self-mentions	77	212	LL=50.98, P<0.0001
Total	1016	1395	LL=47.93, P<0.0001

(8) I *do* think you could improve some of your transitions throughout. (Merc, NES)

(9) Your language is *very* engaging. (Fia, NES)

The fewer use of boosters suggests that the NNES teachers are less likely to reinforce their evaluations on students' papers than their NES counterparts.

In contrast to boosters, hedges are used to withhold writers' full commitment. In written comments particularly, hedges are often used to mitigate the critical force by teachers when they provide negative comments to students' papers, as *a little* in (10) and *perhaps* and *a bit* in (11).

(10) As a reader, the essay is *a little* confusing because the essay does not flow in a coherent order. (Augie, NNES)

(11) You could have *perhaps* gone into *a bit* more depth in analyzing your rhetorical choices/strategies, especially with regard to image-text relationships. (Myers, NES)

The lower use of hedges suggests that the NNES teachers either provide fewer negative comments to students or pay less attention to the threat their negative comments have on the "face" or self-image of students.[8]

Self-mentions are features used to show the explicit presence of the writer in texts and are often realized through first-person pronouns. In written comments, self-mentions, which refer to an explicit intrusion of teachers' identity, are often employed to show teachers' responsibility for their comments and an intimate relationship teachers attempt to establish with their students. As shown in (12), *I* refers to the teacher who gives the comment on the student's paper. The use of the phrase *I think* indicates the teacher's willingness to be accountable for the comment given to the student. In addition, *I think* also makes the comment sound less formal but more personal and conversational, therefore aiding the teacher in building an intimate relationship with the student.

> (12) *I think* this is a really effective build up to this guiding goal for *your paper*. (Lillie, NES)

According to Hyland (2002), self-mentions help writers to show the commitment to their words and therefore set up a credible identity and a relationship with their audiences (p. 1093). The fewer use of self-mentions, then, suggest that the NNES teachers are less comfortable with making commitments to their comments and building an intimate relationship with their students compared to their NES counterparts.

Why do NNES Teachers Comment Differently than NES Teachers?

The findings presented above show that the NNES teachers of FYW in this study do use metadiscourse differently than their NES counterparts, and the difference is manifested mainly through the use of endophoric markers, boosters, hedges, and self-mentions. Specifically, the NNES teachers use more endophoric markers than the NES teachers, whereas the NES teachers utilize more boosters, hedges, and self-mentions that the NNES teachers to a statistically significant degree.

A possible explanation for the NNES using more endophoric markers than the NES teachers could be that the NNES teachers work harder to assure that the comments given are comprehensible and accurate to students because NNES teachers often face more doubts from students than NES teachers. Monika Shehi (2017) has pointed out that NNES teachers of FYW sometimes have difficulties in building their authority in writing classrooms

---

8   See more details about the concept of face in relation to politeness in Penelope Brown and Stephen Levinson (1987).

because NNES teachers are often treated as an "outsider" or "unknowing newcomer" due to social prejudices and therefore are less trustworthy by students in composition instruction (pp. 263–264). Also, previous studies on NNES teachers almost all have indicated that students have doubts about NNES teachers' linguistic competence in teaching FYW (e.g., Liu, 2005; Ruecker et al., 2018; Shehi, 2017; Zheng, 2017). Because of those doubts NNES teachers have encountered, it seems not too surprising that the NNES teachers in this study work harder to ensure that their written comments are accessible to students in order to mediate the distrust they have to face.

Alternatively, it is also possible that the NNES teachers do not have enough confidence as composing their written comments, therefore prioritizing the clarity and comprehensibility of their comments through the use of more endophoric markers, although they have been pretty fluent in English and have gone through several training sessions with their NES counterparts before teaching FYW. In fact, in an interview with a NNES teacher of FYW conducted by Ruecker et al. (2018), they found that the teacher admitted that it perhaps took her longer than her NES counterparts to build confidence in grading, and she also acknowledged that "I feel like I revise my comments a lot more and edit more comments a lot more than a NES" (pp. 626–627).

Similarly, the fewer use of boosters by the NNES teachers could also be explained by the fact the NNES teachers lack confidence in this study. As I discussed earlier, boosters often serve to reinforce teachers' evaluations on students' writing. If the NNES teachers do not have enough confidence in playing their primary role as expert and gatekeeper, it is understandable that they will use fewer boosters that essentially highlight the certainty of their evaluations on students' paper. The NNES teachers' possible lack of confidence, on the one hand, could derive from their self-doubt in their role as expert who is qualified to provide students with feedback, as what Ruecker et al. (2018) found out in their study above. On the other hand, it could also come from students' distrust in teachers who are from a non-English-speaking country, as Xuan Zheng (2017) discovered in her case study.

The fewer use of hedges by the NNES teachers, as I mentioned above, suggests that the NNES teachers either provide fewer negative comments to students or pay less attention to the threat their negative comments have on the "face" or self-image of students. While it could be possible that the NNES care less about alleviating the negativity in their comments on students' papers, given the fact that the NNES teachers are often fluent in English, especially English in academic contexts, and have gone through some mandatory training sessions, it seems more tenable that their fewer use of hedges is the result of fewer negative comments offered to students' writing. Previous research has all indicated that NNES teachers have less credibility than their NES counterparts in FYW classrooms (Liu, 2005; Ruecker et al., 2018; Shehi, 2017; Zheng, 2017), which could put NNES teachers at a vulnerable position where their authority is more likely to be challenged, and the NNES teachers in this study may attempt to mediate the potential challenges they may have to face through providing fewer negative comments on students' writing (which in turn leads to the fewer use of hedges). In fact, NNES teachers' credibility can not only be questioned in FYW classrooms but ESL or EFL classrooms as well, according to Sibel Tatar and Senem Yildiz (2010).

Last, as I mentioned earlier, while self-mentions have a potential to help teachers set up their credibility and build an intimate relationship with students by showing their willingness to make commitments to their written comments and making their comments more personal and conversational, they also put teachers at a risky position because of an explicit connection between their comments and themselves. Hyland (2002) also confirms that despite its rhetorical usefulness, applying self-mentions sometimes is also a risky strategy and is vulnerable to criticism (p. 1104). Therefore, if the NNES teachers in this study have insufficient credibility, it makes sense that they tend to use fewer self-mentions in their written comments so that they can stay distant from explicit responsibilities for their comments, which could potentially make them face fewer criticisms and risks of their authority being challenged. In fact, previous research also has found that NNES teachers' credibility in teaching FYW is sometimes questioned by students because of their nonnative status (e.g., Liu, 2005; Ruecker et al., 2018; Shehi, 2017; Wang-Hiles, this volume; Zheng, 2017). Alternatively, it could also be possible that instead of being doubted by students, the NNES teachers are self-questioned because they are unconfident in playing the role as experts and therefore use fewer self-mentions through which to potentially avoid responsibilities for their comments.

Conclusion and Implications

Through the interpersonal model of metadiscourse, this study found that written comments on students' graded papers by the NNES teachers of FYW do look different from those by their NES counterparts, and the divergence is mainly manifested via the use of endophoric markers, boosters, hedges, and self-mentions.[9] The possible reasons for the NNES responding to students'

---

9   In a larger corpus study where I examined the correlation between metadiscourse and six extralinguistic factors, including location of comments (marginal or end), course context (ENGL 101 or ENGL 102), gender, disciplinary background

writing differently than the NES teachers, generally speaking, are twofold. On the one hand, the NNES teachers in this study may lack confidence in playing the primary role as experts when commenting on students' writing. While, from a quantitative survey conducted among 78 NNES teachers of FYW, Ruecker et al. (2018) found that NNES teachers overall do not lack confidence in teaching FYW and do not see their NNES status as an issue, it seems that, from the results of this study, the NNESTs may still feel less comfortable as interacting with their students through written comments compared to their NES counterparts.

Such a possibility suggests that NNES teachers, at least those in this study, perhaps need more supports from writing programs. In addition to current resources provided to NNES teachers, writing program administrators can offer workshops that focus particularly on helping NNES teachers with providing comments on students' papers and with how to deal with students' doubt or pushback in teaching. In addition, writing program administrators can help NNES teachers raise their confidence by cultivating "translingual teachers" who are able to view their multiple linguistic identities as resources and draw upon their translingual identities as pedagogy in writing classrooms (Zheng, 2017, p. 32).

On the other hand, a second possible reason for the NNES commenting differently than the NNES teachers is that NNES teachers are more likely to be questioned and challenged by students due to their "nonnative English-speaking" status. This possibility seems to suggest that in addition to helping NNES teachers raise their confidence, writing program administrators should cultivate a translingual environment for NNES teachers where students are open to language diversity and various backgrounds of composition teachers. To make this happen, writing courses can engage students in material that challenges their monolingual ideology and develop their translingual disposition, as Jerry Won Lee and Christopher Jenks (2016) suggest. In addition to changes at the classroom level, according to Chris Gallagher and Matt Noonan (2017), it is important for writing program administrators to create a translingual environment at the institutional and programmatic levels as well.

In the end, it must be noted that the findings and their explanations in this study are suggestive rather than conclusive due to a small corpus in size.

(rhetoric and composition, creative writing, or literature), native language, and years of teaching experience, in FYW teachers' written comments through multivariate analysis (mixed-effects model), I found that in addition to native language, all the rest of the factors also affect the use of metadiscourse (Xin, 2021).

Future work could reproduce the study with a larger corpus and with more teachers across institutions. Future studies could also explore from whose written comments, NNES or NES teachers, students benefit more to complement the present study because commenting differently than NES teachers does not necessarily make NNES teachers' responses less effective. It might be possible that students prefer the NNES teachers' written comments because they are easier to process or that comments by both NNES and NES teachers are helpful for students' writing development although the focus of the two groups in written feedback is different in some aspect. Since the practices of written comments often take place behind closed office doors, teachers, as Summer Smith (1997) point out, often have limited opportunities to look at how other teachers respond to students' writing in practice. It would be a good idea for writing program administrators to provide opportunities for NNES and NES teachers to read each other's written comments. Doing so would not only raise both their awareness that written comments can vary according to socio-cultural factors, such as native language, but it would also be a good way for them to learn new or alternative methods of responding to students' writing.

References

Ädel, A. (2006). *Metadiscourse in L1 and L2 English*. John Benjamins. https://doi.org/10.1075/scl.24.

Ädel, A. (2017). Remember that your reader cannot read your mind: Problem/solution-oriented metadiscourse in teacher feedback on student writing. *English for Specific Purposes, 45*, 54–68. https://doi.org/10.1016/j.esp.2016.09.002.

Biber, D. (1990). Methodological issues regarding corpus-based analyses of linguistic variation. *Literary and Linguistic Computing, 5*(4), 257–269. https://doi.org/10.1093/llc/5.4.257.

Biber, D. (1993). Representativeness in corpus design. *Literary and Linguistic Computing, 8*(4), 243–257. https://doi.org/10.1093/llc/8.4.243.

Braine, G. (1999). *Nonnative speaker English teachers: Research, pedagogy, and professional growth*. Routledge.

Brown, P & Levinson, S. (1987). *Politeness: Some universals in language usage*. Cambridge University Press. https://doi.org/10.1017/CBO9780511813085.

Canagarajah, S. (2006). The place of world Englishes in composition: Pluralization continued. *College Composition and Communication, 57*(4), 586–619. https://www.jstor.org/stable/20456910.

Cook, V. (1999). Going beyond the native speaker in language teaching. *TESOL Quarterly, 33*(2), 185–209. https://doi.org/10.2307/3587717.

Ferris, D. (1995). Student reactions to teacher response in multiple-draft composition classrooms. *TESOL Quarterly, 29*(1), 33–53. https://doi.org/10.2307/3587804.

Flowerdew, L. (2004). The argument for using English specialized corpora to understand academic and professional language. In U. Connor & T. A. Upton (Eds.), *Discourse in the professions: Perspectives from corpus linguistics* (pp. 11–33). John Benjamins. https://doi.org/10.1075/scl.16.

Gallagher, C. & Noonan, M. (2017). Becoming global: Learning to "do" translingualism. In B. Horner & L. Tetreault (Eds.), *Crossing divides: Exploring translingual writing pedagogies and program* (pp. 161–177). Utah State University Press. https://www.jstor.org/stable/j.ctt1r6bo8q.

Goldstein, L. (2004). Questions and answers about teacher written commentary and student revision: Teachers and students working together. *Journal of Second Language Writing, 13*, 63–80. https://doi.org/10.1016/j.jslw.2004.04.006.

Guerra, J. (2016). Cultivating a rhetorical sensibility in the translingual writing classroom. *College English, 78*(3), 228–233. https://www.jstor.org/stable/44075112.

Halliday, M. (1994). *An introduction to functional grammar* (2nd ed). Edward Arnold.

Horner, B., Lu, M. Z., Royster, J. J. & Trimbur, J. (2011). Language difference in writing: Towards a translingual approach. *College English, 73*(3), 303–21.

Hyland, K. (2002). Authority and invisibility: Authorial identity in academic writing. *Journal of Pragmatics, 34*, 1091–1112. https://doi.org/10.1016/S0378-2166(02)00035-8.

Hyland, K. (2005). *Metadiscourse: Exploring interaction in writing*. Continuum.

Hyland, K. (2017). Metadiscourse: What is it and where is it going? *Journal of Pragmatics, 113*, 16–29. https://doi.org/10.1016/j.pragma.2017.03.007.

Hyland, K. & Hyland, F. (2006). Interpersonal aspects of response: Constructing and interpreting teacher written feedback. In K. Hyland & F. Hyland (Eds.), *Feedback in second language writing: Contexts and issues* (pp. 206–224). Cambridge University Press. https://doi.org/10.1017/CBO9781139524742.

Hyland, K. & Jiang, F. (2018). "In this paper we suggest": Changing patterns of disciplinary metadiscourse. *English for Specific Purposes, 51*, 18–30. https://doi.org/10.1016/j.esp.2018.02.001.

Hyland, K. & Tse, P. (2004). Metadiscourse in academic writing: A reappraisal. *Applied Linguistics, 25*(2), 156–177. https://doi.org/10.1093/applin/25.2.156.

Johnson, D. & Roen, D. (1992). Complimenting and involvement in peer reviews: Gender variation. *Language in Society, 21*(1), 27–57. https://doi.org/10.1017/S0047404500015025.

Lang, S. (2018). Evolution of instructor response? Analysis of five years of feedback to students. *Journal of Writing Analytics, 2*, 1–33. https://doi.org/10.37514/JWA-J.2018.2.1.02.

Lee, J. W. & Jenks, C. (2016). Doing translingual dispositions. *College Composition and Communication, 68*(2), 317–344. https://www.jstor.org/stable/pdf/44783564.pdf.

Liu, J. (2005). Chinese graduate teaching assistants teaching freshman composition to native English speaking students. In E. Llurda (Ed.), *Nonnative language teachers: Perceptions, challenges and contributions to the profession* (pp. 155–177). Springer. https://doi.org/10.1007/0-387-24565-0_9.

Lu, M. Z. & Horner, B. (2013). Translingual literacy, language difference, and matters of agency. *College English, 75*(6), 582–607.

Matsuda, P.K. (2013). It's the wild west out there: A new linguistic frontier in U.S. composition. In S. Canagarajah (Ed), *Literacy as translingual practice: Between communities and classrooms* (pp.128–138). Routledge. https://doi.org/10.4324/9780203120293.

Phakiti, A. (2015). Quantitative research and analysis. In B. Paltridge & A. Phakiti (Eds), *Research methods in applied linguistics: A practical resource* (pp. 27–48). Bloomsbury.

Reppen, R. (2010). Building a corpus: What are the key considerations. In A. O'Keeffe & M. McCarthy (Eds.), *The Routledge handbook of corpus linguistics*, (pp.31–37). Routledge. https://doi.org/10.4324/9780203856949.

Ruecker, T., Frazier, S. & Tseptsura, M. (2018). "Language difference can be an asset": Exploring the experiences of nonnative English-speaking teachers of writing. *College Composition and Communication, 69*(4), 612–641. http://www.jstor.org/stable/44870978.

Shehi, M. (2017). Why is my English teacher a foreigner? Re-authoring the story of international composition teachers. *Teaching English in the Two-Year College, 44*(3), 260–75.

Smith, S. (1997). The genre of the end comment: Conventions in teacher responses to student writing. *College Composition and Communication*, 48(2), 249–268. https://doi.org/10.2307/358669.

Tatar, S & Yildiz, S. (2010). Empowering nonnative-English speaking teachers in the classroom. In A. Mahboob (Ed), *The NNEST lens: Non-native English speakers in TESOL* (pp. 114–128). Cambridge Scholars Publishing.

Tse, P & Hyland, K. (2008). "Robot kung fu": Gender and professional identity in biology and philosophy reviews. *Journal of Pragmatics, 40*, 1232–1248. https://doi.org/10.1016/j.pragma.2007.02.002.

Xin, W. (2021). *"I'm glad you are addressing this!": Metadiscourse in first-year composition teachers' written comments* (Order No. 28499129) [Doctoral Dissertation, University of Kansas]. ProQuest Dissertations & Theses Global.

Young, V. (2009). "Nah, we straight": An argument against code switching. *Journal of Advanced Composition, 29*(1–2), 49–76. https://www.jstor.org/stable/20866886.

Zheng, X. (2017). Translingual identity as pedagogy: international teaching assistants of English in college composition classrooms. *The Modern Language Journal, 101*(1), 29–44. https://doi.org/10.1111/modl.12373.

9 (Re)framing Uncertainty as Opportunity: A Study of International Teaching Assistants in Writing Classrooms Across the Curriculum

Tamara Mae Roose
CALIFORNIA STATE UNIVERSITY, SAN BERNARDINO

Min-Seok Choi
UNIVERSITY OF LOUISIANA AT LAFAYETTE

Christopher E. Manion
THE OHIO STATE UNIVERSITY

Across higher education institutions in the US, international teaching assistants (ITAs) have come to play a significant role in teaching undergraduate students across disciplines (Chiang, 2009; Gorsuch, 2012). Legislative and institutional policies to ensure the proficiency and preparedness of ITAs suggest that they encounter more difficulty than domestic TAs in their teaching responsibilities because of their different language and culture backgrounds and presumed unfamiliarity with U.S. educational norms (Chiang, 2009; Gorsuch, 2012). ITAs, as nonnative English-speaking teachers (NNESTs), are generally framed in deficit discourses across the literature focusing on the sociocultural, linguistic, and pedagogical challenges they may experience teaching U.S. undergraduate students (Ashavskaya, 2015; Kamhi-Stein, 2018; Kuo, 2002; Ruecker et al., 2018; Yazan & Rudolph, 2018). As a result, Xuan Zheng (2017) has stated that ITAs may face substantial difficulty "positioning themselves as legitimate and competent teachers" (p. 30).

Although new instructors commonly face a variety of challenges (e.g., assessment of student learning, command over instructional content, and authority in the classroom) (Costache et al., 2019), some studies suggest that ITAs will face considerably higher uncertainty due to cultural and linguistic dissimilarities between instructors and students (de Oliveira & Lan, 2012;

Nelson, 1992). While this may be true, it does not mean that greater uncertainty will result in more barriers and constraints among ITAs because they can and very often do "value uncertainty as an occasion for growth and reflection" (Dudley-Marling, 1995, p. 257). In fact, uncertainty can prompt reflection and become the basis for exploration as ITAs may turn uncertainties into valuable resources in constructing their pedagogy and teaching authority (e.g., Tseptsura, this volume).

In light of this claim, the purpose of our qualitative study was to problematize common assumptions surrounding the challenges of ITAs and extend the conversation on NNESTs of writing. To this end, our central research question was: What uncertainties do international teaching assistants of writing experience and how do they perceive these and respond to them?

Conceptual Framework

We adopt Michael Agar's (1994) concept of "rich points" as our approach to understanding how ITAs construct their teaching and student learning. "Rich points" originally refer to moments of frame clash when ethnographers feel something does not go as expected, so they strive to pursue the way insiders view phenomena to better understand what is going on. Because what is taken-for-granted in participating in a particular activity (e.g., cultural expectations and norms for learning in the classroom) is made visible through the clash, Agar (1994) calls this frame clash as a "rich point." In this sense, we see these uncertain moments as rich points because how ITAs perceive and respond to uncertain moments may illustrate how they construct their teaching practices and classroom authority as they gain more understanding of their students' perspectives. In this way, we concentrated on times when these international teaching assistants of writing communicated uncertainty in their teaching due to different cultural and linguistic practices that occur in their classroom contexts.

Across the literature, uncertainty is assumed to be an inherent part of the complexity of the teaching profession because it is centered on social interactions and human relationships (e.g., Floden & Buchmann, 1993; Hasinoff & Mandzuk, 2018; Helsing, 2007; McDonald, 1992). Uncertainty is often associated with discomfort and risk as it can complicate teachers' decision-making and ability to predict, interpret, and assess others' thoughts, emotions, and behaviors (Costache et al., 2019; Hasinoff & Mandzuk, 2018; Helsing, 2007). In reality, "uncertainty is neither intrinsically positive nor inherently negative" (Hasinoff & Mandzuk, 2018, p. 1). Thus, in this study we conceive of uncertainty as a neutral construct and claim that what really matters is how teachers conceive of and relate to their uncertainties over time. Furthermore, uncertainty has been defined as "an unsolved design problem emerging from either a lack of knowing or a doubt when considering a range of alternatives" (Costache et al., 2019, p. 2) and as the inability "to make sense of, assign value to, or predict outcomes of events" (Kosenko, 2014, p. 1425). Drawing upon these definitions and the findings that emerged in our study, we operationalize uncertainty as moments when international teaching assistants are not sure how to interpret, act, or react to a situation or source (whether it be oral or written text) because of the different linguistic and cultural backgrounds of the instructors and their students.

Methodology

Context and Participants

This study reports on a portion of the data collected in a larger ongoing study of writing instructors across the curriculum at a large land-grant Midwestern university, and more specifically, second-year writing (SYW) courses, which are mandatory general education classes often taught by graduate students and offered across thirty different departments within six different colleges. The support, training, and oversight drastically differ across departments— some provide significant resources to instructors teaching SYW courses and others very little to none (Ohio State Writing Across the Curriculum, 2016a). The curriculum also varies widely across and within departments—some instructors follow an established curriculum provided by their supervisors, and others have autonomy to adapt or create their own curriculum (Ohio State Writing Across the Curriculum, 2016b). However, the commonality among the SYW courses is that instructors are asked to address "major topics and writings pertaining to the United States" (College of Arts and Sciences, 1988, p. 7), which potentially complexifies the teaching of these courses for ITAs whose education and experiences may be rooted outside of the US. Furthermore, students in these classes reflect the wider lack of linguistic, racial, and cultural diversity at the institution, with minority enrollment in first-year undergraduate ranging from 18% to 25%, and international enrollment ranging from 5% to 12.5% over the past five years. Only one third of incoming first-year students are identified as coming from outside of the state (Ohio State Office of Student Academic Success, 2019). Overall, ITAs on many levels may see many differences between themselves and their students.

The focus of the current study is on the perspectives and experiences of three international teaching assistants from different countries who were all in their first year of teaching a SYW course: (1) Yasemin, a second-year doctoral student from Turkey in the Department of Education, (2) Pari, a fifth-year doctoral student from India in the Department of Economics, and (3) Jiayi, a third-year doctoral student from China also in the Department of Economics (references to ITAs are pseudonyms). The participant demographics have been summarized in Table 10.1.

Table 10.1. Participant Demographics

	Yasemin	Pari	Jiayi
Gender	Female	Female	Female
Home Country	Turkey	India	China
Department	Education	Economics	Economics
Year in Ph.D. Program	Second year	Fifth year	Third year
Bachelor's Degree	Turkey	India	China
Master's Degree	Turkey	India	US
Home Country Teaching Experience	2 years at the college level; 2 years at the elementary school level	n/a	n/a
U.S. Teaching Experience	One semester at the elementary school level; Second semester teaching this course	Second semester teaching at the university; First semester teaching this course	First semester teaching in general

Yasemin and Pari both earned their bachelor's and master's degrees in their respective home countries, whereas Jiayi earned her master's degree in the US prior to beginning her doctoral studies. Yasemin had four years of prior teaching experience in her home country: two years teaching English language courses at the college level and two years teaching English as a foreign language within elementary schools. She also had more than a semester of teaching experience as an elementary school ESL teacher in the US. She was in her second semester teaching the SYW course at the time of the study. Yasemin's course supervisor, who was also teaching one section of the SYW course provided her with the course syllabus and other teaching materials. Neither Pari nor Jiayi had prior teaching experience in their home countries. Pari previously had taught one economics course in her discipline, but this was her first semester teaching the SYW course. Jiayi had been a teaching assistant in content courses in her department in the past, but at the time of data collection, she had no prior experience as an independent instructor of a course. Both Pari and Jiayi adapted the course syllabus from a former TA teaching the course based on their own experience and expertise.

Data Collection and Analysis

The stances teachers take toward uncertainty greatly vary across individuals as "there are fundamental differences in the ways that teachers describe, interpret, and respond to their uncertainties" (Helsing, 2007, p. 1328). Thus, in this study we privilege the international teaching assistants' individual lived experiences and subjective interpretations of their actions and interactions with their students as the primary evidence of their classroom realities (Smith, 2008). To get access to these insider perspectives, we conducted two semi-structured interviews (approximately 45 minutes each) with each participant, one during the middle and the other at the end of the semester. The interview guide included questions that prompted international teaching assistants to share about the experiences and resources they drew upon in their teaching, the roles the teachers and students took in their classroom, the interactions between teachers and students, and the curricular decisions they made. The interviews were audio-recorded and transcribed by the first two authors and independently coded for emergent themes by all three researchers. The codes were then compared and discussed in order to achieve trustworthiness.

Conceptualizing uncertainty as rich points and applying our operational definition of uncertainty, we identified across the data set three specific components: (1) moments of uncertainty, (2) perceptions of uncertainty, and (3) responses to uncertainty. We restricted our analysis of these moments to when the international teaching assistants voiced uncertainty due to their different cultural and linguistic backgrounds. Drawing upon the coding scheme of Oana Costache et al. (2019), we identified these moments by using their linguistic markers, such as "not sure," "don't know," "unfamiliar with," "couldn't understand," etc. Then, by applying Jochen Kleres' (2011) lexical and structural levels of "linguistic manifestations of emotions" (p. 193), we traced how these ITAs perceived certain types of uncertainty by looking for emotional evidence of their perceptions, such as in the verbal expressions "difficult," "challenging," "kind of worried," "so upset," "not a really big thing," "not a problem," etc. Then we looked for how they responded to these uncertainties through the words and actions they reported about their pedagogical decisions and interactions with their students (e.g., initiating dialogue, prompting reflection, and expanding the curriculum).

Findings

Yasemin: Mutual Learning through Dialogue and Social Interaction

> "They're pushing me; I'm pushing them. So, this is helping us to think and engage more."

As an international teaching assistant of writing in a second-year writing (SYW) course in education focused on social justice issues, Yasemin talked about the uncertainty she initially felt teaching a new course with an unfamiliar student population in a different cultural context. First of all, she expressed, "I was kind of worried to start working with U.S. students because *I didn't know* what to expect. *I didn't know anything* about the undergrad students at [this university] [emphasis added]." Her repetition and word choice here point to her initial worry related to this uncertainty. Moreover, she not only voiced feeling unsure of what to expect of her students but also of what was expected of her as their instructor: "I was kind of nervous because *I wasn't sure* what was expecting me in terms of working with the undergrad students at [this university], because this is the kind of population that *I wasn't familiar with*. And *I didn't really know* what was expecting me." Her negation and repetition here reinforce her initial nervousness and uncertainty as an ITA working with a new student population in an unfamiliar cultural context.

In her interviews, Yasemin also shared about times when she experienced uncertainties in understanding students' writing due to the cultural knowledge they incorporated. For example, she recounted a time when she was working with a small group and had not been sure about what her student was trying to say until she had a conversation with the student and noticed that there were cultural aspects embedded in the student's writing that prevented her from understanding it. Although she recognized that "being a foreigner here" was a possible challenge for her as an international teaching assistant of writing to understand "the cultural things they incorporate in the writing or the things that they discuss in the classroom," she minimized this challenge, framing it as an opportunity for dialogue and interaction with her students: "It's not a really big thing because we can talk about it. And it's also great for me to learn from them. But still it exists." Moreover, she perceived her students whom she was initially nervous and worried about teaching as approachable individuals she could engage in dialogue to clarify things she did not understand: "So most of my students are really nice people. So, they are really polite . . . I just asked them to tell me." Yasemin perceived these uncertainties as "not a problem." Rather, she responded to them as opportunities to learn from her students and grow as an instructor: "So I'm learning a lot from them . . . They're enculturating me in various cultures as well."

In addition to uncertainty regarding students' cultural aspects in their writing, Yasemin shared how she wrestled with understanding students' cultural assumptions in a classroom discussion on a reading about "corruption in the justice system." When confronted with the idea that more African American judges should be appointed to counteract unequal racial sentencing, the students responded negatively, expressing that they thought the judges might "take revenge on White people." Yasemin struggled to understand her students' cultural assumptions: "*I couldn't* think from that perspective . . . *I couldn't* come up with the answer that 'but what if they punish white people?' So, this is one thing that *I couldn't* come [up with], that *I couldn't* like understand their perspective in the first place." Her repetition reinforced the potential challenge this cultural difference presented. However, she responded to this as an opportunity to reflect on her perspective and an opportunity to prompt reflection among students. She went on to say, "But also in the second place, I could come up with an idea that all people should be always thinking about the well-being of all people. . . I think they're pushing me like this also made me to come up with more inclusive solutions. And coming from a more loving perspective to the issue." That is, by suspending her evaluation and reflecting on her students' response over time as indicated by her use of "in the first place" and "in the second place," Yasemin's persistence and effort to understand the cultural clash in perspectives allowed her to turn this source of uncertainty into an opportunity to learn from her students, which could, in turn, prompt her students to ultimately learn more from her as well.

Yasemin's increased confidence in teaching this writing course was largely due to how she perceived uncertainties and responded to them. By shifting her own perspective to that of her students as a means to better understand their ways of thinking and speaking, Yasemin turned her uncertainties into opportunities to learn as a teacher, which leads the class into a mutual learning relationship. She shared, "So they're pushing me, I'm pushing them. So, this is also helping us to think and engage more thoroughly with the reading with the social justice issues, and also, it is, like, intellectually stimulating for us." Throughout Yasemin's interviews, she continuously framed the uncertainties she faced in her writing classroom as rooted in cultural differences yet responded to them as "occasions for reflection and, ultimately, personal and professional growth" (Dudley-Marling, 1995, p. 253). Moreover, Yasemin's ability to build rapport with her domestic students, an area of great interest across ITA literature (e.g., Gorsuch, 2012), was seemingly established through her response to uncertainty—namely, her choice to engage in dialogue and social interaction to seek greater understanding.

Pari: Teaching Through Cultural Resources

> "I think that's where if they have questions I can dig deeper."

As an international teaching assistant of writing in a second-year writing (SYW) course in economics, Pari talked about the uncertainty she initially felt teaching a course that covered such broad content that was often outside of her specialization and at times culturally unfamiliar to her. In her own words: "I think the primary challenge that I face is that, so the topic, the course that I'm teaching is current economic issues in the US. My main challenge is trying to bring in variety in terms of content because I don't specialize in or *I don't know enough* about a lot of these topics, which becomes a little challenging for me." She emphasized that all of the SYW courses in economics were "based on the U.S. market and the U.S. economy" and contained "lots of stuff which [she] was unfamiliar with." As an ITA, Pari faced some uncertainty regarding how to cover this course content: "I'm not from the US. I have done, I've spent most of my life in India and the structure there. The economy there is very different." She considered the broad content to be challenging for her because she believed that if she wanted to bring in a variety of topics on economics in the US, she would need to be well-prepared to do so: "I feel that if I am talking about a topic I should know enough, so that, that for me is the biggest challenge in terms of this course." As a Ph.D. student balancing her own research and writing responsibilities, she felt this would be "very difficult" because it would be very time-intensive: "even preparing one slide on that aspect requires me to read a couple of papers." Throughout her interviews, she mentioned that it was challenging to gain an "understanding of the different things" and "get a variety of topics to discuss." Thus, she experienced a clash between the disciplinary expertise she gained in India and the U.S.-centric course content; however, instead of replicating the approach of the former domestic TA who taught the course, she adapted the materials and her course design to establish her own sense of legitimacy in teaching the class.

Even though Pari identified uncertainty rooted in unfamiliarity with the culturally-based course content and referred to this as her "primary challenge," she did not indicate that this resulted in barriers or limitations in her teaching. In fact, she drew upon her transnational identity and incorporated her own cultural resources into her instructional material. She reported that she would include cultural comparisons between the US and her home country of India, as well as other Southeast and East Asian economies: "You know, something could be different across the two countries, which will have differences in the impacts. So, that's something that I talk about because that's the economy that I know better about. So, yeah, I tried to bring in these comparisons." Pari explained that although she primarily talked about issues in the US, "some of them were like issues in the US as well as elsewhere." For example, she explained, "Inequality is something that's present in the US and is present in other countries . . . So when I was talking about inequality, I spoke about other countries a little, but the focus was primarily on the US and the issues here."

In this way, she developed her course content around topics connected to her specialization and then expanded this scope by drawing on her knowledge of global perspectives to incorporate a variety of topics that she deemed significant current events in the field:

> So, I tried to introduce topics, which I knew better . . . I, first, you know, decided on the topics I wanted to talk about based on what my specialization is. After that I started taking topics, which appealed a little more to me, appeal to general ideas. Like trade was something that was important, something that needed to be addressed in class given the way things are right now with China and so on and so forth. Immigration, you know, these kinds of issues were relevant and for the U.S. context.

In doing so, she extended the boundaries of the course by making connections between what was happening in other parts of the world to the economic issues in the US. Pari's instructional approach addressed the uncertainty she felt with the U.S.-based course content, and she positively evaluated this: "I think, just in terms of content, I have found that if you provide more variety that helps students; they find it very interesting." In other words, she believed that "generally students like to hear about what's happening in other worlds, in the other countries."

Even though Pari was initially concerned about the differences between her disciplinary expertise gained in India and the U.S.-centric course content, she ultimately responded to this as a pedagogical opportunity to draw upon her transnational experiences to incorporate her own cultural knowledge into her teaching. She explained, "The way I approached this particular course was try and speak about what issues I am most familiar with because, you know, I think that's where if they have questions I can dig deeper and go deeper into, so that's the way I was trying to, you know, sort of build the course." Thus, by extending the boundaries of the course content and incorporating her own cultural resources, she agentively responds to the uncertainties she encountered with what content to cover in the course, a common source of uncertainty discussed across the literature (Costache et al., 2019; Floden & Buchmann, 1993). Of greater significance is how Pari perceived this uncertainty not as a liability, but instead, turned it into an asset (Helsing, 2007).

Jiayi: Navigating the Unexpected on the Path to Establishing Teaching Authority

> "There are a lot of unexpected situations and a lot of unexpected questions, but I managed to do that."

As an international teaching assistant of writing in a second-year writing (SYW) course in economics, Jiayi talked about uncertainties as rooted in the "unexpected," times when students' words and actions puzzled her and made her unsure of how to both interpret and appropriately respond to them. The "unexpected situations" were attributed to cultural differences and often framed as difficulties as she strove to establish her authority in the classroom. Across both of her interviews she voiced that the most difficult challenge she encountered was responding to the "unexpected situations," which were most often related to classroom practices and procedures. In fact, the word "unexpected" surfaced seven times in reference to times when her students had what she considered "exceptional" cases that she had not experienced before. She explained, "Some people say how they have a surgery, or they have a car accident, or they have this, they have that." Elaborating on one such unexpected situation, Jiayi explained that when a student who had only shown up once or twice in the semester emailed her a week later that she had been involved in a motorcycle accident, she was not sure if she could trust the students' excuse: "She took a picture of like a [medical] exam sheet, on which I can see which kind of exam she has, but there's no date on it, you know what I mean? It's only a half of a paper. And then I asked her to show me the full page so I can see what if it is accident exam you did last year, right? And then I rescheduled her for like for a presentation two weeks later, which I think is pretty much enough time for her to prepare. She never replied until now." In this situation, Jiayi was uncertain of both what was going on, as well as how she should respond to it. She perceived these student interactions as "unexpected" situations that led to difficulties in classroom management as she tried to maintain course policies (e.g., participation and assessment), while still being understanding of students' personal lives. Jiayi's initial uncertainty with classroom management was tied to her new role as an instructor, "a social authority" in an unfamiliar instructional context (Costache et al., 2019, p. 9), a prevalent uncertainty discussed across the ITA literature (Ashavskaya, 2015; Floden & Buchmann, 1993).

In particular, Jiayi spoke at length about a specific situation in which she faced considerable uncertainty over how to handle a student's "unexpected situation," especially because it affected other students in the class. She shared, "I have one student, he, like after one month of that semester, he said he has some anxiety. I don't know I have mentioned to you, anxiety for speaking." She was unsure how to accommodate the student's needs because a core component of the course was debates and presentations. Jiayi explained, "He said he has been contacting the disability center, but only until the end of semester did I receive like documents." Again, in this situation, she wrestled with how to both interpret and respond to a student's situation, particularly because of his delay in providing evidence and how it affected his group members: "I was having a hard time trying to protect his privacy and dealing with the communication with his group members 'cause he does not want their group members to know, but they should know something. What's going on? Why is the person missing?" How the situation unfolded became a source of tension in her relationship with the student and was a confusing and upsetting experience for her. She explained that when the student found out that she had shared his situation he was quite unhappy about it. She reported, "He said, 'This makes me more embarrassed and more anxious. I'm not going to come to class for a long time, very long time.'" Jiayi shared that "actually, he never showed up after that." She was quite emotionally expressive in recounting this experience indicated by her words, "I feel so upset about that." She also repeated in her interview a couple of times, "I apologized," reflecting her effort to make amends in this situation, and stating, "I know it is my fault, but I didn't mean to do that." Thus, she articulated a clash between her intentions and her student's perception of her actions. This underscores that ITAs from home countries where students are typically compliant may report frustrations and struggles with the attitudes and behavior of domestic students (Kuo, 2002). As Jiayi communicated, her uncertainty with classroom discipline created dilemmas for her and were expressed at times through as a sense of guilt, frustration, confusion, self-blame, and discomfort (Helsing, 2007)

More specifically, Jiayi attributed these "unexpected situations" to disparate value systems of the US and China regarding teacher-student roles and expectations. She explained, "Uh, I think we probably have kind of similar disability center, but the students hardly ever challenge their instructors. The

Chinese students in class like follow the rules and respect their instructors much more than here." Even though she primarily viewed this situation from her own cultural perspective and did not seem to shift her point of view to that of her students, she does exhibit awareness of the clash of classroom norms: "I will say it's [due] to cultural difference in United States. Everyone is important, like individual rights are very important, but in China it's less accentuated." Thus, she primarily voiced uncertainties as rooted in unexpected situations related to cultural differences that, at times, led to confusion and conflict.

However, as Jiayi grew accustomed to the social practices and expectations of her students, the very thing that was the source of her uncertainty and challenge—the "unexpected"—became the greatest source of her sense of growth and pride. At the end of the semester, when asked if there was anything she especially enjoyed about teaching the course, she replied: "The feeling of teaching other people which I think is the most important in my career and also the feeling of being in control, the feeling of being in control of what I'm doing. Yeah, I feel proud of that." She brought up again the uncertainty she faced during the semester but reframed it as beneficial to her personal and professional growth: "Yeah, so it's like, as I mentioned, there are a lot of, a lot of unexpected situations and a lot of unexpected questions, but I managed to do that and I feel like it's important to handle with some unexpected experience so I can learn from it. And then, I mean, whatever situation is either in teaching or even in life, so I enjoyed it." As this final quotation illustrates, even though Jiayi perceived the uncertainties she faced in teaching this SYW course as difficult for her to navigate, they ultimately became sources of strength for her as she felt empowered by the very situations that had challenged her.

Discussion and Conclusion

Across the literature and our dataset, it is apparent that "teaching is evidently and inevitably uncertain" (Floden & Buchmann, 1993, p. 374). Yet, across teachers in general, and for this chapter's purposes, across ITAs as well, the source of these uncertainties differs and so does their perception and response to them. Findings from interviews conducted with these three ITAs of writing across two different departments over the course of a semester suggest that they each identified different uncertainties in their classrooms. Yasemin's uncertainty was rooted in teaching in an unfamiliar context with students who often used local cultural references and held cultural assumptions different from her own. On the other hand, Pari's uncertainty stemmed from her own internal questions about how to address the broad economic course topics rooted in the U.S. cultural context. Jiayi's uncertainties came from unexpected situations that created dilemmas for her as she struggled to find culturally appropriate ways to respond to students' exceptional cases. Despite the uncertainties ITAs voiced, which they generally attributed to cultural differences, they were not constrained by them and each ultimately articulated them as opportunities for growth; indeed, their responses to these uncertainties often were central to how they framed their teaching of these second-year writing (SYW) courses.

Findings from this study suggest that "uncertainty is not a hindrance or something to be embarrassed of. Rather, it may open up learning opportunities that can be translated into positive learning outcomes" (Costache et al., 2019, p. 13). When students respond to teachers in ways that are not anticipated (e.g., with different cultural references, assumptions, behavioral norms, and communication patterns), it can be surprising to teachers and lead to confusion or puzzlement; yet, at the same time, it can also cultivate deeper listening and new understanding (Helsing, 2007). Framing uncertainties as rich points (Agar, 1994) in this study provided a way to challenge deficit-oriented discourses about ITAs. Far from feeling limited by the uncertainties they identify, the instructors in our study constructed more empowering perceptions of themselves and their roles (Zacharias, 2018). As they engaged in dialogue with their students and reflected on their own teaching and learning, this allowed them to draw upon their lived experience and expertise (Choi et al., 2022) to construct their classroom authority and pedagogy (Motha et al., 2012; Wolff & De Costa, 2017).

What's striking is that these instructors referenced little formal training and support that prepared them to specifically address the particular challenges they faced. Pari, for instance, shared,

> We have the liberty to structure the course the way we want to. Um, I was not given specific rules that I have to follow in order to teach it the way I would want to . . . I'm not sure what kind of workshop or what kind of training would have helped me otherwise.

Overall, the ITAs had difficulty identifying any training or support that they would find helpful. Instead, they each seemed to greatly value the autonomy they had in adapting their courses to their experiences and knowledge and expressed pride in their ability to respond to the challenges they faced in their teaching. Thus, instead of relying on formal training and support, we believe that writing program administrators (WPAs) and department supervisors can focus on creating spaces for both ITAs and TAs to reflect and share their lived experiences of teaching with one another (Choi et al., 2022; Wolff & De Costa, 2017), which can reinforce their agency and help them build a diverse repertoire of instructional strategies. For instance, WPAs might incorporate reflective opportunities into ongoing professional development that asks instructors to consider uncertainties they face and share strategies they use over time to address those uncertainties. WPAs can also track and collect common uncertainties and supply resources that might help address them—such as resources for supporting accessibility in the classroom that might have helped Jiayi. Collected reflections on uncertainty and the range of creative strategies responding to them can help decenter predominately monolinguistic, domestic U.S., and White perspectives in writing programs. In doing so, departments can position diversity as a framework that allows for seeing all instructors as resourceful not in spite of, but because of, their diverse linguistic and cultural identities (Motha et al., 2012).

As expressed by Robert E. Floden and Margret Buchmann (1993), "uncertainty is an essential driving force in teaching, not merely a deficiency and worry" (p. 380). In other words, it is not something that should be avoided as "uncertainty is an indispensable step toward genuine questioning," which can lead individual teachers to grow and change (McDonald, 1992, p. 41) and departments to advocate for diversity as an asset. Global perspectives can be powerful resources for student learning because they encourage multiple perspectives in the classroom, broadening students' knowledge beyond their own experience, challenging dominant ways of thinking, and leading to personal growth and learning (Hijazi, this volume; Zhou, 2009). It is important to note the fact that Pari and Jiayi who taught the same course experienced different types of uncertainty and perceived and responded to them in different ways. What this difference may bring to the department may be diverse opportunities for students to learn the content. Thus, WPAs and department supervisors should advocate for global perspectives invoked by policies and practices that promote diversity. In terms of curriculum, the content can be deliberately expanded to include scholars of color and perspectives beyond the US (as Pari demonstrated).

Pedagogically, ITAs ought to be encouraged to use personal examples from their language and culture backgrounds to illustrate points in their teaching (Motha et al., 2012). In fact, Gayle L. Nelson (1992) found in a study of ITAs that use of personal examples led to more positive student attitudes and better recall of the class content. Furthermore, it can help ITAs of writing to anticipate and think through how they might deal with the inevitable uncertainties they will experience in their classroom (as Jiayi exemplified). For example, department supervisors could provide individual or group meetings in which ITAs might share the challenges they face with classroom management and receive more support for navigating unexpected situations. Ultimately, WPAs and department supervisors should support ITAs to be reflective learners of their students (as Yasemin exhibited), while at the same time draw upon their own cultural resources. This can facilitate the development of their teaching authority and pedagogy by providing ongoing occasions for ITAs to reflect on the challenges and uncertainties they face in light of the valuable insight and agency they bring to their teaching (Khor et al., this volume; Reichelt, this volume; Wolff & De Costa, 2017).

Lastly, further research on ITAs' experience of and response to uncertainty from this perspective might reveal a range of strategies that might be of use to their fellow instructors and further solidify understanding of the assets they make use of in the classroom. One particularly important area we unfortunately did not address, and our participants did not discuss (apart from Yasmin's recall of her students' discussion of race and the judicial system)—an area of uncertainty that often asserts itself on non-White ITAs—is how ITAs position themselves and see themselves positioned by U.S. racial and linguistic ideologies. What is their understanding of U.S. racial politics and ideology, and how does it evolve as they work and live in U.S. contexts? How do they situate themselves racially, ethnically, and linguistically in their home countries and regions? How do they negotiate and situate themselves within these cultural formations and systems? While ITAs, particularly non-White ones, likely face hostile uncertainties related to race, they bring their own complex lived experiences and understandings to bear to address or even disrupt their racial positioning (cf. Roundtree's study of Black women GTAs teaching writing, 2019). In doing so, these experiences and understandings can inform how they respond to other uncertainties they encounter in their work and life.

References

Agar, M. (1994). *Language shock: Understanding the culture of conversation*. William Morrow.

Ashavskaya, E. (2015). International teaching assistants' experiences in the U.S. classrooms: Implications for practice. *Journal of the Scholarship of Teaching and Learning, 15*(2), 56–69. https://doi.org/10.14434/josotl.v15i2.12947.

Chiang, S-Y. (2009). Dealing with communication problems in the instructional interactions between international teaching assistants and American college students. *Language and Education, 23*(5), 461–478. https://doi.org/10.1080/09500780902822959.

Choi, M-S., Roose, T. M. & Manion, C. (2022). Navigating identities within liminal spaces: Exploring the teacher identity construction of international graduate teaching associates of second-year writing courses. In R. Jain, B. Yazan & S. Canagarajah (Eds.), *Transnational research in English language teaching: Critical pedagogies, practices, and identities* (pp. 204–222). Multilingual Matters.

College of Arts and Sciences, The Ohio State University. (1988). A model curriculum developed by the special committee for undergraduate curriculum review. https://asccas.osu.edu/sites/asccas.osu.edu/files/ASC-Model-Curriculum.pdf.

Costache, O., Becker, E., Staub, F. & Mainhard, T. (2019). Using uncertainty as a learning opportunity during pre-lesson conferences in the teaching practicum. *Teaching and Teacher Education, 86*, 1–14. https://doi.org/10.1016/j.tate.2019.102890.

de Oliveira, L. C. & Lan, S-W. (2012). Preparing nonnative English-speaking (NNES) graduate students for teaching in higher education: A mentoring case study. *Journal on Excellence in College Teaching, 23*(3), 59–76.

Dudley-Marling, C. (1995). Uncertainty and the whole language teacher. *Language Arts, 72*(4), 252–257. https://www.jstor.org/stable/41482192.

Floden, R. E. & Buchmann, M. (1993). Between routines and anarchy: Preparing teachers for uncertainty. *Oxford Review of Education, 19*(3), 373–382. https://doi.org/10.1080/0305498930190308.

Gorsuch, G. (2012). International teaching assistants' experiences in educational cultures and their teaching beliefs. *TESL-EJ, 16*(1), 1–26.

Hasinoff, S. & Mandzuk, D. (2018). Exploring uncertainty. In S. Hasinoff & D. Mandzuk (Eds.), *Navigating uncertainty*, (pp. 1–16). Brill Sense. https://doi.org/10.1163/9789004368484_001.

Helsing, D. (2007). Regarding uncertainty in teachers and teaching. *Teaching and Teacher Education, 23*(8), 1317–1333. https://doi.org/10.1016/j.tate.2006.06.007.

Kamhi-Stein, L. D. (2018). Challenges faced by NNESTs. In J. I. Liontas (Ed.), *The TESOL encyclopedia of English language teaching*. Wiley. https://doi.org/10.1002/9781118784235.eelt0010.

Kleres, J. (2011). Emotions and narrative analysis: A methodological approach. *Journal for the Theory of Social Behaviour, 41*(2), 182–202. https://doi.org/10.1111/j.1468-5914.2010.00451.x.

Kosenko, K. (2014). Uncertainty management theory. In T. L. Thompson (Ed.), *Encyclopedia of health communication* (pp. 1426–1427). Sage Publications Ltd.

Kuo, Y. (2002). International teaching assistants on American campuses. *International Journal of Curriculum and Instruction, 4*(1), 63–71.

McDonald, J. P. (1992). *Teaching: Making sense of an uncertain craft*. Teachers College Press.

Motha, S., Jain, R. & Tecle, T. (2012). Translinguistic identity-as-pedagogy: Implications for teacher education. *International Journal of Innovation in English Language Teaching and Research, 1*(1), 13–28.

Nelson, G. L. (1992). The relationship between the use of personal, cultural examples in international teaching assistants' lectures and uncertainty reduction, student attitude, student recall, and ethnocentrism. *International Journal of Intercultural Relations, 16*(1), 33–52. https://doi.org/10.1016/0147-1767(92)90004-E.

Ohio State Office of Student Academic Success. (2019). New first year student trend data. http://oesar.osu.edu/pdf/admissions/NFQF_Au_15thday_web.pdf.

Ohio State Writing Across the Curriculum. (2016a). Cultures of support for second-level writing a survey of 2367 instructors. https://cstw.osu.edu/sites/default/files/2021-05/2016_WAC_White_Paper_on_2367_Cultures_of_Support.pdf.

Ohio State Writing Across the Curriculum. (2016b). Strategies to unlock student engagement across disciplines: A study of second-level writing course documents at Ohio State. https://cstw.osu.edu/sites/default/files/2021-05/WAC_White_Paper_2_Course_Docs.pdf.

Roundtree, S. V. (2019). *Pedagogies of noise: Black women's teaching efficacy and pedagogical approaches in composition classrooms* [Doctoral dissertation, The Ohio State University]. OhioLINK Electronic Theses and Dissertations Center.

Ruecker, T., Frazier, S. & Tseptsura, M. (2018). "Language difference can be an asset": Exploring the experiences of nonnative English-speaking teachers of writing. *College Composition and Communication, 69*(4), 612–641. https://www.jstor.org/stable/44870978.

Smith, J. K. (2008). Interpretive inquiry. In L. M. Given (Ed.), *The Sage encyclopedia of qualitative research* (pp. 459–461). Sage.

Wolff, D. & De Costa, P. I. (2017). Expanding the language teacher identity landscape: An investigation of the emotions and strategies of a NNEST. *The Modern Language Journal, 101*(S1), 76–90. https://doi.org/10.1111/modl.12370.

Yazan, B. & Rudolph, N. (2018). Introduction: Apprehending identity, experience, and (in)equity through and beyond binaries. In B. Yazan & N. Rudolph (Eds.), *Criticality, teacher identity, and (in)equity in English language teaching: Issues and implications* (pp. 1–19). Springer.

Zacharias, N. T. (2018). Attitudes of NNESTs toward themselves. In J. I. Liontas (Ed.), *The TESOL encyclopedia of English language teaching*. Wiley. https://doi.org/10.1002/9781118784235.eelt0007.

Zheng, X. (2017). Translingual identity as pedagogy: International teaching assistants of English in college composition classrooms. *The Modern Language Journal, 101*(S1), 29–44. https://doi.org/10.1111/modl.12373.

Zhou, J. (2009). What is missing in the international teaching assistants training curriculum? *Journal of Faculty Development, 23*(2), 19–24.

10 Identity and Professional Development of First-year NNES Teachers: Two Case Studies

Xin Chen
INDIANA UNIVERSITY BLOOMINGTON (IUB)

Given the large population of international students pursuing graduate degrees in the US and thus becoming graduate instructors in U.S. institutions, it is critical to study how those non-native English-speaking (NNES) teachers construct their identities and develop their profession in the new discourse communities, especially during their first year of teaching. The complexity of academic socialization, which involves negotiating various cultures, competence and power relations (Her, 2005; Pavlenko, 2003), has warranted research into NNES teachers' experiences in English-speaking countries, and a great deal of this research focuses on identity issues. Furthermore, teacher identity has been recognized as a critical issue in teacher education with "identity" used as analytical lens to better understand teachers' development (Beauchamp & Thomas, 2009). In the literature of teacher education, Myron Friesen and Susan Belsey (2013) see an increasing emphasis on "the teacher as a person, and the interaction of personal and professional selves" (p. 23). Studies also show that the development of teacher identity is conducive to a teacher's decision-making (Beijaard et al., 2004), effectiveness (Sammons et al., 2007) and educational philosophy (Mockler, 2011). However, not many teacher identity studies focus on how NNES graduate instructors, who were not enrolled in teacher education programs, negotiate their identities as both students and teachers to develop their profession as educators in particular. For those instructors, their teacher identity can be more complex because they have not been systematically trained to be teachers but rely more on the learning from their own teaching experience and interacting with colleagues for professional development. Thus, their interactions with students and other peer NNES graduate instructors also play an important role in their teacher identity formation, but we still have insufficient understanding of how they learn to teach and develop their teacher identity.

Taking this into account, this research aims to explore the relationship between NNES teachers' identity formation and professional development, especially during their first year teaching. It focuses on two NNES graduate instructors who were teaching their first language (Chinese and Japanese respectively) and English academic writing simultaneously. Their unique experiences provided rich data for case studies of NNES teacher's identity construction and reconstruction along with their professional development. By positioning themselves differently in different classrooms the two focal graduate instructors constructed and reconstructed their teacher identities and developed professionally through individual efforts as well as peer support.

Because teachers' pedagogical decision-making is based on both institutional and biographical factors (Duff & Uchida, 1997), understanding the process of first-year NNES teachers' identity formation will also shed light on how those teachers improve their instructional strategies. The research adopted an interactionalist approach to explore how NNES teachers form identities and develop professionally by focusing on their interactions with peer instructors and students. Through those interactions, the first-year NNES teachers made sense of their own experiences and socialized themselves into the new discourse communities of teaching and studying. In addition, they employed individual agency to negotiate their identities through positioning themselves strategically in different interactional contexts.

A Dynamic View of Teacher Identity and NNES Teachers' Agency

Teacher identity has been a subject of interest in research on teacher education and development because learning to teach "involves not only discovering more about the skills and knowledge of language teaching but also what it means to be a language teacher" (Richards, 2010, p. 110). Recently, there has been an increase of research focused on language teachers' identities (Barkhuizen, 2016; Cheung et al., 2015; Kayi-Aydar, 2019; Norton, 2016; Trent, 2010). Although challenges are found in defining the concepts of identity and teacher identity (Beauchamp & Thomas, 2009), literature on language teacher identity has three primary characteristics: 1) it understands identity as multidimensional and shifting; 2) identity is situated in social, cultural and political contexts; 3) and identity is constructed and negotiated through discourse (Zacharias, 2010). This line of research helps develop new interpretations of "identity," which is recognized as not static, unitary or internally coherent; rather it is pluralistic, shifting, and even in conflict (Miller, 2009; Tsui, 2011). Such understanding of teacher identity foregrounds the importance of agency in identity formation and provides the premise for teacher identity research, i.e., that teachers are internal beings who can actively pursue the identities they want to achieve and transform the identities that are negatively assigned to them (Park, 2012; Reis, 2011; Zhang & Zhang, 2014). In this particular study, the examination of first-year NNES teachers' identity and professional development also relies on this dynamic view of teacher identity. It focuses on how NNES teachers construct and reconstruct multiple identities through their discourse and practice (Varghese et al., 2005) during their first year teaching English academic writing. Identity in this research is operationalized as the ways in which NNES teachers talk about themselves, their roles and their teaching practices, as well as how they position themselves in the social and political contexts of work.

Identity is closely related to social, cultural and political contexts (Duff & Uchida, 1997; Mockler, 2011), which means that researchers need to take into consideration the contextual elements of teacher identity construction such as interlocutors, academic settings and the political environment. This view of identity is also relevant to the study of NNES teachers' identity because many NNES teachers tend to experience professional and social marginalization both inside and outside schools through different discourses (Casanave & Schecter, 1997; Johnston, 1999; Widodo et al., 2020; Yazan & Rudolph, 2018). Accordingly, Laura Ahearn's (2001) construct of agency—"the socioculturally mediated capacity to act" (p. 112) is useful in studying NNES teachers' identities because language, culture, and society are mutually constituted and agency could also contribute to identity construction and reconstruction. Although the validity of the dichotomy between NES and NNES has been problematized by many scholars (e.g., Faez, 2011b; E. Lee & Canagarajah, 2019; Liu, 2013) and the assumption that the ideal teacher of English is a NES has been criticized as the "native speaker fallacy" (Phillipson, 1992, p. 185), the dominant "either/or discourse" (i.e., NES or NNES teacher) in English language teaching unavoidably results in negative impacts on NNES teachers' self-esteem (Faez, 2011a; Selvi, 2009). It divides English language teachers into two social categories that enjoy different power and status, and NNES teachers are "constantly reminded of their NNES group membership in their own comparison with peers, their confidence about academic work, and interaction with faculty and students" (Varghese et al, 2005, p. 25).

Manka Varghese's (2004) study reinforced the agency of individual teachers in the process of identity formation to ease the tension between assigned identity and claimed identity. In the case of NNES teachers, re-imagination and repositioning of themselves allows teachers "not only to view themselves positively but also to transmit these views to others and to engage in active attempts to reshape the surrounding contexts" (Pavlenko, 2003, p. 266). Research has demonstrated that NNES teachers benefit more from a friendly environment with collegial support in terms of confidence gaining and professional development (e.g., Braine, 2010; Mahboob, 2010). Nevertheless, from a poststructuralist view, individuals as agents are able to develop alternative understanding of self and visions about the world. The environment may impose authoritative discourse upon NNES teachers (e.g., they are not as competent as NES teachers or don't have the legitimacy to teach the English language) but they can also develop a sense of agency to open new possibilities for understanding their teaching as well as their self.

Moreover, many new teachers struggle to reconcile their conflicting identities as student and teacher (Britzman, 1991; Friesen & Belsey, 2013). Similarly, for NNES graduate instructors of English academic writing in this research, they face more challenges to balance their multiple identities such as a learner of English language while also a teacher of English writing. The attitudes of the people around them will considerably influence their consciousness of their status as NNESs. Therefore, seeking membership in a group that is supportive will help NNES teachers forge a positive identity as a teacher (Johnson, 1992; Norton, 2016). In this research, the focal NNES teachers joined a study group in which they exchanged teaching resources with other NNES teachers and supported each other intellectually as well as emotionally. This study group played an important role in those NNES teachers' self-identification and development of professional identity.

Drawing upon Vygotskian sociocultural theory, Davi S. Reis (2011) explored how a NNES teacher developed his professional identity and established his legitimacy as a qualified English writing instructor against the native speaker (NS) fallacy. He found that a teacher preparation program with a supportive environment would enable NNES teachers to reshape their instruction "in response to more empowering conceptualizations of self" (Reis, 2011, p. 141). The NS fallacy often causes a sense of professional inadequacy for NNES teachers to become confident instructors (Llurda, 2005), but Lia D. Kamhi-Stein (2013) argued that NNESs could achieve positive professional identity with legitimacy by being empowered to recognize and contest ideological discourses that discriminate and marginalize them implicitly or explicitly. Furthermore, researchers and teacher educators have proposed collaborations between NES and NNES teachers to build a positive and productive learning community for both (e.g., de Oliveira & Clark-Gareca, 2017; Matsuda, 1999). The collaborative model can also be applied to NNES teachers among themselves, where NNES teachers are given voice about their stories and are empowered by interactions with peers.

A sociocultural perspective on identity construction and transformation indicates that one's identity arises from the dialectical relationship between the individual and the social context (Cheung et al., 2014; Valsiner, 1998; Wetherell & Maybin, 1996). The professional development of NNES teachers involves their awareness of how they position themselves as teachers and how they are positioned by the public discourse: "as teachers develop new beliefs and acquire new attitudes to their practice, as they adopt new pedagogies, and as they see themselves taking on certain roles in their work contexts, they construct new identities as teachers" (I. Lee, 2013, p. 331). Through critical reflection and collaborative inquiry about their belief and attitudes towards the public discourse, teachers might have a better idea of how to position themselves in both the local and the broad contexts. In particular, NNES teachers can benefit from social mediation and collaboration in conceiving of and internalizing identity options that lead to more professional agency (Reis, 2011). Thus, how individuals dialogically engage with hegemonic ideologies and confront them with instructional strategies is also crucial in the identity formation for NNES teachers.

Methodology

This study on how NNES teachers develop professionally is guided by the following questions: 1) How do first-year NNES graduate instructors negotiate multiple identities (e.g., from graduate students to graduate instructors and from NES language teachers to NNES writing teachers) by positioning themselves in different classrooms? 2) How do they construct and reconstruct teacher identities and develop professionally through individual efforts and peer support?

This chapter comes from a larger qualitative study, which investigated how a group of graduate instructors of English academic writing at a research university in the Midwestern US constructed and reconstructed their identities to improve themselves in the first year of teaching. It looks closely at the cases of two focal teachers who were teaching their first language (as NES language teachers) and English academic writing (as NNES writing teachers) at the same time. My work focuses on the links that teachers see between their previous educational experiences, their multiple identities, and their teaching practices in the classroom.

Research Setting

The setting of this study is a first-year writing (FYW) course for ESL (English as a second language) students. This course is offered in the same program as regular FYW courses, but includes a stronger focus on helping students address particular linguistic concerns. Accordingly, the instructors of the ESL version of this course are expected to have knowledge of second language writing and pedagogy. The FYW course is required for all undergraduate students at the university and only those students whose English placement test scores meet the departmental standard are eligible to take it. The ESL FYW students completed previous studies in languages other than English and most of them are international students. The course takes place for 50 minutes three days a week and the enrollment cap for each class is 15 students.

Participants

Rachel (self-chosen pseudonym) and Jason (self-chosen pseudonym) were two graduate instructors of this course. Both of them are NNES and taught the ESL FYW course for the first time when the study was conducted. Meanwhile, they had been teaching their first language (Chinese and Japanese respectively) at the same university. They were selected as the focal teachers for this chapter because of their unique experiences of teaching first language and second language simultaneously. In particular, I looked into how their identities shifted and transformed when they were positioned as NNES and NES in different language classrooms.

Rachel is from China, in her early thirties. She came to the US for graduate school and already got a master's degree in Chinese language pedagogy from the university where she was studying and working. During her master's studies, she taught Chinese language to college students as a graduate instructor. Rachel was pursuing a Ph.D. degree in English language education when she participated in this study. Although it was her first year teaching English academic writing at college level in the US, she had been teaching the Chinese course in the same university for two years.

Jason is from Japan, in his late twenties. He received an MA in education in another university in the US and came to the university where this study was conducted to pursue his Ph.D. in the same program as Rachel did. Jason had extensive experience teaching Japanese as a foreign language in different U.S. universities and was teaching Japanese courses when he was assigned to teach the ESL FYW course for the first time.

Neither Rachel or Jason had experiences of teaching English academic writing at college level before, and they were enrolled in a practicum on teaching of composition when interviewed for this study. The practicum is required for all first-year graduate instructors of FYW but the instructors of the ESL version would be trained with a focus on working with ESL students.

Data Collection and Analysis

To understand how the focal teachers position themselves in the social context of their work, I observed the writing classes that the participants taught, spending five hours in each classroom throughout the semester. The Chinese and Japanese language classes were not observed due to lack of permission, but both the teachers talked about their language classes in the interview to provide an idea about how they teach their first language. Evaluative observation forms and ethnographic field notes are used for each observation. Those forms and notes documented the teachers' teaching practices and interactions with students in the classroom. I also conducted audio recorded interviews with the instructors at the end of the semester asking about their relationship with the students, experiences in the classroom, self-development, and their perspectives on the teacher identities. Each interview lasted about 90 minutes. Interviews were transcribed verbatim, after which I coded each transcript and sorted codes into overarching themes including teacher role and positioning, instructional practice and self-reflection, individual efforts and peer support for professional development. Additionally, I selected classroom data that exemplified trends in improvement of instructional strategies that I observed. For example, how the teachers used plain English rather than the sophisticated language in the textbook to explain a point of knowledge in composition so as to make it easier for ESL students to understand, and how they pose analytical questions to facilitate students' discussion and learning. Then I combined my observations with the interview data to illustrate how first-year NNES teachers develop professionally with individual efforts as well as peer support.

Findings

Rachel and Jason's multiple identities (such as NNES and NES, doctoral students and graduate instructors) shifted and transformed during their first year of teaching English academic writing but they had navigated their own ways to negotiate the conflicting identities and constructed positive teacher identities to develop themselves professionally. This section will discuss how the two focal teachers constructed and reconstructed teacher identities by positioning themselves differently in different classrooms (NES language teachers vs. NNES writing teachers) and how they developed professionally through individual efforts as well as peer support. Looking into the two NNES teachers' experiences of first-year teaching also sheds light on what influence teachers' attitudes, beliefs and decision-making process in their everyday classroom practices (Zacharias, 2010).

Negotiating and Reconstructing Teacher Identities

Previous educational experiences will, to a great extent, shape teachers' perception of good teaching and influence their self-positioning in the classroom. As international graduate students functioning in their second language, Rachel's and Jason's experiences enabled them to shuttle between different teaching contexts and be sympathetic with the ESL students they were teaching. More importantly, their dual identity as student teachers made them tend to consider teaching from students' perspective. In the interview data, teacher-student relationships stood out as a major concern in their teaching. Both of the participants wanted to be the kind of teacher that they longed to have as a student and the differences between the teacher-student relationship in their home country and that in the US also had an impact on their expectation of the relationship with their own students. As Jason related,

> ... back in my country, teachers have more authority ... so it's hard to reach to our professors in Japan. I mean, it's OK to ask questions but not, not many people do that just because they feel more distance between students and teachers. But here, ... we get to interact with each other more often. I think that's makes our relationship closer.

Similarly, Rachel also felt the distance between teachers and students during the college years in her home country:

> I have never had instructors who are graduate students because in my college it's always professor ... older professor ... I have questions to ask and I really cannot find the answer then I might go to them but not for other concerns. ... If it is not necessary, I don't want to bother them because I think ... they are professors and I feel there's a distance between me and them so if I never had that kind of relationship ...

From those quotes, we can tell that both Rachel and Jason wanted to make themselves accessible and supportive to the students. Jason used the words "friendly" and "open" to describe the ideal relationship he would like to have with his students while Rachel described her as a "cheerleader" in class and positioned herself as a mentor rather than an instructor: "I try to be more like a mentor because I experienced a process they are going through right now so I think from that perspective I know what they are thinking ..." It is worth noting that although they preferred to have stronger teacher-student relationship, Rachel and Jason embraced mixed feelings about the closeness with the students, which sometimes would also result in students' trying to challenge them or negotiate about the course policies. As Rachel noted, "I'm trying to be helpful but they would think they can negotiate with me and that would be one weakness in managing the class." Jason felt that students often did not respect him as a teacher, though he enjoyed greetings from the students when they ran into each other outside the classroom. As can be seen from these examples, it became apparent that a crucial part of the two participants' teacher identity construction concerned their roles as teachers and students and how to position themselves in the classroom in a way that balanced authority with approachability.

Interestingly, the interviews with Rachel and Jason also revealed that they felt the same level of comfort teaching their first language courses (as NES teachers) as compared with the English writing course (as NNES teachers). Rachel admitted that she felt more confident teaching Chinese while Jason felt that he had more authority when teaching Japanese as a native speaker.

> Rachel: It's because I'm the native speaker so I feel comfortable even tell them I don't know this or I never heard about this but you might be right . . . but I don't feel comfortable to say that in the English writing class. I don't feel comfortable to tell them I have never heard about this . . . I try to make them feel or believe like I know everything you are talking about, which is not true.

> Jason: . . . when I teach Japanese, especially this semester, I teach Japanese 101. So they are zero level. So everything I say they believe it . . . But in the English class, they already know some maybe basic English or some of them are more proficient in terms of speaking. So, when I explain something, . . . I sometimes feel that they don't really believe me because . . . I speak less fluently than some of them do . . . And also I'm a native speaker of Japanese, so I have more authority (in the Japanese class).

Both the participants were more confident teaching their first languages, and they recognized that the experiences of teaching their first language influenced their pedagogy of teaching English academic writing as an NNES teacher.

Research shows that many NNES teachers feel their confidence and authority in the classroom is threatened and they are often disempowered by their students' stereotype of an authentic English teacher (e.g., Widodo et al.,

2020; Zhang & Zhang, 2014). The authoritative discourse of the program they study or teach in constructs them as NNES teachers with low status and less power, but marginalized individuals such as NNES teachers can actively change the status quo through local teaching practice and at the same time develop themselves professionally (Simon-Maeda, 2004).

Self and Peer Support for Professional Development

Despite the challenges in first-year teaching, the participants in the study illustrated how they improved their teaching practice through both individual and collective efforts. Such improvement also helped them to construct more positive teacher identities for their teaching career. On top of that, the instructional strategies that those teachers adopted (based on either personal experience or peer support) reflected their identity transformation during the process of professional development.

As NNES teachers in the US, Rachel and Jason agreed that winning students' trust and establishing legitimacy was very important for them, especially when they faced negative judgements due to their accents. They had attempted to deal with student prejudice by sharing personal stories as second language learners with the ESL students and referencing authorities in the field. Personal experience learning English, a unique asset of NNES teachers, served as a way of demonstrating their development from a novice language learner to a successful one. It also enabled Rachel to form a stronger bond with the students: "I guess my strength (of being an NNES teacher) is I also experienced (what the students have experienced) so I know why they are doing that and what they might think difficult in doing that, so they would buy what I say because I know what you are thinking." In addition, Jason tapped into pedagogical theories that validated language difference in the classroom. With these strategies, Rachel and Jason were able to build a positive relationship with their students and gain credibility in their own classrooms.

Since teaching writing to ESL students also involves teaching culture, Rachel and Jason had to research into specific elements of U.S. culture that they had little knowledge about in the textbooks and spent more time preparing lessons in order to teach with better understanding of the content. For example, when teaching the five analytical moves (from *Writing Analytically by Rosenwasser and Stephen*)—Suspend Judgement, Define Significant Parts & How They Are Related, Make the Implicit Explicit, Look for Patterns, and Keep Reformulating, which are based on a Western epistemology, Jason designed a series of visuals himself to help students understand the concepts such as suspending judgement, and making the implicit explicit. Moreover, they would ask NES colleagues about the cultural references that they did not know. Jason found this collaboration very helpful and not only beneficial to them but also to the NES teachers, because the NES teachers could also figure out what part of the teaching materials might not make sense to their students from different cultures. Most of the time, Rachel and Jason would look for examples that were relevant to their students' culture and life rather than adopting the exact examples in the U.S.-centered textbook. As Tyrone Howard (2001) suggested, culturally relevant teaching can promote students' motivation and NNES teachers have advantages in terms of cross-cultural competence.

The participants' strategy to deal with anxieties as first-year NNES teachers was to build self-confidence as well as rapport with the students. For example, one student in Jason's class also wanted the instructors to help him improve vocabulary complexity, sentence variety and stylistic choices of writing. However, as an ESL writer himself, Jason knew it was not something an NNES can learn within a short period of time. Explaining this to his students, he provided more resources along with guidance in using them in hope that students could develop their writing over time. Rachel also shared her own experiences as an ESL student and told the students that they were learning together and she was more than willing to help them with all her capacity. Through reflecting on their experience as teachers in different language classrooms and as students in different countries, the participants employed agency to negotiate and reconstruct the multiple and even conflicting identities across contexts. As their teacher identities shifted and transformed in different teaching contexts, they were also able to build positive relationship with students and became more confident NNES teachers in the US.

> Rachel: I think it's getting better and better. The first a few weeks were more difficult as I felt myself not ready even though I spent the whole summer preparing for this course. I was very self-conscious as an NNES teacher in the FYW class and always worry about how my students perceive me. Do I know enough about the English language and English writing? What if the student asked a question and I don't have the answer? Because in many Asian countries including my home country, teachers are like "sages" who are expected to know everything . . . But now, I realized that if I am being sincere and supportive, students are willing to learn with me, not "through" me.
>
> Jason: The first semester (of teaching a new course) is always challenging because you are not familiar with the (teaching)

content. For me, it is also a different group of students and I need to think more about what they need. In my Japanese classes, students want me to teach more about the language techniques and maybe also Japanese culture, because they see me as a native speaker, an expert on the language and the culture behind it. But in the FYW class, most of them are international and ESL students, and I need to overcome the tendency to see my NNES background as a disadvantage, which often makes me nervous. In fact, I noticed that my ESL students appreciated I sharing my own experiences of learning English academic writing as an NNES. My understanding of their linguistic challenges also made them trust me.

Moreover, both Rachel and Jason were enrolled in the practicum on teaching FYW and they formed a study group with other first-year NNES teachers for peer support. The members of the study group met regularly to check in with each other, and they developed teaching materials together. They also shared resources and exchanged ideas about curriculum and pedagogy. The study group, as a supplement to the practicum, contributed to the professional development of those first-year teachers in many ways. While the study group created a discourse community where NNES teachers could share their experiences and feel valued, both Rachel and Jason still expected more guidance from the practicum. They sought explicit directions from the program director and advanced teachers, who were all NES teachers. Rachel explained,

> They've got lot of resources over there. We don't even know when to use that . . . and also we don't really know whether we are doing the right thing because all of us (first-year teachers of English academic writing) are guessing but I mean we as a group is very helpful, like the way we support each other.

Here Rachel was saying that they were offered many teaching materials from the classic version of FYW, which is usually taught by NES teachers to NES students. Nevertheless, those materials were not necessarily making sense to NNES students or even teachers due to cultural or linguistic barriers. Therefore, the NNES teachers in the study group worked together to adapt those materials and made them more helpful to ESL students.

> Rachel: For example, when teaching visual analysis, the teacher (of the classic version of FYW) shared with me a few posters she used as examples to guide students to analyze the visual el-

ements. I appreciate it that she shared her lesson plan, but those posters contain some cultural signs that many students who are not from the US would not get the meaning. So, we (NNES teachers in the study group) worked together to find some other posters from different cultures so that students from various cultural backgrounds could feel them more relevant. I myself also felt more comfortable teaching with the posters we found because they reflected a wider range of cultural perspectives and some of them aligned with my cultural identity.

Jason acknowledged the usefulness of the practicum as well as the study group, but he also pointed out that more sharing and communication with the experienced teacher, most of whom happened to be NES teachers, can be added to improve the practicum. On the contrary, he was completely satisfied with the study group consisting of NNES teachers and had no further suggestions on that.

> I learned a lot from both practicum and this study group . . . I have no suggestion for the study group, but practicum . . . maybe it's sometimes better to have more experienced (NES) teachers…so that we can see what they are saying based on their experience.

Discussion and Conclusion

Teacher identity has now been widely recognized as a crucial component in teaching and classroom practice (Tsui, 2011; Zacharias, 2010). The identities that teachers bring with them into the classroom will influence the learning dynamic and the interpersonal interactions in the class (Boomer, 1998). As Lawrence Jun Zhang and Donglan Zhang (2014) pointed out,

> teachers' identities are constructed by their own practice in conjunction with the professional knowledge and expertise they bring to the workplace and the work they do. Meanwhile, their identities are also constructed by their students through the words students use and the behaviors and actions that embody their attitudes toward their teachers. (p. 119)

Ultimately, Rachel and Jason had more commonalities than differences in their experiences as NNES teachers. It can be seen that the NNES identity stood out in their multiple teacher identities. Bonny Norton and Kelleen Toohey (2011) argued that language can be a site of struggle in NNES teachers' journey of professional development. Nevertheless, both of the participants managed to transform the drawbacks related to this identity into strength in teaching. Although they faced many challenges as first year NNES writing teachers in the US, Rachel and Jason spared no effort to become the ideal teachers that they wanted to have when they were students. Douwe Beijaard and colleagues (2004) contended that teachers develop their professional identities through interpretations and reinterpretations of who they are and who they would like to become. They built on their experiences of teaching their first language and drew upon cross-cultural competence to improve their teaching practice. They also adapted the U.S.-centered teaching materials to make them more inclusive and suitable for ESL students with different cultural and linguistic backgrounds, which demonstrated that NNESs had their own advantages and could tap into the resources they bring with them transnationally into the classroom.

More than often, NNES teachers have lower professional status than NES teachers because English language teaching as a profession has positioned NES as the ideal English teacher (Moussu & Llurda, 2008). As Zhang and Zhang (2014) contend, when standards of English are defined in favor of native speakers, NNES teachers' identities are closely related to how NES colleagues and students regard their performance and competence vis-à-vis the legitimacy of their professional practice. Although NNES teachers have been acknowledged to have more metalinguistic awareness due to their language learning experiences, they usually lack the confidence and information to navigate the sociopolitical contexts in which they teach English (Park, 2012). Moreover, the NNES/NES dichotomy tends to neglect the multiple identities of NNES teachers that might be drawn upon as strengths. Therefore, NNES teachers often struggle to gain credibility for themselves as qualified English language teachers. Pursuing graduate degrees in English-speaking countries and learning from NES colleagues are common ways NNES teachers (e.g., the participants in this study) take to seek credibility and reconstruct their identities as English language teachers. However, they sometimes tend to underestimate their own linguistic and cultural assets which could actually become their advantages in teaching English. In this study, both Rachel and Jason had made good use of their multilingual and multicultural background to adapt teaching materials developed by NES teachers. Meanwhile, they were also eager to work with NES teachers and learn from them.

Furthermore, the findings of this research reinforced that teacher identity also plays an important role in professional development. Especially for NNES teachers, they usually have to negotiate and reconstruct their identities according to the different contexts they are studying and teaching. Carla Dawn

Nelson (2003) found that attention to NNES teachers' shifting identities can help enhance their confidence and give them a sense of wholeness of life. For instance, the teachers in this study drew upon their own identities to enrich their teaching resources and built a healthy relationship with their students, which has been shown to ultimately be more effective than clinging to NES norms (Amin, 2005; Morgan, 2004). In addition to their individual efforts, it is worth mentioning that peer support is also vital for those teachers to develop professionally. In the study group formed by their cohort of NNES teachers, they shared resources, exchanged ideas and met regularly to make sure no member was isolated or left behind. The study group created a discourse community where those teachers helped each other to gain confidence and built on their own identities for instructional improvement rather than just following the NES norms.

Critical theories inform the complexities of the construction of NES and NNES, which involves power relationship among different language status and races of the speakers. Many researchers have proposed that critical pedagogy and cross-culture competence need to be encompassed in the curriculum of teacher education programs (e.g., Kamhi-Stein, 2013; Pavlenko, 2003). Narges Sardabi and colleagues (2018) found in their study that the teacher education program attempting to help novice teachers develop a critical perspective could empower them to "be engaged in the effort to shape their values and beliefs, and to produce their own critical philosophy of teaching" (p. 621). Besides, cross-culture competence needs to be promoted in teacher education because it will enable teachers to better understand how students' way of learning and knowing are shaped by their native or home culture and enhance their instructional practice accordingly (Woolworth & Thirumurthy, 2012). This chapter argues that cross-cultural competence and critical self-reflections are essential for NNES teachers' professional development. The environment may impose authoritative discourses upon NNES teachers, which sometimes affects their identity formation negatively. Nevertheless, engaging with critical reflections on their own experiences of teaching and learning across different cultural contexts will "open up new discourses and offer new identity options" (Ilieva, 2010, p. 362) that allow them to develop agency as professionals. The sense of agency will also provide opportunities for NNES teachers to develop "alternative instructional practices that are compatible with positive imagined identities" (Ilieva, 2010, p. 362).

In addition to practicum and formal workshops for teacher training and development, program administrators should encourage and provide more opportunities for NNES teachers to communicate and collaborate with each other. NNES teachers can work together to collect more resources for students and share effective teaching practices to improve their profession collaboratively.

It is also important for NNES teachers, especially first-year teachers, to support each other psychologically and construct positive teacher identities against the negative public discourse which tends to marginalize them. Those opportunities could be informal meetings or a shared working space where teachers are able to socialize among themselves. It will be also beneficial to encourage collaborations between NNES teachers and NES teachers (de Oliveira & Clark-Gareca, 2017; Matsuda, 1999), which would support teachers in building a positive and productive learning community for all.

References

Ahearn, L. M. (2001). Language and agency. *Annual Review of Anthropology, 30,* 109–137. https://doi.org/10.1146/annurev.anthro.30.1.109.

Amin, N. (2005). Nativism, the native speaker construct, and minority immigrant women teachers of English as a second language. In L. D. Kamhi-Stein (Ed.), *Learning and teaching from experience: Perspectives on nonnative English speaking professionals* (pp. 61–80). The University of Michigan Press. http://www.catesoljournal.org/wp-content/uploads/2014/07/CJ13_amin.pdf.

Barkhuizen, G. P. (Ed.). (2016). *Reflections on language teacher identity research.* Routledge. https://doi.org/10.4324/9781315643465.

Beauchamp, C. & Thomas, L. (2009). Understanding teacher identity: An overview of issues in the literature and implications for teacher education. *Cambridge Journal of Education, 39,* 175–189. https://doi.org/10.1080/03057640902902252.

Beijaard, D., Meijer, P. C. & Verloop, N. (2004). Reconsidering research on teachers' professional identity. *Teaching and Teacher Education, 20,* 107–128. https://doi.org/10.1016/j.tate.2003.07.001.

Boomer, G. (1998). *Metaphors and meanings: Essays on English teaching.* Australian Association for the Teaching of English.

Braine, G. (2010). *Nonnative speaker English teachers: Research, pedagogy, and professional growth.* Routledge.

Britzman, D. P. (1991). *Practice makes practice: A critical study of learning to teach.* State University of New York Press.

Casanave, C. P. & Schecter, S. R. (Eds.). (1997). *On becoming a language educator: Personal essays on professional development.* Lawrence Erlbaum Associates, Inc.

Cheung, Y. L., Said, S. B. & Park, K. (Eds.). (2014). *Advances and current trends in language teacher identity research.* https://doi.org/10.4324/9781315775135.

de Oliveira, L. C. & Clark-Gareca, B. (2017). Collaboration between NESTs and NNESTs. In J. De Dios Martinez Agudo (Ed.), *Native and non-native teachers in English language classrooms: Professional challenges and teacher education* (pp. 317–336). https://doi.org/10.1515/9781501504143-016.

Duff, P. A. & Uchida, Y. (1997). The negotiation of teachers' sociocultural identities and practices in postsecondary EFL classrooms. *TESOL Quarterly, 31,* 451–486. https://doi.org/10.2307/3587834.

Faez, F. (2011a). Are you a native speaker of English? Moving beyond a simplistic dichotomy. *Critical Inquiry in Language Studies, 8*(4), 378–399. https://doi.org/10.1080/15427587.2011.615708.

Faez, F. (2011b). Reconceptualizing the native/nonnative speaker dichotomy. *Journal of Language, Identity & Education, 10*(4), 231–249. https://doi.org/10.1080/15348458.2011.598127.

Friesen, M. D. & Besley, S. C. (2013). Teacher identity development in the first year of teacher education: A developmental and social psychological perspective. *Teaching and Teacher Education, 36*, 23–32. https://doi.org/10.1016/j.tate.2013.06.005.

Her, Y. (2005). Identity construction in literacy practices in L2: A case study of three Korean graduate students in a TESOL program. *Second Language Studies, 23*(2), 102–137. http://www.hawaii.edu/sls/wp-content/uploads/2014/09/8-Her-Younghee.pdf.

Howard, T. C. (2001). Telling their side of the story: African-American students' perceptions of culturally relevant teaching. *The Urban Review, 33*(2), 131–149. https://doi.org/10.1023/A:1010393224120.

Ilieva, R. (2010). Non-native English-speaking teachers' negotiations of program discourses in their construction of professional identities within a TESOL program. *The Canadian Modern Language Review, 66*, 343–369.

Johnson, K. E. (1992). Learning to teach: Instructional actions and decisions of preservice ESL teachers. *TESOL Quarterly, 26*(3), 507–535. https://doi.org/10.2307/3587176.

Johnston, B. (1999). The expatriate teacher as postmodern paladin. *Research in the Teaching of English, 34*(2), 255–280. http://www.jstor.org/stable/40171475.

Kamhi-Stein, L. D. (2013). Preparing non-native professionals in TESOL: Implications for teacher education programs. In G. Braine (Ed.), *Non-native educators in English language teaching* (pp. 167–180). Lawrence Erlbaum Associates. https://doi.org/10.4324/9781315045368.

Kayi-Aydar, H. (2019). Language teacher identity. *Language Teaching, 52*(3), 281–295. https://doi.org/10.1017/s0261444819000223.

Lee, E. & Canagarajah, S. A. (2019). Beyond native and nonnative: Translingual dispositions for more inclusive teacher identity in language and literacy education. *Journal of Language, Identity & Education, 18*(6), 352–363. https://doi.org/10.1080/15348458.2019.1674148.

Lee, I. (2013). Becoming a writing teacher: Using "identity" as an analytic lens to understand EFL writing teachers' development. *Journal of Second Language Writing, 22*(3), 330–345. https://doi.org/10.1016/j.jslw.2012.07.001.

Liu, D. (2013). Training non-native TESOL students: Challenges for TESOL teacher education in the West. In G. Braine (Ed.), *Non-native educators in English language teaching* (pp. 197–210). Lawrence Erlbaum Associates. https://doi.org/10.4324/9781315045368.

Llurda, E. (Ed.). (2005). *Non-native language teachers: Perceptions, challenges, and contributions to the profession*. Springer.

Mahboob, A. (Ed.). (2010). *The NNEST lens: Non-native English speakers in TESOL*. Cambridge Scholars Publishing.

Matsuda, P. K. (1999). Teacher development through NS/NNS collaboration. *TESOL Matters, 9*(6), 1–10.

Miller, J. (2009). Teacher identity. *The Cambridge Guide to Second Language Teacher Education, 4*, 172–181. https://doi.org/10.1017/9781139042710.023.

Mockler, N. (2011). Beyond "what works": Understanding teacher identity as a practical and political tool. *Teachers and teaching, 17*(5), 517–528. https://doi.org/10.1080/13540602.2011.602059.

Morgan, B. D. (2004). Teacher identity as pedagogy: Towards a field-internal conceptualization in bilingual and second language education. *International Journal of Bilingual Education and Bilingualism, 7*(2–3), 172–188. https://doi.org/10.1080/13670050408667807.

Moussu, L. & Llurda, E., (2008). Non-native English-speaking English language teachers: history and research. *Language Teaching, 41*(3), 315–348. https://doi.org/10.1017/S0261444808005028.

Nelson, C. D. (2003). *"Stories to live by": A narrative inquiry into five teachers shifting identities through the borderlands of cross-cultural professional development*. [Doctoral thesis, University of Alberta]. National Library of Canada. https://tinyurl.com/3zv63bar.

Norton, B. (2016). Learner investment and language teacher identity. In G. Barkhuizen (Ed.), *Reflections on language teacher identity research* (pp. 88–94). Routledge. https://doi.org/10.4324/9781315643465-17.

Norton, B. & Toohey, K. (2011). Identity, language learning and social change. *Language Teaching, 44*, 412–446. https://doi.org/10.1017/S0261444811000309.

Park, G. (2012). "I am never afraid of being recognized as an NNES:" One teachers' journey in claiming and embracing her non-native speaker identity. *TESOL Quarterly, 46*(1), 127–151. https://doi.org/10.1002/tesq.4.

Pavlenko, A. (2003). "I never knew I was bilingual": Re-imagining teacher identities in TESOL. *Journal of Language, Identity and Education, 2*(4), 251–268. https://doi.org/10.1207/S15327701jlie0204_2.

Phillipson, R. (1992). *Linguistic imperialism*. Oxford University Press.

Reis, D. S. (2011). Non-native English-speaking teachers (NNESTs) and professional legitimacy: A sociocultural theoretical perspective on identity transformation. *International Journal of the Sociology of Language, 2011*(208), 139–160. https://doi.org/10.1515/ijsl.2011.016.

Richards, J. C. (2010). Competence and performance in language teaching. *RELC Journal, 41*(2), 101–122. https://doi.org/10.1177/0033688210372953.

Rosenwasser, D. & Stephen, J. (2015). *Writing Analytically*. Cengage Learning.

Sammons, P., Day, C., Kington, A., Gu, Q., Stobart, G. & Smees, R. (2007). Exploring variations in teachers' work, lives and their effects on pupils: key findings and implications from a longitudinal mixed-method study. *British Educational Research Journal, 33*(5), 681–701. https://doi.org/10.1080/01411920701582264.

Sardabi, N., Biria, R. & Golestan, A. A. (2018). Reshaping teacher professional identity through critical pedagogy-informed teacher education. *International Journal of Instruction, 11*(3), 617–634. https://doi.org/10.12973/iji.2018.11342a.

Selvi, A. F. (2009). A call to graduate students to reshape the field of English language teaching. *Essential Teacher, 6*(3–4), 49–51.

Simon-Maeda, A. (2004). The complex construction of professional identities: Female EFL educators in Japan speak out. *TESOL Quarterly, 38*(3), 405–436. https://doi.org/10.2307/3588347.

Trent, J. (2010). Teacher education as identity construction: Insights from action research. *Journal of Education for Teaching, 36*(2), 153–168. https://doi.org/10.1080/02607471003651672.

Tsui, A. B. M. (2011). Complexities of identity formation: A narrative inquiry of an EFL teacher. *TESOL Quarterly, 41*(4), 657–680. https://doi.org/10.1002/j.1545-7249.2007.tb00098.x.

Valsiner, J. (1998). *The guided mind: a sociogenetic approach to personality*. Harvard University Press.

Varghese, M. (2004) Professional development for bilingual teachers in the United States: A site for articulating and contesting professional roles, *International Journal of Bilingual Education and Bilingualism, 7*(2–3), 222–237. http://doi.org/10.1080/13670050408667810.

Varghese, M., Morgan, B., Johnston, B. & Johnson, K. A. (2005). Theorizing language teacher identity: Three perspectives and beyond. *Journal of Language, Identity, and Education, 4*(1), 21–44. https://doi.org/10.1207/s15327701jlie0401_2.

Wetherell, M. & Maybin, J. (1996). The distributed self. In R. Stevens (Ed.), *Understanding the self* (pp. 150–175). Sage.

Widodo, H. P., Fang, F. & Elyas, T. (2020). The construction of language teacher professional identity in the Global Englishes territory: "We are legitimate language teachers." *Asian Englishes, 22*(3), 309–316. https://doi.org/10.1080/13488678.2020.1732683.

Woolworth, S. & Thirumurthy, V. (2012). Promoting cross-cultural competence and awareness in teacher education: Toward the integration of Western and non-Western perspectives. *Northwest Journal of Teacher Education. 10*(1), Article 11. https://doi.org/10.15760/nwjte.2012.10.1.11.

Yazan, B. & Rudolph, N. (2018). Introduction: Apprehending identity, experience, and (in)equity through and beyond binaries. In B. Yazan & N. Rudolph (Eds.), *Criticality, teacher identity, and (in)equity in English language teaching* (pp. 1–19). Springer. https://doi.org/10.1007/978-3-319-72920-6_1.

Zacharias, N. T. (2010). The teacher identity construction of 12 Asian NNES teachers in TESOL graduate programs. *The Journal of Asia TEFL, 7*(2), 177–197.

Zhang, L. J. & Zhang, D. (2014). Identity matters: An ethnography of two nonnative English-speaking teachers (NNESTs) struggling for legitimate professional participation. In Y. L. Cheung, S. B. Said, K. Park (Eds.), *Advances and current trends in language teacher identity research* (pp. 116–131). Routledge.

11 NNESTs, Teacher Education, Language Diversity, and Equality

Melinda Reichelt
UNIVERSITY OF TOLEDO

In this chapter, I describe my experience as the director of an ESL writing program, including my role preparing NNESTs and NESTs to teach ESL writing. I am a NES who completed my undergraduate and graduate degrees in the US. In my graduate work, I focused on linguistics, ESL, L2 writing, and rhetoric/composition. My research and publications have centered primarily on L2 writing, including ESL writing, EFL writing, and writing in non-English L2s. I have also published some work related to world Englishes. Since 1990, I have taught college-level writing, mostly ESL writing. Currently, I am a professor in the English department at the University of Toledo, where I have worked since 1997. Since 2005, I have directed my department's ESL writing program.

To understand the context of my work, it is important to understand the institution where I am employed. The University of Toledo is a public university located in the U.S. Midwest. It enrolls approximately 20,000 students, including about 16,000 undergraduates. It accepts about 94% of its undergraduate applicants. Approximately 870 undergraduate international students attend the university. Until recently, most international undergraduates entered through the university's intensive English program and were allowed to matriculate with a score of 450 on the paper-based, institutional TOEFL. (The score range for this test is 360–677.) Recently, the university has decided to waive this requirement to allow students who graduate from the intensive English program to matriculate without a TOEFL score. In the last several years, more international students have been enrolling in the university without attending the intensive English program; they must achieve a 71 on the iBT (internet-based TOEFL) or equivalent to matriculate. Until recently, all sections of ESL writing at the University of Toledo were taught by TAs earning an MA-TESOL at the University of Toledo through the English department. Typically, eight to 12 ESL TAs taught in the program in any given year, many of whom were NNESs. In most cases, NNES TAs were in the minority, but during some periods, half or more of the ESL TAs were NNESs.

In my university's now-defunct MA-TESOL program, I taught various linguistics courses and courses about ESL pedagogy. Just as the MA-TESOL program was ending, my department started a new MA program in English with a concentration in writing studies. My colleagues in the writing studies concentration were eager to have me continue to teach *Issues in ESL Writing* and *Sociolinguistics* as two required courses in the writing studies concentration.

During more than 17 years as the director of the English department's ESL writing program, I have worked with many NNES TAs. Before I started directing the ESL writing program, I had read some of the NNEST literature and was attuned to such issues as the "native speaker fallacy" (Phillipson, 1992). I had also worked alongside NNES TAs during my graduate studies. However, as the supervisor of the TAs teaching ESL writing at the University of Toledo, I did not initially set out to address the needs of NNES TAs in particular. Rather, my goal was to support all TAs, and frankly, I did not see NNESTs as needing extra help, perhaps because I had never experienced the challenges of being a NNEST myself. I was also influenced by the fact that almost all of the NNES TAs in our program had already taught, typically in their home countries, when they started their MA-TESOL—and thus often seemed more competent than their NES TA counterparts, who rarely had previous teaching experience. Thus, rather than having an explicit plan to support NNES TAs, I found myself adjusting my practices over time to try to meet the needs of the TAs I had—many of whom happened to be NNESTs.

Over the years, I have drawn several conclusions about the needs of NESTs who are preparing to teach writing or currently teaching it. In this chapter, I make several recommendations about the preparation of writing instructors, especially NNES writing instructors, drawing on my years of teaching ESL writing and directing my university's ESL writing program. My recommendations are also based on my background in L2 writing research and sociolinguistics. I argue that in-service and pre-service education for writing instructors, including NNESTs, should focus explicitly on teaching L2 writing. Additionally, I argue that pre-service and in-service writing instructors should also receive in-depth education about issues of language variation and diversity. Finally, I argue that during teacher education and professional development related to writing instruction, NNESTs and NESTs should be treated as equals by their supervisor, who should foster a sense of equality among all TAs.

The Importance of Coursework Related to L2 Writing

Almost all teachers of writing will encounter NNES writers in their courses, whether those courses are mainstream writing courses or courses aimed at

NNES students. Thus, it is important for all future or in-service writing instructors, including NNESTs, to take a course that focuses on teaching ESL writers. It should not be assumed that NNESTs are qualified to teach ESL writers simply because of their own NNES status.

In fact, many NNESTs I have encountered in my years of teaching have received most or all of their English-language instruction outside the US, where English-language writing instruction is often the least-emphasized language skill. According to previous work (Cerezo et al., 2020; Reichelt, 2020), when writing is assigned in foreign language contexts, its purpose is typically to support the overall acquisition of English, especially grammar and vocabulary, rather than to teach academic written genres. Additionally, I have found in my research (Reichelt, 1996; 2005a; 2020) that NNESTs may or may not have received writing instruction in their first language(s), as writing instruction is not necessarily a part of the L1 curriculum in various countries around the world (See also Hatasa, 2011). And even if NNESTs have received L1 writing instruction, differences in pedagogical approach and genre expectations may make the U.S. writing classroom and teaching approaches unfamiliar to NNESTs (Clachar, 2000; Hargan, 1995; Lee, 2013; Naghdipour, 2016; Reichelt, 1996, 2009b, 2020). Thus, NNESTs need instruction about teaching ESL writing in U.S. academic contexts.

When the MA-TESOL TAs I supervised were teaching ESL writing courses at the University of Toledo, all of them were required to take my course *Issues in ESL Writing*. I still offer the course, which is now required for students pursuing our new MA in English with a concentration in writing studies. The primary source for course readings is Dana Ferris' and John Hedgcock's (2013) textbook *Teaching L2 Composition: Purpose, Process, and Practice*. I use relevant articles and book chapters to supplement the textbook. The course provides a brief summary of historical trends in L1 and L2 writing pedagogy and overviews the various writing theories on which current ESL writing pedagogy draws. Additionally, my course *Issues in ESL Writing* overviews the various types of ESL writers who appear in ESL writing courses and provides information about course and task design; feedback and assessment of ESL writing; plagiarism concerns; and tutoring ESL writers in the writing center. In the course, we also compare and contrast ESL with (E)FL writing instruction, drawing on Ilona Leki (2001) and ideas from my own work EFL writing around the world (e.g., Reichelt, 1997, 2005a; 2009a; 2009b; 2009c; 2013). This topic is especially relevant to NNESTs because of differences in approaches to L2 writing instruction in various geographical contexts.

Many of the readings, discussions, and activities I use in the course are intended to help students view linguistic diversity in a positive light, undercutting the idea that the purpose of writing is simply to display grammatical accuracy. This is crucial, especially for NNESTs, whose English-language education in their home countries may have focused on grammatical correctness in writing assignments. In *Issues in ESL Writing*, we discuss holistic approaches to reading student writing, focusing primarily on higher order concerns such as genre appropriateness, audience awareness, content, organization, and development of ideas. In the course, I also expose students to the holistic procedures for scoring ESL writing placement tests for our ESL writing program, examining and scoring sample tests with them. Many NNESTs have commented on the usefulness of learning to view writing holistically rather than focusing on errors, noting that it helped them with grading. These NNESTs had been students (and in many cases, teachers) of English as a foreign language in their home countries and had focused on writing as a means of practicing and reinforcing English vocabulary and grammatical structures—rather than focusing on the broader quality of a piece of writing.

Additionally, since grading is often a very difficult aspect of teaching, especially for new teachers (Ferris & Hedgcock, 2013), as part of the course activities, we practice grading several ESL writers' papers, sometimes in class, sometimes in groups, and sometimes as at-home assignments. NNESTs in the course have commented on the usefulness of this approach, noting that it was especially helpful because they had not taken an English-language writing course in the US and thus weren't sure how to approach grading student papers. I provide students in the course with grading rubrics for each paper, ones that I have developed over many years of teaching. The rubrics emphasize higher order concerns and are designed to remind the grader of each assignment's focus as well as the priorities of the course in general. I especially emphasize that graders should not penalize students for difficult-to-acquire aspects of language such as prepositions and articles, which rarely interfere with meaning (See Casanave, 2017, pp. 157–164 for a discussion of the error correction debate in L2 writing). I use this approach because, based on my years of teaching ESL writing and my own experience as a writer of several non-English L2s, I believe it is the best way to respond to the writing of ESL students. My choice of this approach isn't based on concern that NNES TAs will mark such errors inaccurately; however, this approach may allay the fears of some NNES instructors if they experience linguistic insecurity about grading papers, especially responding to linguistic errors. Additionally, and perhaps more importantly, it offers NNESTs more experience with approaching papers holistically.

The course *Issues in ESL Writing* places NNES and NES TAs on equal footing in multiple ways. Since no one in the program has previously taken coursework in second language writing, everyone in the course is a novice, each exploring a body of unfamiliar theory, research, and ideas about pedagogical practices. One of the first assignments for the course is a reading-writing autobiography. I have been assigning reading-writing autobiographies in various courses for around 30 years. In this course, the reading-writing autobiography assignment highlights the strengths of NNES TAs, even as the NESs express their own writing insecurities in these narratives. Through sharing their reading-writing autobiographies, the NNESTs and NESTs learn about each other's experiences as well as perceived strengths and weaknesses as writers. Often, the NESTs are impressed with the NNESTs' breadth of reading and writing experiences in multiple languages and express admiration and respect. In addition, NNESTs learn from their NEST counterparts' autobiographies that even NESs struggle with aspects of academic writing in English. Although the main purpose of this assignment is to allow students to reflect on their own literacy experiences and goals, the reading-writing autobiography also allows everyone in the course to learn more about each other. As Lia Kamhi-Stein (1999) writes in a discussion of preparing NNESTs, analyzing NNESs language-learning histories not only offers NESs the opportunity to learn about their peers' L2 learning processes, but it also helps NNESs see themselves as sources of information. This can counter any sense that NNESTs are inferior to their NNES counterparts simply by virtue of being native speakers of English. Additionally, during peer review, NNESTs are able to showcase their ability to provide useful feedback on their NNEST and NEST peers' work, again reinforcing their competence and value.

NNESTs' strengths and experiences also surface during other class discussion in this course, especially when NNESTs report to the class on their own experiences with English as a foreign language (EFL) writing—as students and often as teachers—in their home countries. Often, this has led to NESTs being impressed by the NNESTs' knowledge of writing instruction practices in various contexts around the world—and realizing that NNESTs are valuable sources of information about how the NESTs' own ESL students may have experienced writing instruction in their home countries.

The Importance of Coursework Related to Sociolinguistics, Including Language Diversity

Todd Ruecker et al. (2018) recommend providing courses to NNESTs that explore issues of language diversity. Because of my background in linguistics in general and my research background in sociolinguistics (e.g., 2005b, 2006;

Sánchez & Reichelt, 2021), I am able to offer a course in sociolinguistics. *Sociolinguistics* was a required course for the defunct MA-TESOL and is now a required course for the MA-writing studies concentration. In the course, language variation and diversity is addressed in detail. The main source of readings for the course is Rajend Mesthrie et al.'s (2009) textbook *Introducing Sociolinguistics*. The course includes discussion of non-standard dialects of English, including African American English, Chicano English, Appalachian English, and varieties of English spoken by indigenous people in the US, e.g., varieties spoken on the Ute reservation in northeastern Utah. It is important for NNESTs, who may be unfamiliar with these varieties of English, to learn about them because they may encounter them when teaching mainstream or ESL writing. Many NNESTs enrolled in *Sociolinguistics* have not been familiar with these dialects. Interestingly, some NNESTs seemed more open than some of their NES counterparts to the notion that social dialects like African American English or regional dialects like Appalachian English are legitimate dialects of English. This is perhaps because the NNESTs did not grow up in a society that is biased against these varieties of English. The NNESTs' more objective perceptions of these dialects proved useful for class discussion.

Sociolinguistics also includes discussion of world Englishes (Canagarajah & ben Said, 2009; McKay & Bokhorst-Heng, 2017). Since NNESTs may have feelings of self-doubt because of their status as nonnative speakers of English (Liu, 2005; Reis, 2011), it is helpful to all TAs to learn about and respect the many varieties of English that are spoken across the globe. I want all students in their course to know that linguists view different varieties of English as legitimate, especially given my role as an authority figure in their program. In our discussion of world Englishes, we engage in debunking the myth that native speakers are always the best teachers. Like Kang, a NNEST in Davi Reis' (2011) study, both NNESTs and NESTs are able to question their "blind belie[f] in the native speaker mode" (p. 146).

NNESTs as Equals and Experts in Their Roles as TAs

It is important that NNESTs be on equal footing with their NEST counterparts, not only in their coursework, but also in their work as TAs. NNEST participants in Ruecker et al.'s (2018) study indicated that they felt supported by professors who noted their interest in writing and were neutral or positive about their NNES status, and I hope I live up to that characterization. In fact, because NNEST TAs in our MA-TESOL program had previous teaching experience before starting our program, it was easy for me to see them as valuable resources. Especially as NNESTs gained more experience in the program, they confidently asserted their competence in our ESL writing TA staff meetings. During these meetings, the TAs usually wanted to discuss classroom management issues like attendance, tardiness, late papers, and plagiarism although we also discussed ideas about teaching the course material. Classroom management can be challenging for all new TAs because of their novice status, but markedly for NNES TAs, especially if students question a NNEST's authority or credibility (Kamhi-Stein, 1999; Ruecker et al., 2018; Thomas, 1999). Our fairly informal discussions allowed TAs to pool their knowledge and experience in a collegial environment.

While all TAs seemed to benefit from staff meeting discussions, I believe these meetings particularly benefitted NNES TAs. The meetings seemed to de-emphasize TAs' language backgrounds and instead put the focus on expertise (see Kasztalska & Maune, this volume, for more about WPAs emphasizing instructor knowledge and skills when working with NNESTs). Despite their NNES status, second-year NNES TAs were typically seen as experienced experts by their first-year counterparts. Second-year NNES TAs quickly realized that after a year in the program, they were much more oriented to teaching writing at the U.S. university level than new TAs, whether those new TAs were NNESs or NESs. The fact that most of the NNES TAs had prior teaching experience (in their home countries), while the NES TAs rarely did, increased their clout in the eyes of their NES counterparts. Additionally, in staff meetings, NNES TAs learned that their NES TA counterparts were also experiencing teaching difficulties and that they, the NNESTs, often had the expertise to provide productive solutions, especially once they had a year's experience in the program. All of this, I believe, helped undermine any hierarchies among TAs that related to their linguistic status.

In Jun Liu's (2005) study of NNES TAs, participants indicated that they wished they had been provided more opportunities to observe the class they would eventually teach; Liu thus recommends that NNES TAs receive hands-on training during their first semester rather than teaching their own class immediately. In our ESL writing program, both NNES TAs and NES TAs experienced such hands-on training when they began teaching in the program. In their first semester, all TAs assisted an experienced TA with teaching an ESL writing course. The new, assisting TA attended all class sessions, worked with students during class, and met informally with the lead TA about classroom issues. As the semester progressed, the assisting TA became more involved, teaching some class sessions, working with the lead TA to grade papers, and/or meeting with the lead TA and individual students for conferences. When a TA began teaching their own class during their second semester, the TA they had assisted was a convenient peer with whom to discuss teaching ideas and problems. This arrangement was useful to NNESTs, who typically had little or no experience in writing classes in higher education in the US. Additionally, NNES TAs may have felt more comfortable approaching a peer for advice rather than exposing weaknesses to me, their supervisor. As many authors point out, NNESTs may be particularly self-conscious about their weaknesses, based on their linguistic and cultural status (e.g., Liu, 2005; Reis, 2011). Being able to approach a peer informally is one solution to this problem.

This arrangement sometimes involved me assigning a second-year NNES TA to mentor a NES TA. This highlighted the notion to all TAs that it was expertise and competence, not linguistic status, that is important in teaching. In fact, new NES TAs seemed to take it in stride when they were assigned a NNES TA as a mentor. All new TAs often expressed feeling like they weren't prepared to teach ESL writing, and they appeared eager to learn from their more experienced peers, whether NNESs or NESs. Experienced NNES TAs typically acted with confidence and authority in mentoring new TAs, drawing on what they had learned in their first year in the program.

Discussion and Conclusion

The specific ways in which these strategies were implemented at the University of Toledo can be adopted, perhaps in modified form, at other institutions. Since new TAs found it helpful to shadow experienced (second-year) TAs instead of teaching their own course right away, other WPAs might consider advocating for this practice at their own institutions if it's not already in place. At the University of Toledo, the practice started initially in the mainstream writing sections, with new MA-literature students—who were also TAs—shadowing full-time mainstream writing instructors. We soon followed suit in the MA-TESOL program, with new ESL writing TAs shadowing second-year ESL writing TAs. If this approach isn't feasible, new TAs, whether NNESs or NNESTs, might also shadow permanent, full-time instructors—although this can place an unwanted burden on such instructors, who typically have heavy workloads. If this approach is adopted, those instructors should participate voluntarily and should receive a course release and/or monetary compensation. WPAs could argue that the temporary loss of the TA labor during one semester of training is balanced out by the fact that TAs are likely to provide higher-quality instruction after such an opportunity. If it is impossible to allow new TAs to forego teaching their own class during their first semester, TAs might be provided with opportunities to shadow a more-experienced instructor for several weeks while teaching their own class.

Allowing new TAs to assist an experienced TA is ideal because it creates a natural mentoring system. However, if such team teaching cannot be implemented, WPAs can also pair new TAs with more-experienced TAs, even if they are not teaching a course together. This pairing should be done for all TAs, not just NNES TAs, and the pairing should be based on experience and expertise, not linguistic status. When pairing individuals, WPAs can consider strengths, weaknesses, and individual personalities in order to foster positive mentoring situations. WPAs can also consider assigning TAs to groups of three rather than pairs if that is logistically preferable. These pairs/groups can support each other, exchange teaching ideas, compare notes about grading, and discuss classroom management issues. While WPAs can always help with such issues, TAs are often more likely to consult each other than a supervisor, partly because TAs see each other more often, and partly because they may not want to show their weaknesses to a supervisor. While such pairs/groups can be good for all TAs, they may especially benefit NNES TAs, who may have more difficulty making informal connections with their TA peers and who may perceive themselves to be at a disadvantage compared to their NES counterparts.

TAs teaching writing should have the opportunity to take coursework focusing on teaching and research in ESL writing and on sociolinguistic issues (see Matsuda et al., 2013, who describe the need for professional preparation opportunities regarding L2 writing instruction for in-service and pre-service mainstream writing teachers.) Requiring a sociolinguistics course is the best option, but if that is not feasible, TAs should take a course in linguistics that places special emphasis on language variation and on linguistic diversity, including world Englishes and other varieties of English that TAs might encounter in the writing classroom, including, for example, African American English, Chicano English, and varieties of English spoken in native American communities.

Some of the activities and readings described above can also be used in staff meetings or workshops. In such sessions, participants can be asked to share their experiences writing in their first and second (and third, etc.) languages. This would highlight the expertise and experiences of NNESs and allow NNESs to learn that NESs also struggle with writing in English (Kamhi-Stein, 1999). WPAs might also arrange for a session focusing on non-standard varieties of English in the US and on world Englishes, perhaps asking a colleague in linguistics to lead it if the WPA is not familiar with the body of work in this area (See Casanave, 2017, Ch. 4, for a discussion of world Englishes as related to L2 writing instruction). Such a session can emphasize the legitimacy of all varieties of English and undermine the notion that NNESs are always the best teachers of English and of writing.

In my experience, key aspects of preparing and supporting NNESTs for teaching writing courses include the following:

9. Requiring a course focused on teaching ESL writing
10. Requiring a course that offers opportunities to gain understanding and appreciation of the many varieties of English used within the US and around the world
11. Treating NNESTs as equals to their NEST peers
12. Offering shadowing/mentoring opportunities for all TAs, ones in which NNESTs sometimes serve as mentors
13. Helping NNESTs and NESTs appreciate the resources that NNESTs bring to the ESL writing classroom and to their peer group of new writing instructors.
14. Providing opportunities for NNESTs to serve as sources of information about their own experiences learning to write in L2 English, and about the cultural and educational contexts in which L2 writing takes place around the world.

Practices such as these can help us provide quality teacher education for NNESTs.

References

Canagarajah, S. & ben Said, S. (2009). English language teaching in the outer and expanding circles. In J. Maybin & J. Swann (Eds.), *The Routledge companion to English language studies* (pp. 169–182). Routledge. https://doi.org/10.4324/9780203878958.

Casanave, C. P. (2017). *Controversies in second language writing: Dilemmas and decisions in research and instruction.* University of Michigan Press. https://doi.org/10.3998/mpub.8876881.

Cerezo, L., González-Cruz, B. & Mercader, A. (2020). English as a foreign language writing teacher education and development in Spain: The relevance of a focus on second language writing as a tool for second language development. In L. Seloni & S. Henderson Lee (Eds.), *Second language writing instruction in global contexts* (pp. 222–249). Multilingual Matters. https://doi.org/10.21832/seloni5860.

Clachar, A. (2000). Opposition and accommodation: An examination of Turkish teachers' attitudes toward Western approaches to the teaching of writing. *Research in the Teaching of English,* 35(1), 66–100.

Ferris, D. & Hedgcock, J. (2013). *Teaching L2 composition: Purpose, process, and practice.* Routledge. https://doi.org/10.4324/9780203813003.

Hargan, N. (1995). Misguided expectations: EFL teachers' attitudes towards Italian university students' written work. *Language and Education,* 9(4), 223–232. https://doi.org/10.1080/09500789509541416.

Hatasa, Y. A. (2011). L2 Writing instruction in Japanese as a foreign language. In T. Cimasko & M. Reichelt (Eds.), *Foreign language writing instruction: Principles and practices* (pp. 98–117). Parlor Press.

Kamhi-Stein, L. (1999). Preparing non-native professionals in TESOL: Implications for teacher education programs. In Braine, G. (Ed.), *Non-native educators in English language teaching* (pp. 145–158). Lawrence Erlbaum Associates. https://doi.org/10.4324/9781315045368.

Lee, I. (2013). Becoming a writing teacher: Using "identity" as an analytic lens to understand EFL writing teachers' development. *Journal of Second Language Writing, 22*(3), 330–345. https://doi.org/10.1016/j.jslw.2012.07.001.

Leki, I. (2001). Material, educational, and ideological challenges of teaching EFL writing at the turn of the century. *International Journal of English Studies, 1*(2), 197–209.

Liu, J. (2005). Chinese graduate teaching assistants teaching freshman composition to native English-speaking students. In E. Llurda (Ed.), *Non-native Language Teachers* (pp. 155–177). Springer.

Matsuda, P. K., Saenkhum, T. & Accardi, S. (2013). Writing teachers' perceptions of the presence and needs of second language writers: An institutional case study. *Journal of Second Language Writing, 22*(1), 68–86. https://doi.org/10.1016/j.jslw.2012.10.001.

McKay, S. & Bokhorst-Heng, W. (2017). *International English in its sociolinguistic contexts: Towards a socially sensitive EIL pedagogy.* Routledge. https://doi.org/10.4324/9781315092553-7.

Mesthrie, R., Swann, J., Deumert, A. & Leap, W. (2009). *Introducing sociolinguistics.* Edinburgh University Press.

Naghdipour, B. (2016). English writing instruction in Iran: Implications for second language writing curriculum and pedagogy. *Journal of Second Language Writing, 32*, 81–87. https://doi.org/10.1016/j.jslw.2016.05.001.

Phillipson, R. (1992). *Linguistic Imperialism.* Oxford University Press.

Reichelt, M. (1996). *An investigation of first language and second language (English) composition theory and pedagogy at the secondary level in Germany* [Unpublished doctoral dissertation]. Purdue University.

Reichelt, M. (1997). L2 writing instruction at the German "Gymnasium": A 13th-grade English class writes the "Abitur." *Journal of Second Language Writing, 6*, 265–291. https://doi.org/10.1016/s1060-3743(97)90015-1.

Reichelt, M. (2005a). English-language writing instruction in Poland. *Journal of Second Language Writing, 14*(4), 215–232. https://doi.org/10.1016/j.jslw.2005.10.005.

Reichelt, M. (2005b). English in Poland. *World Englishes, 24*, 217–225.

Reichelt, M. (2006). English in a multilingual Spain. *English Today, 22*(3), 3–9. https://doi.org/10.1017/s0266078406003026.

Reichelt, M. (2009a). Bibliography of sources on foreign language writing. In R. Manchón (Ed.), *Learning, teaching, and researching writing in foreign language contexts* (pp. 281–296). Multilingual Matters. https://doi.org/10.21832/9781847691859.

Reichelt, M. (2009b). A critical evaluation of writing teaching programmes in different foreign language settings. In R. Manchón (Ed.), *Learning, teaching, and researching writing in foreign language contexts* (pp. 183–206). Multilingual Matters. https://doi.org/10.21832/9781847691859.

Reichelt, M. (2009c). Learning content in another context: English-language writing instruction in Germany. *Issues in Writing, 18,* 25–52.

Reichelt, M. (2013). English-language writing instruction in Poland: Adapting to the local EFL context. (2013). In Majchrzak (Ed), *PLEJ2: Psycholinguistic Explorations* (pp. 23–42). University of Łódź Press.

Reichelt, M. (2020). Preparing teachers to teach writing in various English as a foreign language contexts. In L. Seloni & S. Henderson Lee (Eds.), *Second language writing instruction in global contexts* (pp. 288–304). Multilingual Matters. https://doi.org/10.21832/seloni5860.

Reis, D. (2011). Non-native English-speaking teachers (NNESTs) and professional legitimacy: A sociocultural theoretical perspective on identity transformation. *International Journal of the Sociology of Language, 2011*(208), 139–160. https://doi.org/10.1515/ijsl.2011.016.

Ruecker, T., Frazier, S. & Tseptsura, M. (2018). Language difference can be an asset: Exploring the experiences of nonnative English-speaking teachers of writing. *College Composition and Communication, 69*(4), 612–641. https://www.jstor.org/stable/44870978.

Sánchez, U. E. & Reichelt, M. (2021). English in Cuba: English in the media, workplace, and education. *English Today, 37*(1), 3–12. https://doi.org/10.1017/s0266078419000233.

Thomas, J. (1999). Voices from the periphery: Non-native teachers and issues of credibility. Braine (Ed.), *Non-native educators in English language teaching* (pp. 5–13). Lawrence Erlbaum Associates. https://doi.org/10.4324/9781315045368.

12 Building Confidence as NNESTs of Writing through Pre-service Training and Professional Development

Anastasiia Kryzhanivska
BOWLING GREEN STATE UNIVERSITY

Tetyana Bychkovska
INDEPENDENT SCHOLAR

Entering a classroom as a novice writing instructor may be challenging, but starting to teach as a NNEST sometimes adds additional difficulties. Previous research has revealed that NNESTs may experience a lack of confidence in a classroom and doubt their credibility due to their linguistic or cultural backgrounds (Floris & Renandya, 2020; Li, 1999; D. Liu, 1999; Long, 2003; Reis, 2011; Thomas, 1999; Wolff, 2015; Worden-Chambers & Horton, 2020). NNESTs of writing in particular sometimes have their nonnative status highlighted by their students and colleagues (Braine, 1999; Ruecker et al., 2018), which, as a result, can make NNESTs self-conscious about their professional skills. Therefore, confidence building becomes an essential part of NNESTs' preparation for writing instruction.

While challenges of NNESTs have been discussed in previous research, less attention has been devoted to examining solutions. Existing suggestions for supporting NNESTs of writing in confidence building include, for example, encouraging writing programs to receive more education about NNESTs' experiences and capitalize on NNESTs' strengths (Kasztalska, 2019; M. Lee et al., 2017; Ruecker et al., 2018; Selvi & Rudolph, 2017; Thomas, 1999; Worden-Chambers & Horton, 2020; Zheng, 2017). Enhancing general pre-service teacher training has also been offered as a solution (e.g., Kasztalska, 2019; J. Liu, 2005); however, few studies have provided an extensive discussion of such training or additional professional development (PD) activities used to support NNESTs of writing.

The purpose of this chapter is to present a collaborative reflection on the elements of training and PD activities in which we, two master's program NNES graduates, participated during our graduate program in the US.

These activities contributed to our sense of confidence as academic writing instructors, which was invaluable as we began teaching as graduate assistants and then transitioned into full-time jobs at two different U.S. universities. This chapter begins with a review of existing research on NNESTs' of writing training. Then, we introduce our reflective method and provide a brief overview of our backgrounds. After presenting the reflection on the barriers to our confidence, we discuss how they were addressed through training and PD activities. Based on our findings, we provide recommendations for NNESTs' trainers.

Training and Professional Development for NNESTs of Writing

Research examining experiences of NNESTs of writing provides insights into their training and PD. Before starting to teach, NNESTs of writing typically receive a short one-week or multi-day pre-semester training (Chen, 2021; Kasztalska, 2019; Ruecker et al., 2018). This short training sometimes leaves NNESTs feeling "ill-prepared" for writing instruction (Kasztalska, 2019, p. 165) since many of them start teaching in their first semester of graduate school as international students, lacking familiarity with the composition pedagogy in the U.S. context. As a result, studies recommend providing more extended training (e.g., Kasztalska, 2019) or, as J. Liu (2005) strongly argues, delaying teaching until the second or later semesters to allow for sufficient NNES teacher training, which "could greatly reduce anxiety and boost their confidence" (p. 174).

Concurrent with teaching in their first semester or year, NNESTs are sometimes supported through a graduate-level course on teaching writing and/or a mentoring program (Chen, 2021; Connor, 1999; Kamhi-Stein, 1999; Kasztalska, 2019; Li, 1999; J. Liu, 2005; Ruecker et al., 2018; Snow et al., 2006). While teacher training in global contexts often includes required academic communication courses to improve English proficiency (Snow et al., 2006), such courses are either rarely offered in the North American contexts or are electives (D. Liu, 1999). NNESTs of writing in the US rarely enroll in these electives, with only one participant in Zheng (2017) mentioning taking such a course. This is despite almost all participants in NNEST research sharing concerns and difficulties with adjusting to the new language and culture.

The importance of promoting discussions about the relationship between language and identity, the native speaker fallacy, and translingualism through training is emphasized by NNEST participants and recommended by researchers (Kasztalska, 2019; J. Liu, 2005; Ruecker et al., 2018; Selvi & Rudolph, 2017; Selvi & Yazan, 2021; Snow et al., 2006; Worden-Chambers & Horton, 2020; Zheng, 2017). Most NNESTs of writing report gaining confidence and feeling empowered through such discussions. Early-career professionals also report that membership in professional organizations has allowed for their identity (re)construction and supported professionalization (Kamhi-Stein, 1999; Kim & Saenkhum, 2019). Exposure to writing samples by NES students early in training is also recognized as useful for building NNESTs' of writing confidence since these samples demonstrate that NES writers are not "perfect" and that NNESTs can help NES students improve writing skills (Kasztalska, 2019; Ruecker et al., 2018).

Gaining training through working as tutors is not typically discussed in research on NNESTs of writing; this activity was only briefly mentioned in Todd Ruecker et al. (2018) and Xuan Zheng (2017). The lack of such discussion might be explained by tutoring being an uncommon component of new composition instructor training. However, it is also possible that the discussion of tutoring and perhaps other aspects of NNEST education was out of scope for the reviewed studies as their main focus was on general experiences of NNESTs of writing, and not specifically on their training. To contribute to a more complete understanding of the education that NNESTs of writing may receive, we present a range of training and PD activities that we, two NNESTs, engaged in as a way of overcoming early-career challenges.

Method

To name the elements of training and PD activities that helped us address our initial challenges as NNESTs of writing, we employed a duoautoethnographic approach (Rinehart & Earl, 2016), which refers to a critical analysis of how two researchers' "own lived experiences contribute to broader understandings of a sociocultural situation or a social phenomenon" (Mirhosseini, 2018, p. 3). Thus, this collaborative self-study aimed to narrate our stories and draw conclusions for a larger audience.

To generate categories for the elements of training that contributed to our confidence building, we first independently created lists of activities we engaged in. The lists, as we discovered upon comparison, appeared similar to a large extent. We had many experiences that overlapped (e.g., taking the same coursework, tutoring at writing labs), but also each of us had unique experiences (e.g., Tetyana working on a feedback coding project as a research assistant, or Anastasiia teaching in several contexts). We then collaboratively discussed the lists of activities and grouped them into six categories:

classroom learning, tutoring writing and training tutors, observations, collaboration and mentoring, teaching experience, and additional PD activities. To recall specific details of our experiences, we consulted multiple artifacts from our master's program, including our CVs last updated right after our graduation; major course papers and instructor feedback on them; course materials; and even personal photos. In the process of writing this manuscript, we had in-depth discussions of the training details, during which it became apparent that each element of training and PD helped us address specific challenges that we initially experienced as NNESTs of writing. Thus, the discussion of challenges is also introduced in this manuscript.

Before presenting our joint reflection, we should acknowledge that our experiences should be interpreted in light of intersectionality (Crenshaw, 1989; Norton & De Costa, 2018). The experiences that we had intersect with other aspects of our backgrounds (e.g., race, religion, gender, prior jobs); not all NNESTs having gone through similar training or PD might have the same experience as we did. Therefore, we introduce our backgrounds below.

Author Background

Anastasiia and Tetyana are both white females, born and raised in Mykolayiv, Ukraine. We are native speakers of Ukrainian and Russian. We received bachelor's degrees from the same university in Mykolayiv, where Anastasiia majored in English and German translation and interpretation and Tetyana in foreign philology (teaching of English and German as foreign languages and world literature). In Ukraine, each of us had around seven years of experience tutoring and a year teaching general EFL to children and adults. When we started our master's program in applied linguistics at Ohio University (OU), we were in our early 20s, with Anastasiia joining the program one year earlier than Tetyana. Despite studying at the same university in Ukraine, it was not until Tetyana applied to OU that we were introduced to each other via email by the OU linguistics program's graduate chair.

After graduation from OU, Anastasiia started a full-time job as an instructor at Bowling Green State University (BGSU). She has been teaching ESOL writing for graduate and undergraduate NNES students along with other skill-based and teacher-education classes. Tetyana, after finishing the program, was hired full-time as a faculty ESL specialist at George Mason University's (GMU) writing center. Tetyana's job responsibilities included training tutors, tutoring, facilitating writing groups, and teaching writing. Currently, Anastasiia is an associate teaching professor and T/ESOL program director at BGSU, and Tetyana is an independent scholar.

Barriers to Confidence: Our Initial Challenges

Before describing elements of the training that helped us build confidence as future writing instructors in the US, we first present challenges that we encountered at the start of the master's program.

Before OU we knew little of the U.S. writing conventions, which is not uncommon for NNESTs (Connor, 1999). Our pre-OU experience with writing in English mostly consisted of extensive translation practice or short essay composition, both following the conventions of Ukrainian writing. It was not until around the second year of our undergraduate program in Ukraine that we learned about writing the "American way," which included composing texts with a clear structure and a thesis statement. We then encountered this type of writing again several years later in TOEFL preparation materials, when applying to U.S. universities. Still, these brief introductions to writing expectations in the US were insufficient for us to gain comprehensive knowledge necessary for teaching this subject matter. When we started our program at OU, a graduate academic writing course was available as an elective; however, neither of us chose to take it since we had little time left outside of our required coursework, assistantship-related activities, and additional jobs, all of which were vital for supporting us financially and making our stay in the US possible. It was through the elements of training described below that we started to learn about expectations for advanced academic writing in the U.S. context, the knowledge essential for teaching writing with confidence.

Having little knowledge of the U.S. writing conventions, we had even less understanding of how academic writing can be taught (e.g., what a curriculum may look like, how to provide feedback). Even expectations for teaching in the U.S. academy in general (e.g., pedagogy, engagement, establishment of authority) were new for us. It is clear that without the knowledge of writing, writing pedagogy, and general pedagogy expected in the US, we would be unable to teach academic writing at the university level effectively and confidently. While fortunately we did not have to do so, we have heard anecdotally, however, from other NNESTs that they had to start teaching university-level writing in their first semester, which had a negative impact on their perception of their professional ability, mental health, self-esteem, and even willingness to continue a teaching career. Similar accounts were also documented in previous research (Chen, 2021; Kasztalska, 2019; J. Liu, 2005; Ruecker et al., 2018).

In fact, Anastasiia experienced some of these negative consequences during her first semester of graduate school, when she was assigned to teach middle school beginning pull-out ESL students. While teaching in this context was less demanding than teaching university-level academic writing, it was still challenging because Anastasiia had to support her students who did not know the English alphabet while adjusting to a new educational context herself. Because her supervisor had a heavy workload administering the ESL curricula in several school districts, he was unable to provide his teaching assistants with extensive training before the start of their assignments or offer observation opportunities. The lack of feedback on Anastasiia's teaching performance led her to question her teaching practices and resulted in teaching anxiety. To compensate for the lack of training and support, Anastasiia spent long hours with her graduate school colleagues trying to understand K-12 standards and brainstorming lesson plans.

Although not having to teach during her first year, Tetyana encountered a challenge when tutoring at the writing lab. After Tetyana's first semester of tutoring, she received only average evaluations from students with comments stating that she was "unclear" in sessions. Having little experience with tutoring practices in the US, she felt frustrated that she was unable to provide writers with the support they needed. Challenges related to Tetyana's tutoring or Anastasiia's teaching occurred despite our previous work experiences in Ukraine.

Another barrier to our confidence was our belief that our NNES status was a limitation in the U.S. educational context. Coming from Ukraine, where the target of language learning was a native speaker, we were not familiar with the ideas of the native speaker fallacy, world Englishes, and linguistic diversity. This led us to experience impostor syndrome when we began tutoring in the first semester: "Who am I to give recommendations about English writing to students if I'm not even a native speaker?" Thus, we believed that one has to be a native speaker to have authority in providing English writing instruction or take on leadership positions. This led us to experience the feeling of inferiority and doubt our value as educators, a challenge also described in previous studies (Li, 1999; Thomas, 1999).

Finally, as other international students new to the U.S. context, we experienced linguistic challenges (Lui, 1999). When Tetyana just arrived in the US, it was sometimes difficult for her to comprehend and be understood by others, especially those with non-American accents. In the first semester, she was even once told that she sounded like "a textbook" when speaking, which perhaps was because writing and reading were emphasized over speaking and listening in her EFL classes in Ukraine. These communication challenges emerged despite her learning English since the age of five and scoring well on the TOEFL. Anastasiia also had a memorable incident related to linguistic issues when through a conversation with her classmates, she realized that she used an unconventional word order in noun clauses (e.g., "I don't know what state standards *should I* use"). It is clear that without the ability to communicate clearly with students we would be unable to teach confidently, and having many language issues when speaking with or writing to students would negatively affect our credibility as writing instructors (Thomas, 1999).

Building Confidence as NNESTs of Writing: Addressing Challenges through Training and Professional Development

In this section, we outline and reflect on the most impactful activities from our master's program pre-service training and PD that helped us overcome our initial challenges. As demonstrated below, it was a variety of experiences, some of which we took initiative to seek out independently, that helped us develop necessary skills for teaching writing, thus contributing to our confidence building as NNESTs.

Pre-service Classroom Learning

Coursework offered through our graduate program greatly supported our confidence development. A course that was directly relevant to teaching English writing was reading and writing pedagogy. We discussed writing as a process with its various stages (e.g., drafting, revising, editing), peer review, individual teacher-student conferences, collaborative writing, pedagogical use of corpora, and principles of providing feedback on various aspects of writing (e.g., content, organization, language use). Another course that impacted the development of our writing content knowledge was an elective, English for specific purposes (ESP). For the major project in this class, Anastasiia and Tetyana chose to collaboratively reassess an academic business writing course for undergraduate international students offered at OU. Our research findings translated into specific recommendations for changes in the course. Learning that writing can be taught as a process and that teachers can conduct a needs analysis to develop or improve a course was influential in developing our pedagogical writing knowledge as NNESTs since these ideas were not present in our previous educational contexts.

Besides learning from course content, we had first-hand experience with different educational materials, pedagogical strategies, and written feedback practices that our professors used while teaching us; thus, we developed cultural understanding of pedagogy through coursework (D. Liu, 1999). When we started our program, we were surprised by how "informal" and approachable professors were, making jokes, sharing personal stories, some sitting cross-legged on a teacher's desk, and learning our names before the first day of classes, all of which were uncommon in our previous educational experiences. High interactivity of classes and frequent use of multimedia were also considerably less prevalent in Ukraine. Therefore, being exposed to a university classroom environment and practices helped us understand the expectations that our own students might have in this context.

In feedback on our papers, our professors helped us enhance our linguistic proficiency by pointing out issues related to language use, especially possessives, articles, and word choice. While this feedback was invaluable for improving our accuracy in written English, the type of feedback that was the most influential in building our confidence as NNESTs was positive comments. We first encountered this type of feedback in the second language acquisition course, when we wrote our first substantial paper in graduate school. Our professor provided detailed comments on what we did well in our drafts and focused on content, which was unusual for us since previously we had primarily received only corrective feedback on language use. Receiving such inspiring comments in our first semester and then throughout the program from other professors substantially strengthened our confidence as NNES writers and served as a model for our own assessment practices later. The importance of professors' feedback for building confidence in writing is supported by previous autoethnographic accounts of NNESTs (Li, 1999).

Tutoring Writing and Training Tutors

Tutoring at writing labs at different levels during our first year was also instrumental in developing our content and pedagogical knowledge. Anastasiia worked at undergraduate, graduate, and intensive English program writing labs in addition to her assistantship; Tetyana also pursued tutoring opportunities at the graduate writing lab on her own, while undergraduate lab tutoring was a part of her assistantship. The majority of students visiting the undergraduate lab brought writing assignments from the same course Tetyana would teach in her second year. This way Tetyana became familiar with this course's assignments and interacted with students from the same population that she would encounter later in her classes.

The required training that we received at the writing labs was especially useful for building our knowledge of English writing conventions. During unbooked hours and student no-shows, we read academic writing handbooks (e.g., Swales & Feak, 2012) and writing style manuals (e.g., APA) as well as completed online grammar modules. This self-study in the first semester of graduate school addressed our lack of confidence related to limited knowledge of English writing conventions and eliminated the need to take an elective graduate writing course.

Tutoring also helped us address impostor syndrome, which we both experienced, especially when working with graduate or NES students. Anastasiia's first tutoring session with a graduate student was on a dissertation about corrosion, a topic she hardly understood. She, however, still had a successful session and helped the student address sentence structure, his major session request. Working at writing labs led us to understand that we can address language use, content clarity, organization, or other aspects of writing without the topic or disciplinary knowledge. This work also allowed us to see that we could tutor (and consequently teach) all students—undergraduate and graduate, beginning and proficient, native and nonnative English-speaking—even if they were more academically or linguistically advanced than us.

At the end of every semester, we received performance evaluations from our students. In her first semester, Tetyana was described by students as "unclear" in sessions. After consulting with her mentors and recalling her previous observations of tutors, she realized that she misinterpreted the training she received. She believed that providing "answers" to writers is wrong pedagogy and relied only on indirect tutoring techniques (e.g., asking open-ended questions) at the expense of student understanding. While some literature on writing tutoring pedagogy does prohibit directive tutoring and even sentence-level work in general (e.g., Ryan & Zimmerelli, 2016, with the foundation laid by North, 1984), Tetyana's training did not adopt these orientations. Instead, the misunderstanding arose from the concept of "editing," which is commonly misinterpreted by tutors, as Tetyana later learned as a faculty ESL specialist at the GMU's writing center (Bychkovska & Lawrence, in press). "We do not edit" could mean "we do not work at the sentence level at all," "we are not allowed to be directive and sometimes tell writers how to change wording," and "we do not take over a student's paper and correct everything for them without a conversation." While the latter was implied in her lab training at OU, Tetyana had the second interpretation in mind. Eventually, after learning from evaluations and adding more directive techniques to her repertoire, Tetyana received high performance evaluations the following semester. Student feedback from the writing lab helped us understand which knowledge and skills needed further development in our tutoring practices and consequently future teaching.

In our second year of working at the undergraduate writing lab, we were promoted to assistant coordinators (i.e., graduate administrators), a position available only to one graduate student in a cohort. Anastasiia's assistant coordinator evaluations highlighted the effectiveness of her leadership, her ability to create a collegial work environment, and her guidance during norming sessions. Such feedback helped reinforce the idea that we do not have to be native speakers to have a leadership position or authority in teaching English writing, which contributed to our confidence building. This position allowed us to transition to the roles of mentors and facilitate tutor training, thus sharing and deepening the knowledge about academic writing that we had gained through our training.

Observations

In addition to implicit observations of our professors during our coursework, we engaged in explicit observations, some as a requirement from our assistantships or jobs and some independently, which aided the development of our confidence in teaching writing.

We completed required tutor observations, first as fellow tutors and then as writing lab assistant coordinators. We also watched instructors teach the classes that we were assigned to teach the following semester. For example, Anastasiia chose to attend and observe most class meetings of introduction to linguistics in her free time before she started teaching it in her second year at OU. Tetyana observed every class meeting for two semesters—one semester for credit as a part of her teaching practicum and another semester in her free time—as a preparation for teaching a first-year composition for international students. While time-consuming, class observation was a crucial step for us to build confidence since we learned about the curriculum that we were required to teach in advance.

By observing experienced teachers, we had a chance to notice the techniques they used to promote student learning and engagement as well as establish their authority. For example, one instructor made sure to explicitly list their relevant qualifications at the beginning of the course and highlight them throughout the semester. This made it clear to students that despite this teacher looking young, they were competent in teaching the subject. To us, as NNESTs, this also meant that presenting our qualifications could help prevent a possible lack of student trust due to our linguistic and cultural backgrounds, something that NNESTs often have to address strategically (Subtirelu, 2011). While observing, we filled out observation forms with guiding questions to explicitly reflect on instructor practices and decide which practices could be integrated into our teaching.

Finally, we benefited from the requirement of being observed first as tutors and then as instructors. While teaching, we both received suggestions to improve the clarity of our instructions for in-class activities; Anastasiia was advised to increase waiting time after asking her class a question; Tetyana's mentor provided a helpful tip of starting a class with a small writing activity to prevent tardies. We found conversations with our mentors and peers particularly helpful for building our confidence since they helped us determine whether our tutoring and teaching met the expectations of the U.S. educational context.

Collaboration and Mentoring

We were actively seeking collaboration and mentoring support from our faculty which, in autoethnographic accounts of other NNESTs, has been regarded as an important confidence-building practice (Connor, 1999). For example, during Tetyana's first year in the master's program, she was a research assistant, helping her mentor code teachers' feedback on student writing in a course she would be assigned to teach in her second year. She observed that some professors provided direct error correction by fixing students' papers, mostly focusing on grammar, and others asked questions, offered explanations, and provided examples on all aspects of writing. This allowed her to be exposed to possible types of written feedback she could provide in the future. During this assistantship, she also had required weekly meetings with her mentor, who informally discussed with her various aspects of academic writing and writing pedagogy.

We also offered mentoring support to others, which helped further build our confidence as educators. Anastasiia became an unofficial mentor to two of her co-teachers in the community English class, and she was required to mentor Tetyana, an incoming writing lab assistant coordinator. In turn, Tetyana in her final semester coached another tutor trainer to replace her after graduation and provided peer mentorship for a student who would teach the same writing course as her a year later.

Teaching Experience

Throughout our graduate careers, we had multiple graduate teaching assistant positions and completed a teaching practicum class. These experiences allowed us to bridge the gap between theory and practice and teach in real-life contexts. In her first year of graduate school, Anastasiia taught pull-out ESL students at a middle school. Lack of training support during this assistantship led Anastasiia to independently prepare for her next teaching position the following year as an instructor of record of the introduction to linguistics class. The preparation included observations and an extensive review of previous materials. In her final semester, when taking a teaching practicum course, she co-taught a community English class at OU. Different teaching contexts, student populations, and class structures required adjustment and flexibility, the skill that helped Anastasiia when she transitioned to teaching writing, among other subjects, after graduation.

Tetyana was also an instructor of record in her second year but taught first-year composition for international students, a course directly related to developing her skills and confidence as a writing instructor. Numerous activities prepared her for teaching: coding feedback on students' papers as a research assistant, tutoring the same student population, conducting research on writing produced by this population, observing each class meeting of this course for two semesters, and attending presentations on writing at conferences. Therefore, she felt extremely confident when she started teaching. Class observations prepared Tetyana to expect that, for example, students from East Asian countries, which comprised the majority of her classes, might be less likely to participate in whole-class discussions. Had she not known that this is common, she would have questioned her pedagogical competence and considered her NNES background to be a culprit of students' reticence. To address students' needs, she practiced other methods of promoting engagement rather than directing questions to the whole class. Thus, with her teaching delayed until the second year, Tetyana's transition to teaching was smooth and less stressful than that of Anastasiia who started teaching during her first year.

Delayed teaching for Tetyana also preempted possible linguistic challenges and stressful situations of not understanding or being understood while teaching the whole class. The ability to "re-calibrate" her speaking and listening skills in the ESL environment by working in the "safe" one-on-one space of the writing lab, taking a phonetics and phonology course, and just conversing in in- and out-of-class settings were instrumental for her linguistic confidence building.

As a result of Tetyana's extensive training a year prior to starting to teach, she received high student evaluations both semesters she taught at OU. Since Tetyana taught exclusively international students, her NNES and international student status was highlighted in evaluations, but only in a positive light: some students appreciated that Tetyana has gone through similar experiences as them and thus could understand their academic and personal needs and relate to them. Anastasiia also received high student evaluations in her second year of teaching. Her NES students did not focus on her NNES background in the evaluations; instead, they commended her for engaging and interactive lessons, well-organized material, and willingness to work individually with students to help them understand linguistic concepts. Through the evaluations, it became apparent to us that with sufficient training and support, the NNES status is not a barrier to effective teaching, and in some cases, it might even be an asset.

Additional Professional Development Activities

To continue learning beyond our master's program and pursue initiatives recommended by our mentors, we engaged in many additional PD activities. These activities included extracurricular readings, engagement in professional organizations, publications, and presentations.

Apart from readings assigned in classes, we read additional research articles and books on academic writing independently. Throughout the program, Tetyana's advisor shared with her readings, including eight books from his personal library related to ESP and academic writing discourse for Tetyana to read during her first winter break. The most impactful reading for Anastasiia was suggested to her by her mentor, the writing lab coordinator. During one of their conversations in her first semester of tutoring, Anastasiia mentioned that she felt like an impostor, questioning her ability as a NNES to help students. To support Anastasiia, her mentor suggested that she read an article by Tetyana's mentor that built upon previous research arguing that one does not have to be a NES to be an accomplished writer, tutor, or teacher (J. Lee, 2005). This knowledge contributed considerably to Anastasiia's confidence as a NNEST. Tetyana also read this and other articles on the strengths of NESTs and NNESTs independently.

To further promote our learning and confidence building, we became members of professional associations such as TESOL. Memberships allowed us to follow important debates related to writing pedagogy through newsletters and forums, thus supporting our teacher identity formation (Kim & Saenkhum, 2019). Professional community membership also, in part, contributed to our engagement in research that later resulted in publications (e.g., Bychkovska & Lee, 2017; Kryzhanivska, 2017). Data for Tetyana's published empirical projects were collected from previous sections of the same course that Tetyana would teach in her second year, which allowed her to analyze the language use and needs of the student population she would encounter. Working on publications strengthened our confidence as NNES writers since we again recognized that the NES status does not define our writing effectiveness or chances of publication. Also, by going through the process of publication ourselves, we gained the skills that would allow us as instructors to coach advanced writers working on their publications.

Finally, our conference experiences were an important aspect of our PD. Since our first semester of the master's program, we attended and presented at state, national, and international conferences (e.g., Computer Assisted Language Learning (CALL) Conference, Ohio TESOL, International TESOL), which supported our professionalization (Kamhi-Stein, 1999). We attended presentations about writing, including ones on plagiarism, genre-based writing, and feedback practices. Upon graduation from OU, we had delivered over 10 presentations each, in which we focused on our projects from master's courses or independent research with mentors. Seeing the positive feedback and support of the professional community encouraged us to pursue PD even further and helped us improve our professional confidence. Additionally, after attending Ohio TESOL once, we made friends that we were looking forward to seeing at other conferences and after graduation. It created a personal connection to the professional community and fostered a sense of professional selves that contributed to our confidence building.

These additional PD activities helped us follow recent research on writing, learn about cutting-edge pedagogical practices, and feel a part of a global community of writing teachers. In fact, it was through engaging in additional readings and attending conference presentations that we learned extensively about the topics of native speaker fallacy, linguistic diversity, and language ideology, which we remember to be only briefly covered in our coursework. Explicit learning of these topics helped us understand our strengths as NNESTs and complimented our observations that in comparison to our NES peers, we had greater explicit knowledge of grammar (since we learned English rather than acquired it) and understanding of NNES writers' needs (since we were NNES writers ourselves). This knowledge felt empowering and contributed to our confidence building as NNESTs of writing.

The described training and PD activities also contributed to us obtaining employment after graduation. A wide range of activities that we engaged in as a program requirement and that we sought out independently helped us add valuable experience to our CVs and demonstrate competence in other job application materials or during the interviews. In fact, it was during the community English class that Anastasiia wrote her first teaching philosophy and recorded a teaching demo to use in job applications. Close interaction with our mentors and their encouraging feedback also led us to receive help with job application documents and obtain recommendation letters in support of our candidacy. In general, the described training and PD gave us, NNESTs of writing, enough confidence to believe that despite our accents and different cultural and linguistic backgrounds, we have the necessary qualifications to teach writing.

Discussion

Based on our reflection above, we present the following implications for trainers of NNESTs of writing.

Training in writing pedagogy. Provide opportunities for NNESTs of writing to take a pedagogical writing course. Such a course should be required and include both theoretical foundations and practical teaching advice. Unfortunately, previous research (e.g., Kasztalska, 2019) shows that some NNESTs' formal education in writing pedagogy is limited to short pre-semester training, which is insufficient for developing writing teacher competencies. While NESTs would also benefit from such a course, they have the advantage of taking at least one first-year writing course in college and observing it from a student perspective. NESTs are also more likely to have had opportunities to notice pedagogical strategies used by their professors and develop their meta-awareness while completing other courses. Most NNESTs, however, would lack this experience.

Delaying teaching. Allow NNESTs to start teaching later—in their second semester or second year—unless they already have prior teaching experience in the US. Some states (e.g., Virginia, Texas) have a legal requirement that graduate students must complete a certain number of course credits—typically a year's-worth of full-time coursework—before they are allowed to teach; such delayed teaching can also be possible in the states without this law, as Tetyana's experience in Ohio demonstrates. While preparing for teaching, NNESTs can work, for example, as tutors or research/program/administrative assistants. Because Anastasiia was required to start teaching in her first semester of the master's program, her experience was more stressful than that of Tetyana who had an opportunity to prepare for teaching by conducting observations, tutoring writing, and engaging in other activities. Delayed teaching can also positively contribute to NNESTs' implicit linguistic competency development, which is crucial for effective communication with students. This recommendation is supported by research both for NESTs (Kanno & Stuart, 2011) and NNESTs (J. Liu, 2005; Wolff, 2015). However, delaying teaching is especially valuable for the latter because of linguistic, cultural, and pedagogical adjustments necessary for many NNESTs. This would allow them to feel more confident in the classroom and avoid traumatizing experiences such as the ones described in George Braine (1999).

Tutoring writing as a teacher education component. Encourage NNESTs to engage in tutoring writing to gain pedagogical, assessment, and content knowledge necessary for teaching. This recommendation is consistent with the literature that argues that the writing center is an effective training ground for composition instructors and regards it as a crucial experience for teachers-in-training before stepping into their writing classrooms (Broder, 1990). Because some NNESTs might be coming from a context where writing centers are not an established practice, explicitly recommending writing center tutoring to them is important for teacher education.

Leadership positions. Advise NNESTs to apply for leadership positions at the writing center or in a writing program, if such are available, after a semester or two of tutoring. Developing leadership and mentoring skills while working in the writing center is an unparalleled opportunity for graduate students (Hewerdine, 2017), and NNESTs in particular. Tetyana was hired for her first full-time job to a large extent due to this experience, and in Anastasiia's current administrative role, she heavily relies on the skills gained through her tutor training role at the writing center. The realization that one does not need to be a NES to assume a leadership role may build NNESTs' confidence and support their professional growth (Braine, 1999).

Observations. Provide multiple opportunities for structured observations (i.e., with an observation form or protocol and post-observation discussions) of experienced writing instructors. Both Anastasiia and Tetyana attended and observed every class meeting of the courses they were about to teach, mostly in their free time, which was time-consuming but crucial for their sense of preparedness. When NNESTs of writing start teaching, observe them several times per semester, offering constructive feedback and highlighting their strengths. Recommendations to include observations, in person or through video recordings, in teacher training are supported by previous research (e.g., Long, 2003; Snow et al., 2006; Wolff, 2015). This recommendation for NNESTs might help address cultural, educational, linguistic, and pedagogical differences and expectations of teachers-in-training.

Mentoring and collaboration. Work closely with NNESTs of writing to collaborate and support their development. Provide NNESTs-in-training with opportunities for both formal mentoring where they would work with a professor or experienced mentor and informal opportunities to discuss teaching practices with peers. This accords with previous recommendations for NNESTs (e.g., Floris & Renandya, 2020; Kamhi-Stein, 1999; Kasztalska, 2019; Kim & Saenkhum, 2019; Li, 1999; Ruecker et al., 2018; Snow et al., 2006; Wolff, 2015). Formal and informal mentorship can address the unique needs of NNESTs in various domains: content, pedagogical, curricular, and assessment.

Additional Professional Development. Encourage NNESTs of writing to engage in PD activities such as reading additional literature, becoming involved with professional organizations, publishing research, and attending and presenting at conferences (Connor, 1999; Kamhi-Stein, 1999). Inviting a student to collaborate on a research project and guiding them through the presentation and publication processes may be helpful for building NNESTs' confidence as academic writers and provide them with the expertise necessary to teach or tutor graduate students working on publications. While most novice teachers, including NESTs, would likely benefit from this recommendation, NNESTs of writing, in particular, can gain additional conference and public speaking experience that NESTs might already possess.

Building connections between language and identity. Provide opportunities to learn about the strengths of NNESTs, linguistic diversity, and language ideology through graduate coursework. This recommendation is supported by previous research that emphasizes the importance of promoting discussions of these topics in graduate pedagogical writing courses (Kasztalska, 2019; J. Liu, 2005; Ruecker et al., 2018; Zheng, 2017). Self-reflections, autoethnographic projects, and personal narratives can be incorporated (Kryzhanivska & Hunter, 2021; Li, 1999; Selvi & Yazan, 2021; Worden-Chambers & Horton, 2020) to help NNESTs develop knowledge of self (Kamhi-Stein, 1999; Wolff, 2015).

While we encourage trainers of NNESTs of writing to consider implementing our recommendations, it is important to acknowledge the impact of the programmatic, financial, or wider structural constraints they operate within. Not every aspect of the training we mentioned may be possible to implement in every context. It might not even be necessary to do so since teacher trainers should avoid overwhelming NNESTs of writing who might deal with multiple obligations and stressors in their academic or personal lives. We did not engage in every aspect of our training all at once; the required and additional activities we participated in were spaced out throughout the two years of our program. We also find it important to acknowledge that we do not think that the responsibility of building NNESTs' confidence should fall exclusively on NNESTs and writing program administrators; university administration at all levels needs to work on addressing issues in this area. It is also important for linguists to engage in more public-facing work to address beliefs about NNESTs among students and the general population (Floris & Renandya, 2020; Kang et al., 2015).

Conclusion

This chapter presented activities that two pre-service NNESTs of writing engaged in to overcome initial challenges and build their professional confidence as novice instructors. An obvious limitation of this paper is that it is based on a self-reflection of only two NNESTs. While there is value to this account of our experiences, more research with a larger number of participants is needed. A larger-scale study would help uncover other aspects of training that NNESTs of writing from other contexts or backgrounds found useful for confidence building. Future research may also systematically collect advice or strategies for success unrelated to training or PD, such as, for example, the strategy of sharing the relevant experience with students at the beginning of the semester to establish authority or other strategies (e.g., Subtirelu, 2011).

We hope that this discussion can help the trainers of NNESTs at the graduate level support beginning instructors more effectively. Our account in this chapter may also be useful to NNESTs of writing who seek possible activities to develop their skills to enter a writing classroom with confidence.

References

Braine, G. (1999). From the periphery to the center: One teacher's journey. In G. Braine (Ed.), *Non-native educators in English language teaching* (pp. 15–27). Lawrence Erlbaum Associates.

Broder, P. (1990). Writing centers and teacher training. *Writing Program Administration, 13*(3), 37–45.

Bychkovska, T. & Lawrence, S. (in press). Tutors' perspectives on their work with multilingual writers: Changes over time and in response to revisions in training. *The Writing Center Journal.*

Bychkovska, T. & Lee, J. J. (2017). At the same time: Lexical bundles in L1 and L2 university student argumentative writing. *Journal of English for Academic Purposes, 30*, 38–52. https://doi.org/10.1016/j.jeap.2017.10.008.

Chen, W. (2021). *Teaching in a foreign land: Portraits of international teaching assistants in English composition classes and students' evaluations* [Doctoral dissertation, The University of Memphis]. ProQuest Dissertations Publishing.

Connor, U. (1999). Learning to write academic prose in a second language: A literacy autobiography. In G. Braine (Ed.), *Non-native educators in English language teaching* (pp. 29–39). Lawrence Erlbaum Associates.

Crenshaw, K. (1989). Demarginalizing the intersection of race and sex: A Black feminist critique of antidiscrimination doctrine, feminist theory, and antiracist politics. In K. T. Bartlett & R. Kennedy (Eds.), *Feminist legal theory: Readings in law and gender* (pp. 139–167). https://doi.org/10.4324/9780429500480-5.

Floris, F. & Renandya, W. (2020). Promoting the value of non-native English-speaking teachers. *PASAA: Journal of Language Teaching and Learning in Thailand, 59*, 1–19.

Hewerdine, J. M. (2017). *Conversations on collaboration: Graduate students as writing program administrators in the writing center* [Doctoral dissertation, Southern Illinois University at Carbondale]. ProQuest Dissertations Publishing.

Kang, O., Rubin, D. & Lindemann, S. (2015). Mitigating U.S. undergraduates' attitudes toward international teaching assistants. *TESOL Quarterly, 49*, 681–706. https://doi.org/10.1002/tesq.192.

Kamhi-Stein, L. (1999). Preparing non-native professionals in TESOL: Implications for teacher education programs. In G. Braine (Ed.), *Non-native educators in English language teaching* (pp. 145–158). Lawrence Erlbaum Associates.

Kanno, Y. & Stuart, C. (2011). Learning to become a second language teacher: Identities-in-practice. *The Modern Language Journal, 95* (2), 236–252. https://doi.org/10.1111/j.1540-4781.2011.01178.x.

Kasztalska, A. (2019). International teaching assistants in the composition classroom: From world Englishes to translingualism and beyond. *Journal of Language, Identity and Education, 18*, 161–175. https://doi.org/10.1080/15348458.2018.1545584.

Kim, S. H. & Saenkhum, T. (2019). Professional identity (re)construction of L2 writing scholars. *L2 Journal, 11*(2), 18–34. https://doi.org/10.5070/l211242088.

Kryzhanivska, A. (2017, July 24–28). *Do you also see what I see: Russian-Ukrainian conflict in European, Ukrainian and Russian media* [Paper presentation]. Corpus Linguistics Conference 2017, University of Birmingham, Birmingham, UK. https://www.birmingham.ac.uk/Documents/college-artslaw/corpus/conference-archives/2017/general/paper80.pdf.

Kryzhanivska, A. & Hunter, L. (2021). The person in personal narrative: Two ESOL instructors teaching away from home. In R. Jain, B. Yazan & S. Canagarajah (Eds.), *Transnational Identities and Practices in English Language Teaching* (pp. 38–54). Multilingual Matters. https://doi.org/10.21832/9781788927536-004.

Lee, J. J. (2005). The native speaker: An achievable model? *Asian EFL Journal, 7*(2), 152–163.

Lee, M., Schutz, P. A. & van Vlack, S. (2017). Non-native English-speaking teachers' anxieties and insecurities: Self-perceptions of their communicative limitations. In J. de D. M. Agudo (Ed.), *Native and non-native teachers in English language classroom* (pp. 119–138). De Gruyter Mounton. https://doi.org/10.1515/9781501504143-007.

Li, X. (1999). Writing from the vantage point of an outsider/insider. In G. Braine (Ed.), *Non-native educators in English language teaching* (pp. 43–55). Lawrence Erlbaum Associates.

Liu, D. (1999). Training non-native TESOL students: Challenges for TESOL teacher education in the West. In G. Braine (Ed.), *Non-native educators in English language teaching* (pp. 197–210). Lawrence Erlbaum Associates.

Liu, J. (2005). Chinese graduate teaching assistants teaching freshman composition to native English speaking students. In E. Llurda (Ed.), *Non-native language teachers: Perceptions, challenges, and contributions to the profession* (pp. 155–177). Springer. https://doi.org/10.1007/0-387-24565-0_9.

Long, K. (2003). *Self-perceptions of non-native English speaking teachers of English as a second language* [Master's thesis, Portland State University]. PDXScholar. https://doi.org/10.15760/etd.5179.

Mirhosseini, S. (2018). An invitation to the less-treaded path of autoethnography in TESOL research. *TESOL Journal, 9*(1), 76–92. https://doi.org/10.1002/tesj.305.

North, S. (1984). The idea of a writing center. *College English, 46*, 433–446. https://doi.org/10.2307/377047.

Norton, B. & De Costa, P. (2018). Research tasks on identity in language learning and teaching. *Language Teaching, 51*(1), 90–112. https://doi.org/10.1017/s0261444817000325.

Rinehart, R. E. & Earl, K. (2016). Auto-, duo- and collaborative- ethnographies: "Caring" in an audit culture climate. *Qualitative Research Journal, 16*(3), 210–224. https://doi.org/10.1108/qrj-04-2016-0024.

Reis, D. S. (2011). Non-native English-speaking teachers (NNESTs) and professional legitimacy: A sociocultural theoretical perspective on identity transformation. *International Journal of the Sociology of Language, 2011*(208), 139–160. https://doi.org/10.1515/ijsl.2011.016.

Ruecker, T., Frazier, S. & Tseptsura, M. (2018). "Language difference can be an asset": Exploring the experiences of nonnative English-speaking teachers of writing. *College Composition and Communication, 69*(4), 612–641. https://www.jstor.org/stable/44870978.

Ryan, L. & Zimmerelli, L. (2016). *The Bedford guide for writing tutors* (6th ed.). Bedford/St. Martin's.

Selvi, A. F. & Rudolph, N. (2017). Teachers and the negotiation of identity: Implications and challenges for second language teacher education. In J. de D. M. Agudo (Ed.), *Native and non-native teachers in English language classroom* (pp. 257–272). De Gruyter Mounton. https://doi.org/10.1515/9781501504143-013.

Selvi, A. F. & Yazan, B. (2021). Beyond "native" and "non-native" English-speaking teachers. In Y. Bayyurt (Ed.), *Bloomsbury World Englishes* (Vol. 3: Pedagogies) (pp. 107–125). Bloomsbury Academic.

Snow, M. A., Kamhi-Stein, L. D. & Brinton, D. M. (2006). Teacher training for English as a lingua franca. *Annual Review of Applied Linguistics, 26*, 261–281. https://doi.org/10.1017/S0267190506000134.

Subtirelu, N. (2011). Juggling identity and authority: A case study of one non-native instructor of English. *TESL-EJ, 15*(3), 1–30.

Swales, J. & Feak, C. (2012). *Academic writing for graduate students: Essential tasks and skills* (3rd ed.). The University of Michigan Press. https://doi.org/10.3998/mpub.2173936.

Thomas, J. (1999). Voices from the periphery: Non-native teachers and issues of credibility. In G. Braine (Ed.), *Non-native educators in English language teaching* (pp. 5–13). Lawrence Erlbaum Associates.

Wolff, D. (2015). *All in the same boat?—native and non-native English speaking teachers' emerging selves in a U.S. MATESOL program* [Doctoral dissertation, Michigan State University]. ProQuest Dissertations Publishing.

Worden-Chambers, D. & Horton. A. (2020). Becoming multilingual, becoming a teacher: Narrating new identities in multilingual writing teacher education. *Composition Forum, 45*. https://www.compositionforum.com/issue/45/multilingual.php.

Zheng, X. (2017). Translingual identity as pedagogy: International teaching assistants of English in college composition classrooms. *The Modern Language Journal, 101*(S1), 29–44. https://doi.org/10.1111/modl.12373.

§ Afterword

Mariya Tseptsura
UNIVERSITY OF ARIZONA

Todd Ruecker
UNIVERSITY OF NEVADA, RENO

As we write this, we are excited to see this collection finally heading towards production. It has certainly been a long journey, as we conceived this project in early 2018 when we were still in an advisor/advisee relationship at an institution we have both since moved on from. This collection was initially inspired by our work across writing studies and applied linguistics, combined with our firsthand experiences navigating the politics around native speaker privilege and prejudices—Todd as a White native English-speaker spending time in the Czech Republic and Chile and Mariya as a nonnative English-speaker coming to the US from a very different education system, an experience she details in this collection. We had read the extensive body of work on these issues by TESOL and applied linguistics scholars such as George Braine, Ahmar Mahboob, and Ali Faud Selvi, which we drew on as we began to bring this issue to the writing studies community through a 2018 publication in *CCC* (Ruecker et al., 2018) as well as Mariya's work helping to establish the NNEST SIG at the *Conference on College Composition and Communication*.

Based on our own experiences and the stories that our 2018 study participants shared, we knew there was a need for a more robust resource targeting the field of writing studies audience more specifically. When we sent out the call for proposals for this collection in 2019, we were confident we had a unique idea and would make a meaningful contribution in a field that had increasingly turned its focus to the intersections of language, race, and linguistic justice. Our confidence quickly turned to a quiet slog as we encountered mixed reactions from reviewers—reactions that seemed to push against our efforts to bridge dialogues across TESOL, applied linguistics, and writing studies. Earlier, we experienced similar challenges with our *CCC* article (Ruecker et al., 2018) when the editors did not quite know what to do with it in the face of mixed responses from reviewers situated firmly on either side of the disciplinary divide. We were able to find more unequivocal support with our current publisher, but our four-year-long journey towards publishing this collection is a testament to the divisions between our different subfields that continue to exist despite the valiant work of well-known scholars trying to overcome that divide (e.g., Atkinson et al., 2015; Bou Ayash & Kilfoil, 2023; Matsuda, 2006; Silva & Leki, 2004; Silva & Wang, 2020; Zawacki & Habib, 2014; among others).

Our work as editors of the collection was further complicated and prolonged by the negotiations we had to carry out between our authors and multiple reviewers. In putting together this collection, we made a point of including the work of newer scholars to have a better representation of NNES writing professionals at different stages of their careers. Admittedly, several authors needed a few rounds of feedback and revision to develop various aspects of their chapters. However, at multiple points we had to push back against some feedback that called for certain rhetorical choices that were presented as universal practices rather than an individual's suggestions. Furthermore, as editors we made the choice to respect the variety of Englishes our authors brought to their chapters and consciously strove not to edit their writing beyond minor typos. Todd felt this would be especially inappropriate for him as a White NES to engage in this work (see Kuzhabekova, 2019, for the politics around this editing).

Unfortunately, we were not always able to avoid missteps in negotiating between reviewers, editors, and authors. We would like to give tribute to two chapters that are no longer included in this collection because in our efforts to expedite the publication process, we did not push back against some feedback that was ultimately perceived by the authors as offensive, intruding, or not supportive. We especially regret our lack of caution in passing on this feedback uncritically because these chapters were by NNES BIPOC scholars who were describing their personal experiences with linguistic injustice and prejudice. This experience was a difficult lesson that we as editors need to take principled stands to protect the integrity of our authors' and our own work. We have found guidelines such as The Anti-Racist Scholarly Reviewing Practices (2021) document timely and helpful as we had to push against disciplinary boundaries. We found some of the suggested practices especially relevant to our work, such as the call to validate multiple sources of expertise, including authors' own lived experiences. For instance, we received comments from some TESOL-based reviewers that questioned the autobiographical approaches in some of the chapters in this collection. At the same time, while we did not receive such comments from reviewers working from the writing studies perspective, one reviewer of our earlier 2018 article criticized us for using quantitative data. We hope that more editors and reviewers adopt more inclusive practices such as the recommendations outlined in The Anti-Racist Scholarly Reviewing Practices guide (2021).

Afterword

One theme that has come up at multiple points as we have worked on this collection is that it is disheartening that we are still detailing some of the same experiences that early NNEST scholars in TESOL did in the late 1990s. Whereas it feels that the writing studies field has come a long way since then, the chapters in this collection detail not only prejudice from students but also colleagues and others who should arguably "know better." It is true that writing programs across U.S. institutions (as well as institutions more broadly) have been becoming more diverse in recent decades, and in many cases this growing diversity of the student populations has pushed writing programs to pay more attention to linguistic diversity; the translingual and transnational movements of the past two decades are a testament to that growing awareness. However, not all programs and not all universities are equally diverse, and unfortunately, not all have been equally engaging with scholarship and ideas surrounding linguistic diversity.

When Mariya first started teaching writing as a graduate student at a Midwestern flagship university a decade ago, she was the only international student in the English department, with only a handful of international students who had completed the program before her. The undergraduate student population was (and still is) over 80% White, with a majority of students being in-state. Like many other NNES instructors, Mariya found scholarship on native speaker bias and linguistic justice extremely helpful and instrumental in her professionalization. However, she did not get introduced to that scholarship until she enrolled in her Ph.D. program—despite completing an MA degree in TESOL. The topic of linguistic diversity was largely absent from the TA training she received while teaching in the writing program at her first institution. We hope that this collection will contribute to our collective fields' efforts to ensure that writing programs across the country do not suffer from similar curricular lapses. As many scholars and professionals in our fields strive to "expose and intervene in the dominant ideologies of monolingualism and nationalism that continue to shape compositionists' belief systems and professional practices" (Bou Ayash & Kilfoil, 2023, p. 9), it is our hope that this collection will help writing programs widen their focus to pay closer attention to the scope and potential of linguistic diversity within their instructor ranks and treat that diversity as a resource rather than a liability.

Since we started this collection, our country has become even more divided, and overt displays of racism and other forms of prejudice have become more widely tolerated and even codified into law in many states. Nonetheless, we are heartened to see that the authors in this collection have found strength from work in our field as they have found various ways to navigate, challenge, and overcome prejudices. We hope that this collection will prove itself another such source of strength and help build a sense of community where fellow NNESTs of writing can find support and understanding. Ultimately, the chapters in this collection offer a variety of approaches to shape attitudes of future generations around language diversity. The process of steering this collection to publication has taught us as editors that we need to continually reflect on own actions and words as we strive to curtail the systemic practices of exclusion in academic publishing and the disciplinary divide within our fields.

References

Atkinson, D., Crusan, D., Matsuda, P. K., Ortmeier-Hooper, C., Ruecker, T., Simpson, S. & Tardy, C. (2015). Clarifying the relationship between L2 writing and translingual writing: An open letter to writing studies editors and organization leaders. *College English, 77*(4), 383–386. https://www.jstor.org/stable/24240054.

Bou Ayash, N. & Kilfoil, C. B. (2023). Introduction: Translingual and transnational graduate education in rhetoric and composition. In N. Bou Ayash & C. B. Kilfoil (Eds.), *Translingual and transnational graduate education in rhetoric and composition* (pp. 3– 24). Utah State University Press.

Cagle, L. E., Eble, M. F., Gonzales, L., Johnson, M. A., Johnson, N. R., Jones, N. N., Lane, L., Mckoy, T., Moore, K. R., Reynoso, R., Rose, E. J., Patterson, GP., Sánchez, F., Shivers-McNair, A., Simmons, M., Stone, E. M., Tham, J., Walton, R. & Williams, M. F. (2021). *Anti-racist scholarly reviewing practices: A heuristic for editors, reviewers, and authors.* (2021). https://tinyurl.com/review heuristic.

Kuzhabekova, A. (2019). "There are notable linguistic problems": Publishing as a non-native speaker of English. In T. Ruecker & V. Svihla (Eds.), *Navigating challenges in qualitative educational research* (pp. 193–205). Routledge.

Matsuda, P. K. (2006). The myth of linguistic homogeneity in U.S. college composition. *College English, 68*(6), 637–651. https://doi.org/10.2307/25472180.

Ruecker, T., Frazier, S. & Tseptsura, M. (2018). "Language difference can be an asset": Exploring the experiences of nonnative English-speaking teachers of writing. *College Composition and Communication, 69*(4), 612–641. https://www.jstor.org/stable/44870978.

Silva, T. & Leki, I. (2004). Family matters: The influence of applied linguistics and composition studies on second language writing studies—past, present, and future. *The Modern Language Journal, 88*(1), 1–13. https://doi.org/10.1111/j.0026-7902.2004.00215.x.

Silva, T. & Wang, Z. (2020). *Reconciling translingualism and second language writing.* Taylor and Francis.

Zawacki, T. M. & Habib, A. (2014). Internationalization, English L2 writers, and the writing classroom: Implications for teaching and learning. *College Composition and Communication, 65*(4), pp. 650–658. https://www.jstor.org/stable/43490878.

§ Contributors

Tetyana Bychkovska is an independent scholar who has tutored and taught English academic writing as well as facilitated tutor training at three universities in the US. Her research focuses on second language academic writing, including corpus analysis of lexico-grammatical and discourse-level features in student-produced texts, tutor perspectives on their work with multilingual writers, and multilingual writers' perspectives on language ideology in the writing center. Her work has appeared in the *Journal of English for Academic Purposes* and *System*.

Xin Chen is Lecturer of Communication Skills at the Kelley School of Business, Indiana University Bloomington (IUB). She received her Ph.D. in Literacy, Culture, and Language Education from IUB and holds a Graduate Certificate in Teaching English as a Foreign Language (EFL) & English as a Second Language (ESL). Previously, she taught writing courses in the English department and served as the assistant coordinator of the Multilingual Writing program at IUB. Her research interests include multilingual students' development of English academic literacy and intercultural communication.

Min-Seok Choi is Assistant Professor of Education at the University of Louisiana at Lafayette. His research interests include multilingual students' learning and use of disciplinary literacy practices, identity construction, and communicative repertoires in and out of school. At present, his research is dedicated to understanding how instructional conversations in discipline organize the exchange of advice between multilingual students. His scholarly contributions can be found in publications such as Linguistics and Education, Teaching in Higher Education, as well as several book chapters.

Marcela Hebbard is Senior Lecturer in the Writing and Language Studies Department at the University of Texas Rio Grande Valley where she teaches composition, sociolinguistics and teacher preparedness courses. Her research interests include online writing pedagogy, raciolinguistics, multiraciality, and teacher identity. Her work has appeared in *Across the Disciplines* and the *American Journal of Qualitative Research*. She has also co-published several book chapters.

Nabila Hijazi is Teaching Assistant Professor of Writing at the George Washington University. Her research interests include Muslim and refugee women's rhetoric(s) and literacy practices, writing center theory and practice, and multilingual writing. She teaches classes in academic writing,

writing across the curriculum, writing center theory and practice, and women's studies.

Aleksandra Kasztalska is Lecturer in the CAS Writing Program at Boston University. She received her Ph.D. in linguistics from Purdue University and has taught courses in composition, linguistics, and TESOL. Her research interests include world Englishes, second language writing assessment, English pedagogy and assessment in Poland, and legitimation code theory.

Su Yin Khor is Professor of Writing and Rhetoric and Director of the Writing Program at College of the Atlantic. Her research interests include teacher and learner identities, literacy socialization, and translingual practices that writers use and develop in and across various educational, workplace, and everyday settings. She most recently co-wrote *The Practical Nature of L2 Teaching: A Conversation Analytic Perspective* (Routledge).

Anastasiia Kryzhanivska is Associate Teaching Professor at Bowling Green State University where she teaches English to speakers of other languages, first-year composition, linguistics, and teacher education classes. Her research interests are arts-based pedagogy, second language writing, and multicultural awareness.

Christopher E. Manion is the coordinator of the Writing Across the Curriculum program at the Center for the Study and Teaching of Writing at the Ohio State University. His research focuses on instructor and curriculum development in Writing Across the Curriculum programs. His work appears in *Technical Communications Quarterly* and the *Journal of Teaching Writing*.

Michael Maune is Lecturer in Writing, Rhetoric, and Professional Communication at Massachusetts Institute of Technology. His research interests focus on applications of systemic functional linguistics and legitimation code theory for college writing curriculum and instruction.

Md Mijanur Rahman is Assistant Professor of Writing Studies and English Education Coordinator in the Department of English at California State University, Los Angeles. He received his Ph.D. in English studies from Illinois State University. A teacher-scholar, he brings interdisciplinary expertise in Applied Linguistics and Writing Studies, especially in areas like ESP/EAP, genre theories, language ideologies, L2 pragmatics, NNEST, multilingualism, and translingualism. Before joining Cal State LA, he taught at Illinois State University, Millikin University, Lincoln Land Community College, and Northern University Bangladesh.

Melinda Reichelt is Professor of English at the University of Toledo, where she directs the ESL writing program and teaches ESL writing and linguistics. She has published articles on second language writing and is co-editor, with Tony Cimasko, of *Foreign Language Writing Instruction: Principles and Practices* (Parlor Press, 2011). With Nur Yigitoglu, she co-edited *L2 Writing beyond English* (Multilingual Matters, 2019).

Tamara Mae Roose is Assistant Professor at California State University, San Bernardino in the TESOL Program within the Department of Teacher Education and Foundations. Her research is centered on the intersection of language, culture, and academic literacies. She is particularly interested in how students and educators draw upon diverse language and cultural resources as they develop new academic practices. Her work has appeared in journals such as *Journal of English for Academic Purposes, ELT Journal*, and *Multicultural Learning and Teaching*.

Todd Ruecker is Associate Professor of Rhetoric and Composition and Director of Core Writing at the University of Nevada, Reno. His research focuses on exploring the increasing linguistic and cultural diversity of educational institutions and developing innovative ways to support student and teacher success. His work has appeared in journals such as *TESOL Quarterly* and *College Composition and Communication* and he has published several books.

Cristina Sánchez-Martín is Assistant Professor of English at the University of Washington, Seattle. Her work revolves around investigating how humans understand and navigate composing and language practices in transnational contexts from decolonial perspectives.

Lisya Seloni is Professor of Applied Linguistics in the Department of English at Illinois State University. Her research focuses on ethnographic approaches to second language writing, academic socialization and the politics of English language teaching. Her most recent publications appeared in *Journal of Second Language Writing, English for Specific Purposes, Language Policy* and *Journal of Language and Politics*.

Mariya Tseptsura is Director of the online writing program in the Department of English at the University of Arizona where her work focuses on online writing instruction (OWI). Besides OWI, her research interests include second language writing, writing program administration, and linguistic diversity in higher education. She has taught composition and ESL courses in a variety of settings in the US and abroad.

Lan Wang-Hiles is Associate Professor of English at West Virginia State University, where she also directed the ESL Program. Her research interests include L2 writing, writing center theory and tutoring practice, multilingualism, and non-native English-speaking teacher identity. Her studies have been published as journal articles and book chapters by *New York State TESOL Journal*, MLA, the Michigan University Press, Springer, Multilingual Matters, etc. She is the Chair of the Standing Group of the Non-Native

Contributors

English-Speaking Writing Instructors (NNESWIs) for the Conference on College Composition and Communication (CCCC) and a Higher Education Representative on the West Virginia TESOL Board.

Wen Xin is Assistant Teaching Professor of English at the University of Kansas, where he also received his Ph.D. in English with an emphasis on English language studies and rhetoric and composition. His research draws upon a variety of methods, techniques, and algorithms from statistics, data mining, and natural language processing to explore the use of pragmatic features, such as metadiscourse, stance, and hedges, and variations of those features in writing classrooms.

Demet Yiğitbilek is a Ph.D. candidate at Illinois State University, focusing on applied linguistics and writing pedagogies. She has worked as an EFL instructor internationally at the college level before deciding on pursuing her scholarly development in the US. More recently, she has taught upper-level writing intensive courses, descriptive linguistics, and applied grammar and usage for writers. Her research mainly focuses on multilingual students' positioning in and through writing, and identity representations of multilingual individuals writing in English as an additional language in various academic discourses.

www.ingramcontent.com/pod-product-compliance
Lightning Source LLC
Chambersburg PA
CBHW060558080526
44585CB00013B/608